Meihong Xu joined the People's Liberation Army when she was seventeen and received her BA from the Institute of International Relations in Nanjing. Larry Engelmann is the author of four other books, including the *New York Times* Notable Book *The Goddess and the American Girl*. They live in California.

Daughter of China

The True Story of Forbidden Love in Modern China

by Meihong Xu and
Larry Engelmann

HEADLINE

First published in 1999
by HEADLINE BOOK PUBLISHING

First published in paperback in 2000
by HEADLINE BOOK PUBLISHING

10 9 8 7 6 5 4 3 2

ISBN 0 7472 6278 0

Printed and bound in Great Britain by
Clays Ltd, St Ives plc

HEADLINE BOOK PUBLISHING
A division of the Hodder Headline Group
338 Euston Road
London NW1 3BH

www.headline.co.uk
www.hodderheadline.com

CONTENTS

For all the other daughters of China

ACKNOWLEDGEMENTS

Two individuals contributed to our success in transforming our experiences into a book. Elizabeth Fernandez of the *San Francisco Examiner* wrote the first account of our ordeal eight years ago and suggested the possibility of a book. Our agent, Sandra Dijkstra, was enthusiastic about this project from the moment we proposed it to her and provided constant encouragement and support.

We want to extend our thanks to our family members and friends who were supportive and courageous while we were living the story told in this book. They are Zhong Yuhua, Marya Flood, Tim Flood, Erika Erhart, Mike Erhart, Meifang Xu, Peter Martin, Joan Chen, Peter Hui, Yan Geling, Lawrence Walker, Anchee Min, Li-Young Lee, Jiang Wen, Alice Weixin Zhang, Yvonne Lynott, Greg Lynott, Mao Lei, Mitch Nelson, John Snetsinger, Bruce Burns, Robert Bernell, Bianka Bernell, Al Conetto, Alan Soldofsky, Marilyn Day, Will Day, Bui Huu, Zhou He, Yanan Li, Sue Chen, Jiajun Lin, Feng Weinian, Jiang Lu, Nevin Zhang, Roy Rowan, Tony Paul, Sidney Fine, David Chang, Katherine Dee Robinson, Patrick Freeman, Jeremy Kagan, Susan Zhu, Xiaofei Chen, Vincent Xie, Jose Alvarez, Sudha Alvarez, Sheela Battu, Charu Gupta, Beate Goetz, Fang Li, Kindra Tully, Gu Hua, Frank H. Wong, Yu Lin Mei, George Crance, Hall Gardner, Ruth Kling, Charlotte Ku, Richard Gaulton, Richard Pomfret, Rosemary Prentice, Erik Tibbet, Shen Kun, Jamie Anderson, K.C. Leung, Fox Butterfield, Vincent Leung, James Walsh, George Moore, Mai Le Ho, Lynn Cole, June Yee and Katerina Lok.

Some names must be omitted from this list and other names

within the narrative of the story have been changed to protect them from retribution. All of these people, by their selfless and generous actions helped turn a tragedy into a triumph. We remain grateful to them and will never forget what these people did for us. It is our hope that they will each experience the love and peace in their lives that they helped make possible in ours.

Those special few who paid a very high price for supporting us will remain always in our thoughts and prayers.

But birds, as you say, fly forward.
So I won't show you letters and the shawl
I've so meaninglessly preserved.
And I won't hum along, if you don't, when
our mothers sing *Nights in Shanghai*.
I won't each Spring, each time I smell lilac,
recall my mother, patiently
stitching money inside my coat lining,
if you don't remember your mother
preparing for your own escape.
After all, it was only our
life, our life and its forgetting.

— LI-YOUNG LEE
For a New Citizen of These United States

ONE

Red Aunt

The past, like a cricket in the corner
Whines in its low, persistent voice

— SHU TING

i

The room is small. It's like countless similar rooms I've seen in military barracks scattered across China. At some earlier time the room probably housed eight enlisted men. Tonight there are only four beds in the room – two of them pushed side by side against each of the longer walls. The narrow window has been nailed shut and old copies of *The People's Liberation Army Daily* have been pasted over the glass.

Three female soldiers assigned to guard me perch close together on the bed nearest the door and occasionally whisper to each other. They never divert their gaze from me. Two armed soldiers are pacing back and forth in the hall outside.

Wearing only khaki trousers, a blouse and sandals, I sit on the bed farthest from the door. I fold my arms tightly over my breasts in a futile effort to stay warm. The faint flickering vapor of my breath, as delicate and transparent as life itself, blurs my view of the guards for a moment every time I exhale. Soon, I lose interest in them and stare only at the chipped concrete floor and wait.

Before long, I know, there will be footsteps in the hall followed by an insistent knock on the door. A guard will stand and unlock the bolt with a key fastened to her belt. More guards will then enter the room and announce my name. I will stand and be led from the room and down the hall, surrounded by all the guards, to another door. I can see it happening. We pass through the swinging double doors and into the darkness outside, quickly transformed into mere silhouettes in a grim little parade. We walk away from blades of light that knife through the shaded windows of the barracks to provide the only illumination outside. As if on signal, the guards stop and step away from me. We are in an open space and I face away from the light and wait. I can barely see the ground, which is hard and sharp and shines with a slick skin of ice. The sky is starless. I hear footsteps behind me and then someone pushes me to a kneeling position. My arms are pulled back hard and tightly bound together behind me. I am painfully aware of the sound of my own breathing and I feel the anxious flutter of my heart. The others are impatient. They want to be finished with this unpleasant business and get back inside. I gaze at the ice and wait to hear the rustle of clothing when one of the soldiers raises his hand and holds his pistol a few inches from the back of my head. There is a momentary muted crunch of ice and snow beneath the boots of the others as they step away to avoid being soiled with my blood. Then there is complete stillness. I close my eyes tightly, I think of him one last time – my American. As I remember him – at this moment – will my thoughts fly to him? Will he hear my last unspoken words? Will he whisper my name when I fall? Will he remember me?

My military records will be purged. No documentary evidence of my career or my crime will remain. I will be erased from existence and become a nonperson. My family and friends will be told that I disappeared. They know what that means. They will not ask questions and will not speak my name aloud for a long time. When they mourn me it will be secretly and in silence.

These are my expectations as I sit in this room with my three guards. I force my mind to shuffle quickly through a hundred memories of happier times, searching for something I can hold on to, something to take me away from this room. Yet I can't completely push from my mind the bleak reality of the present.

I find again in my memory the face of the American. His eyes are so blue tonight. He smiles. I see his lips move but I no longer hear his voice. I know I will never see him or hear him or hold him again. His eyes close, his face fades, he is gone.

The sound of footsteps in the hall is the measured rhythm of death approaching. Each second is precious now. I know a few words might save my life, alter my fate. But I can never say those words. I cannot betray those I love, not even to save myself. I am even unable to betray those I now know have betrayed me.

My thoughts come to rest on a familiar memory. Lishi! I see my village – Lishi – and I remember once more the story of the little girls who were lost in the fires. How many times have I heard the tale of their courage in the face of death? How could I have forgotten? Now I wonder if I have that same courage. I think of my aunt in Lishi. In my refusal to betray those I love, aren't I like her? On this night, surrounded by those who denounce me, isolated from everyone I care about, without hope, condemned – do I feel at last what she felt? I sense something like pride and hope rising within me, filling me with strength. I am suddenly comforted. I am not afraid.

ii

We are simple people. Peasants. Our birthright and destiny is hard work. We are each born with a strong back and a strong will and we inherit a tradition of dogged persistence and resiliency. We live by the cycle of the seasons. We know when to cultivate the earth, how to nourish it and renew it. In return, it gives us sustenance.

For sixteen centuries our village, Lishi, has survived in Jiangsu province near the shore of Mirror Lake (Lian Hu) south of the Yangtze River and west of the Grand Canal. The devastations of man and nature – floods, droughts and famines, plagues and earthquakes, wicked warlords, evil emperors, foreign devils, revolutionaries and religious fanatics – have swept back and forth across our land destroying, stealing and carrying away the handiwork of our labor. But we survive. We return to work, repair the damage and plant the grain once more. Life goes on.

We have good fortune as well as bad, our elders constantly remind us. One follows the other, always, like the seasons, they say. Fortune, too, has its cycles. It is the way of the world. We accept it all as part of life. It is fate. And we believe in fate.

We also believe it is important to remember and honor the courage and strength of those who lived and died here before us. Those who struggled, suffered and survived to build and plant again should never be forgotten. Their example inspires and instructs us. Memory is the sacred thread connecting us to our ancestors. Someday it will connect our descendants to us.

There are a few particular memories, however, that are nearly unbearable. Some believe that those memories have the power to poison the present and the future. They must be told – but only with special care. They must be told even when the telling hurts, because they also explain who we are and who we are not.

Such is the memory of December 1937, when a cycle of hope and complacency in Lishi was reversed and hell once again ruled the earth.

It was a time of war. The villagers convinced themselves that the isolation of Lishi would deliver them from destruction. We were unimportant, after all, in the larger scheme of things. We were not a great prize to be fought over and then held up as a trophy for the world to see. We were neither a fortress nor a great walled city like Shanghai or neighboring Nanjing. We were only peasants in a village near a road linking far more important places. We felt safe in our insignificance.

Yet, the Japanese Imperial Army – the short devils (*xiao dong yang*), as we called them – ignorant of our insignificance, passed through our village on their way from Shanghai to Nanjing. They did not stay in Lishi for long – less than one hour, in fact. But we will remember and retell what they did there for a thousand years.

A road linking Shanghai to Nanjing cuts through fields south of the village. It was crowded with refugees and soldiers that December. For days the villagers watched anxiously from their fields as a stream of humanity stretching from horizon to horizon flowed steadily westward along the road. The villagers of Lishi heard tales of the monstrousness of the Japanese soldiers who had long occupied distant parts of our country. Now they were on the move again, pushing all before them as they advanced on the Nationalist capital in Nanjing and on all of the cities and towns of China beyond it.

There were nervous murmurs about the approaching Japanese Army and calls for the villagers to abandon everything and join the mass exodus. Yet there was also uncertainty and fear about leaving the village. 'Is it really necessary?' people asked. 'Where will we go? How will we live? What will we eat? How long will we be gone? Wouldn't it be safer hiding in the fields until the short devils have passed?' The village was far from the main road. Travelers seldom noticed Lishi. If there were no smoke from the cooking fires and if everyone in the village hid from sight, there was the distinct possibility – indeed, the probability – that the short devils would not stop.

Several young villagers, unconvinced of the wisdom of remaining in Lishi, panicked and decided to join the jumble of soldiers and refugees on the road. They quickly packed their possessions in blankets and baskets, bound their children on their backs, said goodbye and departed. None of them returned. Those who remained in Lishi prepared to hide in their homes or to conceal themselves along the dikes or in ruts in the fields and wait for the short devils to pass, exactly as our ancestors had done when barbarian invaders approached and then passed on.

After several days the throng on the road thinned and then disappeared. In the distance, a short time later, the villagers watched thick columns of smoke rise slowly to hang like gigantic black ribbons suspended from hooks in heaven. They listened to the distant deep thunder of big guns and occasionally saw bright flashes of light on the horizon. Again and again they felt the earth trembling beneath their feet. They extinguished all cooking fires so no signs of life could be detected.

As they prepared to go into hiding, some of the villagers saw a lone Chinese soldier, lost and confused, stumbling through the nearby fields. The men chased him down and cornered him. He was just a boy – no more than sixteen years old – and he was terrified and trembling. They attempted to question him, but he could not understand a word of the village dialect. With exaggerated gestures coupled with some common Mandarin idioms they succeeded, they thought, in communicating with him briefly. They were quite sure he said that the short devils had halted and Chinese armies were advancing from the north and east. The short devils were retreating toward Shanghai!

It was possible, they told each other. There were Chinese armies in Nanjing and Zhenjiang under capable commanders. And if those armies were advancing, then there was no reason for the villagers to hide. When the boy left in a hurry, the villagers concluded that he was on his way to rejoin his unit.

They returned to the village with good news. A delegation was hastily assembled to welcome the Chinese troops and to offer them food and assistance. A half dozen elders were selected to carry the message and they hurried across a field, over a dike and down several winding paths to the main road. They were followed by a boy, a grandson of one of the men, who wanted to see the Chinese soldiers.

When the delegation arrived at the road there was no sign of an army approaching from the north. So they waited. After half an hour they saw a long double line of men stretching all the way to the horizon, walking behind a column of trucks and cars and motorcycles approaching them not from the north but from the south. One of the elders said, 'This is impossible. This cannot be happening.' Those were his last words.

In the village people stood together waiting for the elders to return. Then they heard distant gunfire. A few minutes later the boy returned alone, crying and out of breath. There was no Chinese army, he screamed. There were only the short devils, thousands and thousands of them. The elders were all dead. The boy had seen the short devils order them to kneel in the road, and then stab them with long knives and run them over with their trucks. Now the short devils were searching everywhere. They were spreading out across the fields and would be in the village within minutes.

The wives and children of the murdered elders cried out. Some tried to break away and run to the road but were restrained. The important thing now was to save the living.

It was too late to try to run away. One of the older women suggested a plan. Since the Japanese soldiers always looked first for the young girls, they were in the greatest danger, she said. They had to be hidden quickly. The villagers decided to conceal them in the stacks of rice straw around the village.

Everyone else would hide in their homes until the danger passed.

Bundled in extra layers of clothing, all the young village girls were quickly buried inside the haystacks. The youngest girls were placed beside older sisters in the haystacks – two or three of them together – so they could be calmed and kept quiet if they became frightened. The girls were told not to move or make a sound and most important not to come out until their parents returned to uncover them. In only a few minutes, more than fifty girls were buried in the haystacks. The debris that might indicate the stacks had been disturbed was carefully picked up or swept aside. When they were convinced their meticulous deception could not be detected, the villagers scattered to their homes, blocked the doors and huddled under their tables and beds or crouched in corners, clinging together in terror waiting for the short devils to pass them by.

Minutes later they heard the first voices outside shouting in a language they did not understand. A dog barked. There was the sharp report of a rifle and the barking stopped. Then there were more shouts mixed with sudden bursts of laughter. Soldiers entered dwellings, kicked the doors open, turned over tables and pots, broke water jars. A group of soldiers found several large urns of rice in one home. They removed the covers and took turns urinating in the urns. In other homes the soldiers paused long enough to lower their trousers and defecate. Inside their homes, the villagers huddled together in terror and waited for death to find them. Many kept their eyes closed tightly and covered themselves with blankets as if this might in some way ward off the short devils or hasten their departure. The soldiers found them and ripped the covers away and laughed at them, imitated their terrified expressions and then laughed even louder. The frightened villagers whimpered and squealed and clung desperately to each other. The soldiers punched them and jabbed them with their rifles and then kicked them and spit on them. The villagers made no sound except for the chattering of their teeth.

A soldier found a small boy under a large iron wok inside one home. He picked up the boy and carried him to the other soldiers and asked him several questions. The boy stared at them wide-eyed. He understood nothing they said. The soldiers made hand motions, and spoke slowly, scrunching up their faces and speaking in a soft soprano voice like a young girl. The boy said nothing. Suddenly, a soldier noticed something unusual. He carefully plucked several strands of rice straw from the boy's hair and then examined his jacket and shoes, where he found more straw. He said something to the others excitedly, and then pointed to the nearby haystacks. The soldiers laughed again as if they'd stumbled onto the obvious solution to a riddle. They walked to the nearest haystacks. A soldier plunged his arm into the hay, felt around and pulled out nothing but a fistful of straw. He gave his comrades a melodramatic look of disappointment. He walked partway around the haystack and repeated his action. This time he jerked his hand out suddenly, jumped back several feet and gasped, 'Ahhhh!' He examined his fingers and then glared at the haystack while speaking to himself in low angry tones. He shouted at the haystack as if it were a living thing. He listened for a response. Silence. He shouted out an order at the haystack and the unusual shifting tone of his voice indicated that he intended to tease as well as to threaten. Again there followed only a hollow echo of his own words. Then he affixed a bayonet to the end of his rifle and prodded a haystack with it. He found nothing. He shook his head in disgust. Then, impatiently, he stepped to another and jabbed the bayonet in again and again, more forcefully each time. There was no sound, no movement, no resistance to the long pointed blade. But after jabbing a fourth haystack he saw something unusual, examined his bayonet closely and held it out for the others to see. There was a vermilion smear along the entire length of blade. He turned and shouted at the haystack. Again silence. Then he shouldered his rifle, aimed it and fired it into the haystack. There was still no movement. A soldier emerged from a house carrying a can of kerosene. The other soldiers saw him and gave a shout of approval. He sprinkled the kerosene on all of the haystacks and then struck matches and ignited the hay. The kerosene-fed fires blossomed quickly. There was still no sound or movement from the haystacks. After staring at the blazing mounds for several minutes, the soldiers moved on.

A short time later, some of the bolder villagers peered outside. When they were sure it was safe they ran from house to house and shouted to the others that the short devils were gone. Then they saw the smoke and the glowing embers where the haystacks had been. Some of the women screamed the names of their daughters and some fainted and fell to the ground. Others raced to what remained of the haystacks and with pitchforks and shovels and bare hands pawed madly through them. They blistered and burned their hands and arms but didn't feel the pain. A fetid greasy smoke hung in the cold night air and engulfed the fields and the distraught villagers. They breathed the smoke and choked on it and cried and kept calling out the names of the girls and continued digging. Their faces reddened and then blackened and their hair singed and crackled as they dug frantically through the glowing pyres.

The fields were a wasteland of ashes and the charred cadavers of their daughters and sisters. In some places they found a tangle of bones and the blackened flesh of the little girls who had clung to each other as the fires consumed them. Mothers and fathers tried to pick up what remained of the bodies, but it fell apart in their hands like overcooked meat.

They sifted through the debris again and again that night and searched along the dikes and in the fields crying and shouting the names of the girls, hoping to find some little girl who might have escaped. But the round-faced little girls of Lishi were all gone. None escaped.

The remains of the girls were gathered the next day and buried in a common grave on a slight rise overlooking Mirror Lake. The bodies of the murdered elders were also recovered and buried near the girls. The past and future of the village all seemed to have died on the same day.

On that day the village of Lishi became another open wound on the ravaged body of China. In the lives of the villagers who survived the short devils that day there would be an emptiness, an ache, that would, as long as they lived, remind them of their loss.

When my mother was born in the spring of 1941, the burning of the little girls in the haystacks was still a fresh wound. Her parents named her Yingdi. Ying means 'hero' and 'di' indicated that they hoped she might soon be joined by a brother. A cousin born six months later was also a girl. She was named Lingdi, or 'lead to a brother.' There had been an older child in Lingdi's family – a girl – but she was killed in the burning haystacks by the short devils. In the next years both families were blessed with sons and the two girls survived to greet and help raise and serve their younger brothers.

Four years after the defeat of the Japanese, the Communist armies liberated China from the Nationalists. When the liberators passed down the road near Lishi, Yingdi and Lingdi dressed in their finest clothes and danced and sang with other village children and threw flowers at the feet of the soldiers. Later they joined the Young Pioneers and became leaders in the Communist youth movement. In their late teens the girls became members of the Communist Party and prominent pillars in the local red brigade.

In 1960, two years after the start of the Great Leap Forward, the two girls, aged nineteen, left the village, which was suffering from a severe and prolonged famine. In those years many villagers starved to death. Others whose families had survived in Lishi for hundreds of years departed. There was no food, they pointed out, and they chose to beg on the roads or in the streets of Shanghai or Nanjing and survive on handouts rather than to sit and quietly starve to death in the village. Those who left for the cities, like those who fled to Nanjing in 1937, never returned.

Yingdi and Lingdi succeeded in getting train passes and traveled thousands of kilometers away to Shenyang, where they found work in a textile factory. They labored there for three years. Each month they mailed home all but a small portion of their earnings. They ate only one meal each day – a breakfast consisting of thin rice soup. After work they were too hungry and exhausted to do anything but return to their dormitory room and sleep. But the girls gladly made this sacrifice for their families and for the village. They knew that their absence from Lishi was a blessing to the villagers since there were fewer mouths to feed and the money they sent home could be used to buy food on the black market.

They returned to the village in the late spring of 1962 and

both of them married. Yingdi, my mother, married a young man from the village who was trained as a veterinarian. She worked in the fields as a peasant on the collective farm that had been established after liberation. Lingdi, my aunt, married a man from Shanghai who had been a capitalist before liberation. He had been sent by the Communist Party to our village for reeducation through labor in the fields. His family, two generations earlier, had lived in Lishi. He was accustomed to a soft life in the city and was unhappy in our village. He was never a good worker. But the villagers accepted him because his roots were in Lishi. They believed that marriage to Lingdi would help enlighten him, that he would see the necessity and honor of common labor and the wisdom of the dictates of the Party. They thought that in time he would respect the village as Lingdi did and would then carry his own weight.

I was born on December 6, 1963. My younger brother was born in 1965 and my sister in 1968. Lingdi and her husband had no children.

Four years after she had married him, Lingdi's husband announced that he wanted a divorce. A divorce was difficult to obtain in China in those days unless one was a high-ranking Party cadre. A serious complaint was required before officials granted any divorce. But Lingdi's husband, who wanted to return to Shanghai and did not want to take his illiterate peasant wife with him, had just such a complaint.

To all outward appearances, Lingdi was a perfect wife. She was a hard worker and a good cook and always kept her small home clean. She was a leader in community activities. Her only outward shortcoming was that she was childless, a source of deep unhappiness for her. But the inability to bear a child was not considered an acceptable reason for a divorce.

When Lingdi's husband appeared before officials to apply for a divorce he was asked the reason for his petition. 'My wife is not totally a woman,' he said.

A moment of silence followed his blunt allegation. The officials were not sure what to make of his words. One of them asked, 'What do you mean your wife is not totally a woman?'

'I mean she is also a man,' he said. 'And she cannot serve me as a wife and cannot provide me with children. She is neither a woman nor a man. She is both. And I can no longer share a bed with her.'

The officials were stunned and scandalized by this revelation. During the next few hours the story spread quickly. Soon everyone whispered about it, some blushed at the accusation, some shook their heads in disbelief or laughed out loud. Lingdi became an object of curious attention. When she was told of her husband's complaint she went inside her house, closed the door and stayed there for several days, too ashamed to venture into the fields or the market or to attend Party rallies.

Within days a pair of solemn Party officials called at her home to notify her officially of her husband's petition. 'These are serious charges,' they advised her. Lingdi was silent as they described, as delicately as possible, the details of her husband's petition.

She understood little of the things that the two men told her. But she knew enough to be humiliated as she listened to their words. When asked if what her husband said was true, she said nothing.

The officials realized that she would not respond to their questions directly. They said there was a way to demonstrate that her husband's charges were not true. She could visit a physician in Danyang – a female physician, they emphasized – for a physical examination. She had the right, of course, to refuse. But if she refused, she was told, the officials could only assume that her husband's charge was true, and in that case the divorce would be granted.

Ashamed as well as frightened, she stayed in Lishi. Six weeks later, Lingdi's husband was granted his divorce. He departed immediately for Shanghai. We never heard of him again.

In the next years, Lingdi's life was particularly dismal. Villagers whispered and joked about her. Many of them avoided associating with her in any way. Occasionally, when Lingdi was working in her garden or in the common fields on the collective, some of the children threw stones at her when her back was turned, called her names, and ran away. She was suddenly an outcast in the village where her family had lived for centuries and where she had always been a model daughter, Party member, worker and wife.

She never again visited the community bath. She hid her body from the prying eyes of other women. She no longer went swimming with the other village women in Mirror Lake. She became increasingly isolated.

Yet she struggled to remain a perfect Party member. Invariably she was the first to arrive at Party meetings and the last to leave. She worked hard in the fields. Yet fewer and fewer villagers openly expressed praise or admiration for her as they had in the past.

As I grew older, I became aware that Lingdi paid lots of attention to me. She gave me gifts – new shoes and pencils, paper, ink and brushes for school. I had never owned real leather shoes until Lingdi gave me a pair. My favourite gifts were always the children's storybooks she bought for me.

Shortly after the birth of my younger sister, Lingdi visited my mother. She was lonely, she confessed, and her personal life was empty. She wanted a child. 'I would like you to give me Meihong to be my daughter,' she said. She could provide for me better than my parents could, she said. She also pointed out that she needed someone to care for her and provide for her in her old age.

My mother, surprised by the request, promised to discuss it with my father. She said she understood Lingdi's feelings. Everyone needed a child to look after them in their later years. At first my father said he would never give away any of his children. My mother wept out of pity for Lingdi and reminded him of her kindness and her constant loneliness. Finally, my father agreed that if Lingdi would take my younger sister, then perhaps they might come to an agreement.

When Lingdi was offered my sister, she said no. She said she wanted only me. My father refused. So there was nothing more to talk about on the subject. Throughout the years, however, Lingdi treated me as her daughter, providing me with school supplies, books and clothing. Many times she walked me to school and then in the evening walked me home again. On rainy days she held an umbrella over me on the way to school. On holidays she bought special gifts for me. I enjoyed her attention and I responded to it. She took me to Party meetings and often cooked my favorite dishes for me in her home.

My mother had three children to care for and Lingdi's attention to me helped ease her burdens. Sometimes, however, she was uncomfortable with Lingdi's special treatment of me. She asked her several times not to give me so many things. I was being spoiled, she feared, and my younger brother and sister were becoming jealous. Again, my mother offered my sister to Lingdi to raise as her own child. But again Lingdi refused. She only wanted me, she said.

During the Great Proletarian Cultural Revolution, which began in 1966, there was heightened political activity throughout China. Gradually, people everywhere in the nation were swept up in fervent revolutionary rapture. At night there were torchlight parades and rallies and denunciations of revisionists, rightists, capitalist roaders and landlords. Traveling groups of dramatists, dancers, singers and students stopped in the village to perform or harangue or encourage us to be ever more red. Huge banners glorifying Chairman Mao and other leaders decorated the villages. On weekends, children were organized to scour the surrounding area in search of landlords plotting to undermine and overturn the revolution. It was an exciting time to be a child as we formed our own platoons to hunt down the duplicitous monsters in our midst.

Then a troubling series of incidents began. Just as the posters appeared praising Mao and the revolution, counterrevolutionary graffiti appeared in the villages. Some of it was simple: a picture of Chairman Mao or Comrade Jiang Qing, his wife, had an X across it, as if they were executed criminals. Several smaller posters appeared later stating simply, 'Down with Mao. Down with Jiang Qing. Down with the Party.'

The source of these counterrevolutionary signs was a mystery. Mass meetings were held to show the defaced banners and graffiti, and to denounce those responsible.

No one was above suspicion – not even a respected teacher. At this time, one of the girls in my school had difficulty learning to write Chinese characters. We were learning the characters for 'Chairman Mao.' The two characters for 'Chairman' are difficult to make and she always wrote the second one incorrectly. The teacher corrected her writing by putting an X through the incorrect character and then writing the correct one beside it. The next day the teacher was sent into the fields to work as a peasant and was replaced by someone more politically astute.

The anti-Mao graffiti continued. Chairman Mao's names appeared on a wall with a question mark following it. Meetings were called at the school, and we were told that this was a most serious crime. We were asked individually if we had written the counterrevolutionary slogans, or if we knew who might have done this. We were admonished to watch each other, to report any suspicious statements or actions of our classmates and our family.

We attended political rallies each day at school. Regular classes were suspended and political struggle became our obsession. We sang – or rather we shouted – revolutionary songs and denunciations of rightists. Yet the counterrevolutionary graffiti continued. And whenever it appeared all of the students were once again marched outside to examine the signs and slogans and try to identify the handwriting.

Red Guards and Party cadres collected samples of the writing of everyone in the village and studied it for telltale signs of the culprit. But they could not find the guilty party. Teachers were asked to guess who was doing the writing and the individuals named were detained and grilled for hours. Yet nothing seemed to discourage the clever counterrevolutionary.

Then late one night we were awakened by someone pounding on the door of our home. A Party cadre had come to summon my mother to an emergency meeting at brigade headquarters. My mother was chief of the local brigade. My brother and I were so anxious about the unusual midnight caller that we couldn't go back to sleep. We were sure the Americans or the Russians had invaded China and that soon we would be hunting down enemy spies trying to infiltrate our village.

My mother returned several hours later. I listened from my bed as she whispered nervously to my father. She was obviously very upset. I asked what had happened. She refused to tell me. She said only that there would be no school that day and in the morning there was to be a public rally. Everyone in the three villages of the brigade was required to attend.

The rally was held in the large open area where crops were stored and where general Party gatherings were convened. It began at 8 A.M. and everyone in the brigade was in attendance, even infants carried by their parents. Villagers stood around in clusters speaking in low tones or sat on the ground and waited and talked about the mysterious news that was about to be revealed to them. A somber Party official finally appeared, mounted the small wooden stage that stood at one end of the square and announced that the meeting was postponed for one half hour. Later he announced a second postponement and then a third and a fourth. People grew increasingly uneasy and impatient. Each time the official came onto the stage he was very serious. I had seen this demeanor and heard this tone of voice in the past when someone was to be executed or punished severely for counterrevolutionary activities.

Then the Local Party secretary came to the stage. She announced that the criminal responsible for the anti-Chairman Mao graffiti had been identified. This was a serious crime, she screeched through a large megaphone, and the arrest of the criminal represented a great victory for the revolution. She confessed that the Party cadres and Red Guards had never guessed how such a class enemy could be concealed so discreetly in our midst.

Then she shouted out triumphantly, 'The class enemy is – Xu Lingdi! Down with Xu Lingdi! Down with Xu Lingdi!'

There was a moment of silence and a loud gasp of astonishment from the crowd – as if they'd just witnessed some supernatural phenomenon. But within moments everyone joined in the chant 'Down with Xu Lingdi! Down with Xu Lingdi!' which became louder each time it was repeated.

The words, the loud hateful chanting, hit me like fists. I became momentarily dizzy and leaned against my father. I didn't understand. I stood there stunned by the sound of her name. I had never heard her say anything disparaging about the Party or Chairman Mao. On the contrary, she was the model Party member and revolutionary, the model peasant. My red aunt was a counterrevolutionary and an agent of the rightists? She had always been so kind and so generous. Maybe that was why, I thought! She had been attempting to recruit me into the ranks of the counterrevolutionaries all along.

The Party secretary waved to stop the chanting. Then she said, 'Xu Lingdi has admitted her crime. She has confessed! Confessed! And she will be punished severely.'

During the next days details of the arrest and confession spread through the village. From the moment the first graffiti appeared, officials began detaining and interrogating suspects. Some were held in custody for several days. The police initially pursued the most obvious suspects – a group identified as hooligans and troublemakers. These were young men who were seldom serious at rallies, flirted with the girls when they should have been paying attention to speakers, were lax in their fieldwork and did poorly in school. Most of them dressed in a defiantly unrevolutionary style and some even curled their hair. The Party had, in response to this, decreed that no young man who curled his hair could become a member of the Communist Youth League. But the troublemakers laughed at that and told people that they were glad about the policy because they never wanted to join the League anyway. Eventually a dozen hooligans were rounded up, held in the local jail and interrogated over the course of a week. But none of them broke down and confessed, even when they were beaten.

The police were absolutely convinced that this group was guilty of at least some of the crimes and so decided to charge three of the hooligans, including Lingdi's younger brother, with writing and posting the graffiti and to punish them as a warning to the other criminals. The Party and police had no evidence against the young men but they did have their suspicions, which, they concluded, were as good as evidence.

During the first day of the secret trial of the boys, Lingdi appeared before the Party secretary and said that she was the real criminal. The Party secretary refused to believe her. She said she believed that Lingdi, out of a misplaced patriotic desire to save the village from denunciation by higher Party officials, was willing to take the responsibility for the crimes. It was a selfless gesture, she said, but it would not work. The authorities wanted the real criminal. Lingdi was told to return home and to stop being a nuisance by confessing to crimes she could not possibly have committed.

Lingdi persisted, nevertheless. She returned the following day and confessed again and was once more reprimanded and sent home. She returned another time with newspapers from which the pictures of Chairman Mao had been cut. She said that she had cut out the pictures and pasted them up and then x'd them out.

When the Party secretary examined the newspapers she was temporarily dumbstruck. What Lingdi said was true! After several minutes she asked how Lingdi, of all people, could do this? Lingdi only said that she was confessing because she felt that the young innocent men – including her brother – being tried for her crimes should be released. She said her mother's heart was broken by the mistreatment of her son. He was suffering for Lingdi's crimes. Lingdi was placed in a jail cell and the trial of the young men was suspended. They were sternly warned about their shocking unsocialist behavior and sent home.

Several weeks after the meeting announcing the capture and confession of Lingdi another brigade rally was held. This time, the village square was surrounded by red flags the size of bedsheets and by huge posters denouncing the crimes of Lingdi and all other enemies of the revolution. Posters proclaimed in large characters that if she was not severely punished, 'the anger of the people will not cease.' One sign I remember particularly proclaimed: 'Xu Lingdi is a traitor! Death to Xu Lingdi!'

At the start of the rally the Party secretary and other cadres pushed Lingdi onto the stage. She was wearing a tall pointed dunce's cap and from her neck hung a placard with her name x'd out and a description of her crimes. She stumbled when she walked. She was barefoot. Her hands were bound tightly behind her at the wrists and elbows. She was bent forward at an awkward angle with her bound arms pulled up high by two women who stood behind her. She stared blankly at the ground. Whenever she raised her head just a bit, I could see that the left side of her face was swollen and bruised and her eye was completely shut. Her lips also were enlarged and cracked. She'd lost weight, and her clothes hung loosely on her body. One after another the Party cadres stepped forward, denounced her, and then slapped her face. Each time they slapped her, the crowd cheered.

Then the sentence was read: Xu Lingdi was stripped of her Party membership and sentenced to ten years in prison. She was told she was lucky to escape the death penalty.

Lingdi's mother, my mother's aunt, stood in the front row of the rally surrounded by a dozen Red Guards. She was a hardworking widow who had always worried about her childless, divorced daughter. During the denunciations and the slapping of Lingdi she became ill. She fainted and fell to the ground. She was revived and the Party cadre screamed from the stage for her to remain standing. When she tried to look away, one of the Red Guards held her by the ears and kept her facing the stage. They demanded that she denounce her daughter. In a whisper she said what they told her to say: 'Down with Xu Lingdi! Long live Chairman Mao!' Then she fainted again and was once more propped up by Red Guards, who continued to berate her, condemning her for fainting, shrieking that she was betraying her sympathy for a criminal. A Red Guard stepped to the stage and shouted that Lingdi's mother was 'revisionist trash' and should be punished for it.

Finally Lingdi was shoved from the stage. Red Guards dragged her mother home and continued to denounce her for showing sympathy for her traitorous daughter. The next day they checked to see that she was at work in the fields beside her hooligan son, who, several days after Lingdi's arrest, was severely beaten and had his head shaved by the Red Guards. Even though he was not sent to prison, everyone agreed that he should not escape punishment.

I became the leader of the Young Pioneers in school. Each day the students read aloud short articles about things that were happening in the country. The stories always concluded with warnings about the enemies among us and then gave instructions on how to capture rightists and make them confess.

I wrote articles about Lingdi and read them aloud in class. I asserted that I hated her and that all students should hate her. I had copied the articles about other accused criminals from the Party newspaper and simply changed the names. That was accepted as scholarship for the young during the Cultural Revolution. We were instructed to copy official Party publications and put our names on them and were praised for our words. Several students could write word for word the same essay, and all receive the highest grade. The teachers dared not give anything less than an A for such work, or risk their career and their lives. Those students who didn't have access to the newspapers had difficulty putting together sufficiently colorful denunciations. My father, however, received *The People's Daily* at his office and I had no such problems.

In one article I wrote that after the death of Lin Biao I saw Lingdi 'cry as hard as she would as if her own mother had died.' At that time, Lin Biao, formerly a hero of the revolution, was considered an archtraitor to Chairman Mao. I copied the denunciation from the description of another woman in *The People's Daily* and inserted Lingdi's name in it. The teachers, as expected, lauded my plagiarism. But my mother was unhappy with the piece. She asked me to stop writing denunciations of Lingdi. 'Your aunt is guilty of no crime,' she said. 'None!'

I was nine years old and could not comprehend what I heard. Until that moment I thought of my mother as a faithful and spotless revolutionary. Suddenly, I suspected my mother was a covert counterrevolutionary, along with my formerly red aunt. It seemed obvious. They had been so close over the years. They had probably worked together to discredit Chairman Mao.

I became more suspicious when I overheard conversations between my parents late at night, when they thought I was asleep. In public during the day my mother was a proper revolutionary. She was head of the Party's village committee and denounced Lingdi in meetings, but with little genuine enthusiasm, I felt. At night, with my father, I heard her say sympathetic things about my aunt. I knew my mother never lied and what I heard her say about the disposition of Lingdi's case confused me. She said she knew that Lingdi was innocent. She said that it was bored teenage troublemakers who were responsible for all the anti-Mao mischief and that Lingdi took the blame for them. The boys never realized the seriousness and the consequences of what they did. They thought it was fun to stir up all the excitement about counterrevolutionary plots. Lingdi's brother had tearfully told her this, she revealed, and had asked her what he should do. She told him to say nothing more about it, ever. Nothing could be done to help Lingdi now, she said. It was too late. The Party secretary who had turned in Lingdi had become a local hero. She was praised by other Party officials and lauded at public rallies. To contradict Lingdi's tale would only undo the reputation of the Party secretary and make her lose face. That would bring more problems and other accusations. My mother was deeply troubled by the episode and by the impossibility of helping her cousin without hurting others.

She considered visiting Lingdi in prison. My parents discussed what repercussions such a visit might have on their status in the village. My father was against it. But my mother brought it up again and again and pondered the implications of such an action. In the end, she did not make the visit.

Despite what I'd heard my mother say, I remained the leading student in my school in denouncing Lingdi. Not to do so would bring suspicion on myself, I felt. But I was unsuccessful. After one of my more colorful denunciations another girl asked if we should not be suspicious of those who were related to this traitor. We should open our eyes and look around, she suggested, and see who these people are. We should ask if these people might not try to avoid suspicion, despite the fact that they were infected with counterrevolutionary ideas, through their own criticism of Lingdi. I ignored what she said and pretended I didn't understand. But I was terrified by this unexpected turn in the classroom discussions. The other students looked at me differently after that, I felt.

Following the death of Mao and the fall of Jiang Qing and three of her cohorts – the Gang of Four – in the autumn of 1976, when I was twelve years old, thousands of political prisoners appealed to the government and were released. But Lingdi did not immediately appeal. She remained in prison for six years – until 1978. She had been sent to the Li Yang labor camp, about a hundred fifty kilometers from our village, and worked in a factory there making gloves. I heard later that when they were about to set her free she asked to be allowed to remain. 'I have no home but this one,' she told the camp supervisor. If she returned home it would be a shame for her elderly mother, her brother and her cousins to have her nearby. She explained that she had been an outcast in the village long before she was sentenced to the camp. She would suffer more if she was sent home than if she stayed.

The supervisor was sympathetic. But he explained that there was no policy for letting people stay in the camp who had served their time. She must return to her former work unit. The state, which had sentenced her to the camp, required that she go home.

When she came home, I saw she had changed. She was thin and pale, there were streaks of gray in her hair and she stooped slightly when she walked.

As she feared, there was little forgiveness for her in Lishi. She moved into a small dwelling beside the rice paddies. In her spare time she tended her own garden. She visited her mother and cooked for her. My mother visited her, often, late at night. They sat at a table in the dark and reminisced and drank tea. My mother preferred that her visits be kept a secret and we didn't talk about it to others. Why go looking for trouble?

My aunt still liked me very much and often demonstrated it by approaching me when I was nearby and waving or motioning to me to come to her. But I pretended that I didn't see her. I kept my distance. I was warned at school that she had a political disease, and the germs were dormant but still deadly. Anyone close to her might catch the disease and be infected by it. Like almost everyone else in the village, I suspected her and I feared her.

In 1981, I was one of twelve girls selected nationwide to attend the People's Liberation Army (PLA) Institute for International Relations in Nanjing. This meant I was to be inducted into the PLA just before classes began and upon graduation would be commissioned as an officer. All of the village was proud of me and celebrated. When Lingdi heard of my good fortune, she seemed more animated in her joy than anyone else in the village and asked my mother if she might give me a banquet before I left for the military academy. My mother said that the family and other friends had already taken up all of my spare time. Lingdi then suggested that she could buy me new clothing for school. My mother told her I would be wearing a uniform and had no use for new clothing.

Then late one evening as we were preparing for bed, there was a soft tapping on our door. It was Lingdi. She said she had a gift for me, and she pressed a small red envelope into my hand and left as quietly as she had come. I opened the envelope as my father and mother looked on. It contained three hundred yuan. On special celebrations, family members and relatives in the village typically gave a five-yuan gift, which was considered generous given the fact that an average salary in the village was about twenty yuan per month. Lingdi's gift was incredible – a huge amount of money for that time. I, as a young girl, was delighted even at holding this much in my hand. My mother, however, insisted that I could not keep it. So we walked to my aunt's house to return the money. My mother knocked softly on the door and my aunt answered without lighting a lamp. The two cousins, more like sisters, whispered to each other in the dark as I stood beside my mother. They spoke softly and rapidly, sometimes their voices breaking. My aunt didn't understand why I could not keep the money. It was her life's savings, she said. She had no use for it herself. She asked if she could buy me a watch instead. My mother said she had already given me a good watch, a Zhong Shan brand, Chinese made, that cost twenty-five yuan, very expensive. Lingdi begged my mother to let me keep the money. My mother pushed it back again and said I could not accept it. Finally, I heard my aunt's voice break and she started to cry. 'I have always cherished this little girl. I wanted her since the day she was born. She is like my daughter, my only child. I am as proud as you are. I just want to contribute something to make her life easier – easier than my life. If you refuse me this, you are totally rejecting me and you are just like everyone else in this village. I will be deeply wounded.'

I listened to her crying in the dark. My mother stood there, without responding, and I watched her hands gently caress Lingdi's hair. In the starlight I saw the shimmer of tears on my mother's face. And then I heard her say, 'All right. She can keep it.'

Lingdi immediately embraced me and held my hands in hers. As my mother and I walked back to our house my mother told me, 'Never forget your auntie, Meihong. Never.' I could tell without looking at her that she was crying as she said this. 'Remember what you saw tonight. Lingdi has always treated you as her own daughter. Always. No matter what is said about her, she is a good woman. A *good* woman – remember that!'

Three years later, during my junior year at the military academy I received a letter from my mother telling me that Lingdi was about to be married. When I returned home for the spring festival, I learned what had happened.

Lingdi was over forty-three years old at the time. She had confided to my mother a year earlier that she wanted to be married, but there were no suitors. There was a blind man in our village, and he could find no wife. He was very lonely. My aunt let my mother know that she would marry him. My mother agreed to be the go-between and went to this man and his family. But the family felt insulted. 'How dare you?' they said. 'She is not even a woman! How can she marry our son?'

Lingdi's mother also opposed the idea. 'You no longer need a man in your life,' she said. 'You are too old now. Forget it. You have no need for that kind of trouble again.'

One year later – in 1984 – however, a suitor appeared. He was an older man – fifteen years older than Lingdi – who had been born and raised in our village, and then had moved to and worked in Shanghai. He had four daughters who were married and lived with their husbands. His wife had died and left him alone. He wanted a wife from his home village and so he returned to Lishi to find one.

Lingdi was told of the man and she asked to be introduced to him. One afternoon he visited her. They talked all afternoon and into the evening. She prepared dinner for him and the two sat in chairs outside her house talking most of the night. They did not light the lamps when it became dark.

Then the man proposed that rather than return to the home

of his relatives, he stay the night with Lingdi in her house. This was unheard of in our village.

Lingdi, naturally, had fears about this. But it was not the censure of the villagers that gave her pause at this moment. She already had that. She still had doubts, however, about her own feminine nature. Her life had been little more than misfortune and tragedy. But she had strong feelings for this man now, powerful feelings she had never before felt, and she at last said yes, he could stay in her house that night.

The next morning, as always, the adults and children walked to the open market to buy vegetables and meat for the coming day. The man from Shanghai came to the market alone, and people caught glimpses of Lingdi cooking in her house. Had he abandoned her? Was he angry? Disappointed? What had happened? Everyone was curious. But the man made his purchases, said little and returned to her house. They were not seen again that day and that night.

On the following day, again, early in the morning, he walked to the market, bought a few items, and returned to Lingdi's home. Again, they were not seen for the rest of the day and night.

On the next day he walked to the market again. Then he came to our house. He told my mother that he and Lingdi discovered that they liked each other very much. (In the dialect of Lishi there is no word for love. In place of that word, the people use the words 'respect,' 'like,' and 'cherish.' A marriage takes place between a young man and woman who 'like' each other. As husband and wife they 'respect' each other. Children respect their elders, and parents 'cherish' their children. Words expressing stronger affections do not exist in our dialect. Some feelings, we believe, are too profound for words.) 'Thank you for introducing me to her,' he said. 'We plan to marry next month and we would like you to be the witness at our wedding.'

My mother was surprised and delighted. 'Good,' was all she could say. 'Good.' She smiled broadly when she spoke.

'Something else,' he said.

'What is it?' my mother asked.

'About her ex-husband and the stories he told. About the

27

divorce. You know the story,' he said.

'Yes, I heard the story,' my mother admitted, and avoided looking into his eyes.

'Well, I want you to know that man was a lying bastard. He made up that story. And Lingdi has suffered for nearly twenty years because of it. Lingdi is a woman. All woman. More than that. She is a perfect woman.'

In the next days, Lingdi's fiancé gave her a wedding ring. Few people in the village at that time could afford one. They took the train to Shanghai one morning and returned three days later with new clothes and jewelry.

I attended Lingdi's wedding. It was the first time I'd seen her in more than two years. She was smiling and laughing like a girl again. I noticed right away that she walked straight and held her head high. She was happier than I had ever seen her before.

After their honeymoon in Shanghai, Lingdi and her husband came back to the village to live there permanently. Her husband worked in Lingdi's garden with her and in the fields beside her, like a peasant. In the summer, village women customarily carried an umbrella to protect their skin from the sun. He always carried Lingdi's umbrella for her and walked beside her. Most shocking of all, they held hands when they walked in the countryside. Sometimes they even paused and Lingdi's husband kissed her on the hand or on the cheek. The other villagers were scandalized. They had never before seen this sort of brazen public behavior. Indeed, I had never before seen a man and woman embrace or hold hands or in any way publicly reveal romantic feelings in the village. I was utterly fascinated when I watched them.

Naturally, people whispered about them. There was something very different about these two. They made others uncomfortable and jealous.

In the autumn, they walked each night down the winding paths, along the shore of Mirror Lake and past the haystacks piled high in the fields. Now and then they paused and Lingdi told him things she remembered about life in the village. She told him about the time Japanese soldiers came to Lishi and about the little burned girls. One of the girls was her elder sister.

People who watched them couldn't understand why they never seemed to tire of each other's company and why they continued to behave the way they did. It was a mystery. They tried to explain it – but they couldn't.

TWO

Winter

Who fights for communism must be able to
fight and not to fight, to say the truth and not
say the truth, to render and to deny service, to
keep a promise and to break a promise, to go
into danger and to avoid danger, to be known
and to be unknown. Who fights for
communism has of all the virtues only one:
that he fights for communism.

— BERTOLT BRECHT

———◆———

The whisper of the guards slowly draws me from my warm memories back to the cold dreariness of the barracks room. I smile to myself as I retrace in my mind the road that led me to this place. I saw, now, it had been clearly lined with warning signs. For a long time I'd been on the way to this place without even realizing it.

I was never blind to the warnings. But instead of reacting to them in a way the military trained me to react, I dismissed them or disregarded them and behaved at times as if I'd forgotten everything I'd learned. In thrall at that time to unguarded and innocent romantic optimism, I behaved as if I'd earned an exemption from the iron realities of the world in which I'd always lived and operated. I was wrong.

On several occasions I noticed a car parked outside my dormitory at night, engine running, the occupants sitting stiffly inside, the glowing ends of their cigarettes flitting back and forth providing the only evidence that they were not mere mannequins. The vehicles had military license plates. I wondered what they were doing. Were they monitoring transmissions from listening devices inside a nearby residence or listening to tapped telephone conversations? Were they keeping a log of who entered and left a building? Or were they just young officers waiting for their girlfriends?

I began to receive disquieting telephone calls – the caller upon hearing my voice, hesitated for a moment, and then hung up without saying a word. Were they testing a new phone tap? I wondered. Did someone want to know if I was in my room? Why? Letters sent to me by friends took longer to arrive than they had in the past. One friend called to complain that I hadn't responded to her letters and I had to tell her that I hadn't received them. When I returned to my room after a brief walk I noticed a pen or a book I'd placed in a certain way on the chair or a desk had been moved, sometimes only slightly. A letter or note dropped in a drawer wasn't there a day later. Three times I returned to my room and found it unlocked when I remembered clearly locking it or I returned to find myself locked out when I knew I'd left it unlocked.

To an outsider any of these things might arouse suspicion. But there is no right to a private life in China and we grow up with expectations of being under observation. Only a fine line separates the daily aggravations of being under general surveillance from those indicating one is under specific surveillance. And although it is difficult to tell when you have been singled out for special attention, someone like me, trained as an intelligence officer, should always know the difference and take countermeasures.

Once I was targeted my reckless nonchalance must have made me seem a bumbler to those watching me. When I should have doubled back during a short walk to look for familiar faces, I chose not to. I acted as if I didn't notice or didn't care. What an easy assignment I became for those watching me. What a clear target. How they must have enjoyed their success.

I was changing at that time, and wasn't thinking enough about the possible dire consequences of those changes. I was becoming increasingly optimistic about my future – outside the PLA. I sensed new possibilities in my life and felt old fears simply evaporating. I behaved like a child whose eyes had just opened and who was seeing the world for the first time. I experienced a sense of wonder at new possibilities. It felt good to be alive again.

Looking at my reflection in the mirror one morning, I remember having the strange feeling that I truly was no longer Lieutenant Xu Meihong of the People's Liberation Army of China, a trained intelligence officer on her way up. I felt that woman had become a stranger. I was suddenly someone else. I felt again I was just Xu Meihong, the naive girl from the countryside who wanted desperately to live without restraints and to see all the wonders of the world. I felt free for that brief moment and the feeling of freedom made me swoon.

But my timing was all wrong. And in China, timing is often the difference between life and death. Sudden happiness can be a delusion and a snare. I tried to let go of the world that I'd always embraced without realizing that it would not let go of me.

My fate was sealed the moment I first saw the American walking so confidently with his long stride and his big grin down a hallway to his office. When we passed he said hello, and just for a second we looked into each other's eyes. In such a casual way, the last sad act of my career in the army and my life in China began.

Yet the roots of my trouble went deeper than that, back at least to my earliest days in the military academy when my childish ideals began to fracture. The American merely had the misfortune to be pulled into the world of my disillusionment and longing. In his humor and compassion, his loyalty, fearlessness and optimism, I saw a whole new world. In him and through him I found hope. For that we both paid a price.

ii

I was inducted into the People's Liberation Army in China in the summer of 1981, when I was seventeen. I became one of an elite group of twelve girls selected from throughout China to train and study in the most prestigious military intelligence school in the country – the People's Liberation Army (PLA) Institute for International Relations in Nanjing – which trained officers for the Second Bureau (intelligence) in the Army. The selection of the twelve of us at that time was an experiment. China's relations with the United States were expanding. There was a greater need for military intelligence officers proficient in

English who could work with our new American counterparts and friends. Those in charge of military intelligence gathering believed that in some cases specially trained young women might have the capability of making contacts and gathering intelligence from Americans when male operatives could not. So the experiment of training the twelve girls was undertaken in order to test this hypothesis. After the initial group was selected, and if the experiment looked promising, others were to follow in our path. We were the trailblazers.

We were called 'the Twelve Pandas,' indicating that we were the treasures of the Army. During the next four years we were trained intensively in military science, guerrilla and conventional warfare, survival techniques, weapons utilization, Communist Party doctrine, politics, intelligence and counterintelligence operations, formal and colloquial English, technical translation, and Western history and culture. We were reminded every day that we were being prepared to serve our country, our Party, our Army and our family and to bring honor to all of them.

Following graduation from the Institute, we were told that some from our group would be assigned to the office of the defense attaché in our foreign embassy. In that capacity they would be identified openly with the PLA and would serve in uniform.

Others, however, would become part of what the great military philosopher Sun Tzu called China's 'divine skein' – the corps of secret agents who are 'the treasure of a sovereign.' When we heard this, we all experienced a palpable shiver of pride – this was *our* mission.

An elite few would be sent abroad, we were told, to become 'bottom sinking fish' (*chen di yu*). They would put away their uniforms and their open identification with the military and dress and live as civilians. In some cases they might be given new names and identities. They might work for travel agencies, airlines or newspapers or become students or visiting scholars, entrepreneurs or business representatives. Like fish at the bottom of the sea, we would blend into the general population wherever we were sent. Some of the *chen di yu* would be called back within a few years. Then – having made contacts, established information networks and opened avenues of information and identified and cultivated 'friends' of China – they could once more don a uniform and work openly for the nation and the PLA.

One or two of this elite group, however, would be required to keep new identities all their lives, establishing contacts, marrying, taking foreign citizenship and starting families that would be useful in the next generation or even the one after that. These few were 'heroes without names' (*wu ming ying xiong*) because their true undertaking could never be revealed even to their families and friends in China in their lifetime. This sacrifice – leaving our mother country and old lives behind while still secretly embracing old loyalties – was, short of dying for the nation, the ultimate act of heroism.

After we were told of our probable future assignments, we were read a poem by the American poet Robert Frost. His lines, read to us in both English and Chinese, were these:

> *I shall be telling this with a sigh*
> *Somewhere ages and ages hence:*
> *Two roads diverged in the wood, and I—*
> *I took the one less traveled by,*
> *And that has made all the difference.*

Those words, we were informed, described us. The twelve of us had taken the road less traveled and it would make all the difference not only in our own lives but in the life and future of China. We were instructed to commit the poem to memory. I recited it to myself often after that. We never learned anything about the author other than his name and nationality. We believed the poem was specifically about patriots like us and sacrifices gladly made. For several years, I thought Robert Frost was one of the greatest Communist poets who ever lived.

We were assured, also, that no matter which assignment we were given, the thread connecting us with military intelligence would never be severed. It was unbreakable and absolute. No matter where we were sent and no matter what we did and no matter how many years passed, we would never be forgotten.

In time, we would all be heroes. That was why we had been selected and that was our destiny.

When this was revealed to us during our first day at the Institute, we were overwhelmed with patriotic pride. Later, in our barracks, we sat in a tight circle and held hands and talked with great excitement about our future, our journey together down the road less traveled, our assignments and our sacrifices, and about the inevitable day when we would be separated from each other, a few to go underground and never to be seen again by the others. We were intoxicated by the sudden realization that we were literally heroes in training. We sat together long into the night talking and crying, a band of sisters linked by a secret bond and a common destiny. We were young and red and we believed we could do anything.

iii

Then something went wrong. It happened gradually, over the course of several years. We discovered that the longer we served in the PLA, the more our patriotic passion cooled. When we witnessed firsthand the sham machinations and corruption of the gods of our youth – the Communist Party and the PLA – our crisis of faith commenced. We struggled to dismiss what we saw and heard. Sometimes this was easy, but more often it was not.

Naturally, we sought to conceal such sensations from our superiors as well as from each other. We found it nearly unbearable to believe that we might be dedicating – even sacrificing – our lives to a cause in which we no longer believed.

We found some solace and reassurance in the public recitation of officially sanctioned goals – we were heroes in training and heroes don't have doubts. Reflexively we continued to encourage each other. The twelve of us marched and worked and studied and showered and slept side by side by side. We kept diaries, placed them in unlocked drawers in desks in our room (where we were sure our commanding officers opened them and read them regularly) and then weekly went through the ritual of reading the diary entries aloud to the rest of the group. This was followed by self and group criticism. Our every thought became the property of the group. We were never alone.

We meticulously wrote down the proper thoughts, sang the old revolutionary songs when we marched each day, shouted slogans about red heroes and mouthed the requisite oaths of allegiance to our commanders and leaders. We clung desperately to the faith of our youth when we felt it fading and we feared that without it we were nothing.

iv

The overseas assignments the twelve of us expected were not made following graduation. The world had changed, we were told, and further preparation and training was required before we would be called upon to serve our motherland.

So in the summer of 1985 the Twelve Pandas went our separate ways. Some of us were sent to teach at other military institutes while others were given administrative positions within the military. Two were sent to listening posts.

I was assigned to remain at the Institute in Nanjing and became an aide to a brigadier general. In the spring of 1988 I married a former classmate. My husband served as an aide to General Zhang Zhen, president of the National Defense University (NDU) in Beijing. Assignment to the NDU was often a stepping-stone to a higher position within the PLA. Our wedding reception was arranged and hosted by General Zhou Erjun, a two-star general and the nephew of the late Premier Zhou Enlai.

My husband and I lived nine hundred kilometers apart and saw each other twice a year – during summer vacation and the spring festival. But we wrote to each other every day. The arrangement was not unusual for military families. Some classmates stationed in Tibet were unable to see their spouses for years at a time.

In the summer of 1988, in order to prepare for a special program being initiated at the Institute, I was selected to study for one year at the Center for Chinese and American Studies, a two-year-old educational joint venture of Nanjing University and the Johns Hopkins University in the United States. The Center was located within its own walled compound adjacent to Nanjing University. At the Center, intended to be a model of international cooperation, Chinese and American students and faculty lived together in a single large complex of classrooms, apartments, offices, assembly halls and dormitory rooms as well as a library and cafeteria. The Chinese students sent to the Center were customarily mid-career professionals – government bureaucrats, Party officials, junior university professors, military officers, journalists or administrators – who had been out of school several years and were chosen by their work units to have a chance to study English and other academic subjects (history, political science, economics, international relations) with a small group of distinguished visiting American instructors.

American students at the Center were almost all young graduate students from American universities, but also included a few American military officers who came to the Center to study Chinese language and history with selected Chinese instructors.

To the Chinese students at the Center, the facilities were luxurious. Each student room had a private telephone, a Western-style bathroom and hot water part of each day. We were unaccustomed to such convenience. But for the Americans, I learned, conditions in the Center were considered spartan.

In 1988 China restored its military commission system and awarded traditional ranks and insignia to its officers in place of the old Communist system under which no special insignia were displayed. Three female officers from my institute were commissioned. I was one of them. One month after I began my studies at the Center, I returned to my institute to attend a special commissioning ceremony during which I received my stars and became a first lieutenant in the PLA.

V

While I resided and studied in the Center I reported back to the Institute each weekend. I continued to supervise files and carried out other regular duties. I also worked closely with my commanding general, helping plan his trips to Beijing and Shanghai and assisting him in the composition of his briefings, reports and speeches.

At the Center, on the other hand, for the first time in my life I came into close contact with American students and professors who spoke freely about politics and cultural values, who joked openly about their own political leaders, who were unafraid of retribution, who had great hopes and few fears for either the present or the future. The first time one of the American professors told a disparagingly humorous story about one of America's Founding Fathers, we were stunned. We could not understand how he dared to say such things. After showing us a copy of a famous painting of General George Washington crossing the Delaware River, he asked us why we thought General Washington stood up in the boat. The students spent several minutes guessing. When they finally asked for the 'correct' answer, the professor told us, 'Because he knew if he sat down, someone would hand him an oar.' The students were dead silent. The professor said it was a joke. 'Maybe it just doesn't translate well,' he said, and continued on with his lecture.

The Americans were a curious group and we Chinese students talked constantly about them. Participating day after day in discussions at the Center, reading and socializing with these Americans, I felt something inside myself coming loose. I began to laugh at some of the absurdities of the world and the people around me and lost my sense of awe of people in power. I felt I was finding myself – my own identity. I began to think critically and independently. Like all Chinese students, I'd always mistaken memorization for education. I thought there was one truth and one way and one system that was best for all people and that I was part of it. Now nothing was as simple as it once was.

During the last week of November in 1988 three of my colleagues at the Center were summoned to the Institute. They were called individually before the commanding general and asked detailed questions about the Center. On the afternoon they returned, one of them, a close friend, came to my room and described the unusual inquiry. It was strange, she said. There were many questions about little things, details about what the Americans said in class and during meals, who talked to whom and when the lights were turned out and who was in the halls at night. She wasn't sure why any of this could possibly be important.

Before she returned to the Center, she said, the General called her aside and told her to tell me to come back to the Institute immediately. He asked her to deliver the message personally and not to phone it to me. No one else was to know of it. He further directed that I come to his living quarters rather than to his office. Within an hour of hearing his request, I was on my way to see him. I left the Center shortly before dark, walked several blocks and made sure I was not followed and then caught a bus for the first leg of the forty-five-kilometer journey to the Institute. I had to change buses three times and walk the final kilometer. I might have called for a military car to drive me to the Institute – one of my privileges as an officer. But I sensed that if the General didn't want his request telephoned to me he would also not want me to call the Institute to arrange a special ride.

Two hours later I arrived at the General's home.

vi

One of the General's passions was coffee. He'd acquired a taste for it, he explained to his aides, during one of his visits with a Chinese military delegation to the United States. After that he stocked his cupboard with several different

42

brands of coffee. He became a connoisseur of coffee – Kona was his favorite – and when his colleagues traveled abroad he asked them to bring back a local blend.

Following evening meals at home or at official banquets, when he was offered tea he placed his hand over his cup and ostentatiously ordered coffee – 'just like the Americans,' he said – black and unsweetened. It gave him a certain aura that he thoroughly enjoyed. The junior officers watched his after-dinner ritual and envied his cosmopolitan conceit.

When I arrived that night at the General's living quarters, he and his wife had just finished dinner. The General acted surprised upon answering my knock at the door – probably for the sake of his wife. He led me to his study and closed the door. We sat down to talk, in two overstuffed chairs facing each other across a small lacquered coffee table. The General's professional expertise was in Western military history and politics and the shelves of his study were lined with English-language books. The General was a rising star in the PLA and was expected to ascend, in time, to the very top ranks of the military. I felt privileged to serve under him at this point in his career.

His wife brought him a steaming cup of coffee. I accepted the glass of hot tea she offered me. She closed the door behind her upon leaving the room. The General placed his cup and saucer on the table between us, settled back in his chair, and began speaking in a hushed and unhurried voice just above a whisper.

He observed that it was a beautiful night. I agreed. He slowly sipped his coffee. He avoided my eyes. He stared out the window, lit a cigarette, inhaled deeply and watched the smoke waft into the air when he exhaled as if he thought there was something infinitely interesting in the patterns it produced. Not a word was spoken for a minute or two.

Then he asked several detailed questions – questions about the food at the Center, about the food servers and the domestic workers – several of them reported regularly to the National Security Police, he reminded me. I told him I was aware of that. One of our graduates worked in the office of the Ministry of State Security (MSS) near the Center and gathered detailed reports on everything that went on at the Center. The General nodded and said he was aware of that. He remembered the young man, followed his career and thought he would go far.

He asked about visitors, conversations in the hallways, strangers arriving late at night, military vehicles parked along the street outside. He wanted to know about the American students and teachers. What did I think of them? Were they friendly? Competent? Loud?

What about the Chinese at the Center? How were the Chinese instructors and administrators? Did they get along well with the Americans? Had they shown favoritism to any Chinese students? Why did I think so or not? He asked about the lectures the Americans gave. Did any Chinese students tape the lectures? Did they keep the tapes or give them to someone else? He wanted to know what questions the Chinese students asked, who stayed after class to speak to the instructors, who were the visitors from the United States, what movies were shown to the students? Then he turned to questions about me. What were my thoughts? Who did I think was unusual? Interesting? Funny? Friendly? Unfriendly? Suspicious? I chose my words carefully, spoke slowly and tried to read his expressions and gestures to see if they might provide a clue to the answers and comments he was seeking.

He rambled a bit and paid little attention to my answers, as if this was preliminary to something more pressing.

The questions stopped and he was quiet for a time. Then he cleared his throat and said, 'Let me tell you a story, Meihong. A true story.'

He spoke in a slow, steady cadence and a low tone, as if he were lecturing or testifying rather than carrying on a conversation – it was impersonal and deliberate and sounded rehearsed. He'd thought for some time about what he was going to tell me, I concluded.

'There is a student, a young woman, who was studying at the Shanghai Foreign Languages Institute. There is a professor there, an American, teaching English. He is in his forties. The woman is very beautiful, very young, very . . . what is the word? Vivacious. She is vivacious and lively and . . . romantic. Very romantic!

'The professor, of course, noticed her. How could he not notice her? She is so beautiful. They became friends. She was interested in everything he said and in every question he asked. They talked often after class. She gave him tours of Shanghai. They took a train to Suzhou and Hangzhou to see the sights. They went for long walks together, always talking and laughing. People saw them and watched them. She visited his apartment. They became close. She trusted him, completely. And why not? He was merely a language instructor, wasn't he? They became closer and began a relationship. This professor said that he had fallen in love with her. She responded that she too was in love. He made promises to her. Sweet words. He knew all the sweet words. He promised to bring her to America and to marry her. He promised her a good life in America, a family, a home of her own, new friends, new cars, dollars. A bright and sunny future.

'But as she prepared to leave with him, suddenly she disappeared. Just disappeared! And he quickly left China without her.'

The General paused to let his words sink in. He looked directly into my eyes and waited for my reaction. I didn't know what to say. Finally, weakly, I asked, 'What happened?'

'Oh, the State Security Police watched this. They discovered, just in time, that this "professor" was not in fact what he said he was. He was an agent. He worked for the Central Intelligence Agency. And the young woman, of course, was not just any young woman. She was well situated. She had relatives in high positions. He knew this from the start. He lied to her. He used her. There was no truth to anything he said.'

There was another pause as the General put out his cigarette and immediately lit another. He looked around the room lost in his thoughts, only momentarily making eye contact with me before gazing out the window again.

'She is from a good family,' he said again. 'Her father is a PLA general. He holds a very important position. She herself, of course, is not that important, but she has access through her father to certain information and influential people that might be of interest to others.

'But now she's gone. Her father and her family are discredited and under suspicion. Did she know what she was doing?

Did her family? No one can tell yet. No one knows where she is – even her father doesn't know her fate at this moment. Perhaps in time he will be told. But this will always be a stain on his record.'

'Will she stay alive?' I asked.

'I don't know,' the General said. 'It all depends. But I want to emphasize that this is a true story. At the moment, not many people know about it. But it is true. You should know that if the young woman in fact was merely misled by the agent and she did not tell him anything important, if they just had a romantic relationship, an affair, perhaps there is hope for her and she can be saved. She can be rehabilitated. Her connections and her family's reputation may help her.

'But that is only if she did not tell him anything or provide him with information and contacts. If she did none of these things, someday she may reappear. Her activities will be restricted and she will always be watched closely. She will no longer be a student. But she will stay alive.

'On the other hand, if she told him something – anything – or knowingly cooperated with him in any way, out of her unfortunate misguided sense of love, they will find out. And in that case, then . . . then she will be gone! She cannot be helped. She will never reappear.

'That's it,' the General concluded. 'A true story. I thought you should know.'

'Why?' I asked. 'Do I know this woman?'

'No,' the General said. 'No, you don't. But, you know, this sort of thing happens. Young women can be naive. There is a moment of weakness and something feels like romance and then suddenly it's too late. The damage is done. There is no going back. It's tragic and unfortunate. We do what we can to prevent this sort of thing. But now and then it happens.'

I was aware that the General had been called to Beijing the week before. I thought he must have heard the story there and had been asked to make a judgment on it.

'Why are you telling me this, General?' I asked.

Again, he said nothing for a moment and seemed lost in contemplation of the story. He turned to me as though I should know the answer to my own question. While I waited for his response, he put his cigarette to his lips, inhaled for an instant and nervously flicked the ashes into a small dish on the arm of his chair.

Then, in a low nervous voice, barely above a whisper, he said, 'I don't know what has happened to you.'

He paused for a moment after saying this. Then he continued: 'But it seems to me that something has gone wrong in your life. What is it, Meihong? What has gone wrong?'

'Nothing is wrong, General,' I answered instantly. 'What in the world could be wrong? Everything is fine.'

'You told no one your background, did you? You've not spoken to anyone about intelligence matters, have you? You're sure? Not a soul?'

I could not tell the General the truth. If our conversation was being recorded, the truth would destroy us. But I also believed there was no way to explain my life or my feelings or my dreams or my actions to him anymore. Even if I intimated to him what the truth was, I'd alarm him. So I lied, hoping my lie would cover and protect him, and, at the same time, assure him and whoever else might hear my words.

'I don't think so,' I replied. I pretended to be going back over my recent activities in my mind, pausing long enough to fake an effort to recollect conversations and contacts. Then I said, 'No. No, I'm sure I haven't.' He seemed unconvinced, so I tried to reassure him. 'No, I haven't done anything out of line, general.'

'Really?' he asked. Then he warned, 'Be very careful, Meihong. Very careful. These are dangerous times.'

I tried to lighten the tone of the conversation. 'General,' I said, 'you are too nervous. Maybe you drink too much coffee. I've made no mistakes and nothing is going to happen to me!'

He quickly changed the subject. We talked about the celebration of American Thanksgiving at the Center. The Americans imported a huge frozen turkey and prepared a traditional holiday feast for the Chinese students and faculty. Everyone had a wonderful time, I told him. We had also marked Halloween with a costume party and dance and were preparing for traditional American Christmas and New Year's Eve festivities.

'Do you ever study?' he asked with a smile.

We both laughed at his question. 'Very hard,' I assured him. 'Exams are in early January, before the Chinese New Year. Then we have our break and we return in mid-February.'

Our talk ended on that happy note – the holiday season was approaching. We would all return home for the celebration of Chinese New Year. The General stood and brought me my coat to signify that our meeting had ended.

There was still time to catch the last bus to the Center, the General said, glancing at his watch. He offered to accompany me on the walk to the bus stop. We both bundled up tightly in our winter coats and turned up the high fur collars.

We walked down a narrow path, through a grove of trees, along a wall and then out along the shore of a frozen pond and down to a walkway commonly used only by the grounds-keepers. The path skirted two sentry posts. As a result, no one saw us leaving the Institute. During our walk the General again expressed his concern about me.

Without looking at me, he said in a hushed voice muffled by his scarf, 'I need you to promise me that you will never betray me.'

'Never,' I answered instantly in a whisper, 'I am incapable of that.'

'I want you to tell me right now that you love your country. That you love the Army. That you will never ever betray either of them,' he said.

'Never!' I assured him.

We stood side by side at the bus stop until we saw the lights of the bus approaching in the distance. He then turned and placed his hands on my shoulders and gripped them firmly. We looked at each other without saying a word. I could see the worry and fear in his eyes. He slowly loosened his grip, dropped his arms to his sides, turned and walked away, and was swallowed up in the darkness.

Early the following morning I received a telephone call from one of the General's aides. It was a routine checkup call. He didn't seem to know of my meeting with the General on the previous night. I chatted with him for a while and then asked to speak with the General. 'The General is busy right now,' he said. 'But I'll tell him you asked, anyway. Goodbye.' He hung up without waiting for a response from me.

That afternoon I called my friend and former classmate at the nearby station of the Ministry of State Security a few blocks from the Center. Since my arrival at the Center I had met with him in his office several times and had spoken to him on the phone on a regular basis. But I had not heard from him since mid-November. I called his direct personal line. There was no answer. Then I called his office and his secretary said he was unavailable. When she asked for my name I responded that I'd call back later. I called two more times that afternoon. Both times she said he was out and she didn't know when he'd be back. I also called his personal number two more times and there was no answer.

After I concluded that I was not going to be able to reach him, I knew what I had to do. I locked my door and braced a chair against the handle. Then I went through my letters, notes and photographs and meticulously tore them to pieces and flushed them down the toilet. When I was finished I got down on my hands and knees and searched the floor to make sure that no telltale bits remained.

After that I took a short walk alone after dinner to get some fresh air. It was cold and overcast. It felt like rain would fall again soon. The sky was black. As I crossed the street half a block from the Center I saw a military vehicle virtually bristling with antennas parked at the curb. The headlights were off but the motor was running and I could see, by the dim interior lights, that three soldiers were sitting in the car. I looked closely to see if I recognized any of them. I didn't.

I felt uneasy about walking by the car again and returned to the Center by a different route.

vii

It was past midnight, the start of the second day of December 1988. A gentle mist of rain was falling. As the minutes passed, the air outside became tinseled with sleet that glistened like millions of tiny pearls. The sleet hissed as it ricocheted off the concrete in the courtyard three stories below me. I stood at the window in my room watching for something, unsure what it might be. A sound? A sign? A friend?

The long bare branches of tall trees waved to me from the far side of the darkened building nearby. I remained absolutely still, like a spy waiting patiently for a signal from a comrade hidden in the maze of shadows beyond the courtyard. But there was no comrade – no signal.

The sleet slowly became a light rain once more. The ominous hissing faded. Patches of frost on the window beaded up and started to slide down the glass like large tears. The rain faded to a mist and soon even the mist was gone. The air was clear. The night was still as a stone. Suddenly, several gasps of wind shattered the quiet and rattled my window like an intruder testing the lock. The wind, impatient, hurried on. The trees, shaken momentarily by the wind, steadied themselves again.

What time was it? I looked for that first familiar hint of indigo and coral at the edge of the blackness along the horizon. When I saw it I'd know that another day was about to take flight and I could feel secure. But everything was dark. I listened for other sounds but all I heard was my own breathing.

I was alone.

I leaned forward and carefully rested my head against the icy glass of the window. What could have gone wrong? Someone must have betrayed me. Who? How? For what? I went over it all once more. The good soldier remembers every detail.

I turned from the window, switched on a desk lamp and rummaged through my desk drawers making sure that my pictures and notes and letters had been removed. The drawers were empty.

I turned off the lamp and slipped under the covers on my bed. I thought about the last caller. When I picked up the phone and said, 'Hello,' he whispered. 'Be careful!' Of what? Why the low muffled voice and why didn't he say more? 'Be careful' is all he said. 'Who is this?' I asked. 'Who are you?' Without responding he hung up.

My mind replayed the call over and over again. I strained to hear the words he didn't speak. I could not. Be careful! Who is this? What do you know? Wait! Please, wait! Click!

I had trouble falling asleep. I was startled by footsteps in the hall. Seconds later they passed and their echo faded in the stairwell. My heart was racing. What had I forgotten? I told myself to relax and stop worrying. My head ached. Had I been careful enough? I was still waiting for the caller's unspoken words when finally I fell asleep.

In the morning the sky was gray but there was no rain. The air outside was bitter and cold. There are moments in the morning when I am tempted to laugh at my nervousness.

Late that afternoon I was in my room reading when they came for me.

viii

During my English-language class Friday morning, I had been unable to concentrate. I told the instructor I didn't feel well and couldn't stay. I apologized and returned to my room to be alone. I'd lost my appetite. I skipped breakfast and lunch. Most of that morning and early afternoon I sat in a chair staring out the window wondering what was going to happen next.

In the early afternoon I received a call from a friend from my home village who was studying at Nanjing University. She asked if she could visit me and use my phone to call home. It was difficult making the call from a public telephone on campus, she said, and there was more privacy if she called from my room. I invited her over and said I'd welcome her company. I told her I'd be in my room the rest of the day as well as that evening and the guard at the gate to the Center could just ring my room when she arrived.

After her call I tried to take a nap. But I was too restless and anxious to sleep for long and awakened after only ten minutes. I continued to lie on the bed with my eyes closed, trying to calm my nerves. When I checked the clock it was after 3 P.M. Nothing out of the ordinary had happened. I pulled a textbook from my bookshelf and began paging through it, trying to find the section where I'd stopped reading two days earlier. A short time later I was interrupted by a soft knock at my door.

My heart raced. Was this it? When I asked who it was I heard a familiar and welcome voice whisper, 'Me!'

I unlocked the door and let in the American. I sat on the bed and he pulled the desk chair across the room and sat facing me. We looked at each other without speaking for a few moments. Sometimes words are unnecessary and it is comforting just to sit next to someone for whom you care. A peace settled in whenever we were together. In a short time we had shared many peaceful moments, many words, and many secrets.

'You're quiet today,' he said at last. 'I was told you walked out of your morning class. What's wrong?'

He spoke just above a whisper so that someone passing in the hallway would not hear his voice.

I wasn't feeling well, I told him. I'd been up most of the night. I was uneasy. Something was wrong. Something bad was going to happen to me, soon – today or tomorrow. I would have to account for some of my actions in the Center. I was absolutely sure of it. So I was trying to prepare myself.

He noticed I was shaking. He reached out and took my hands in his and told me to stop worrying.

'Nothing is wrong. This has to be your imagination. Everything is fine. You're probably overreacting to something,' he said.

I was not reassured by his innocent confidence.

I reached out and gently pulled his face next to mine so we could whisper into each other's ear. 'I think my room may be bugged. I searched for a microphone last night but couldn't find it.'

'No. That's impossible.'

'I'm sure,' I said. 'Absolutely sure. They probably know everything we talked about, everything we said. They know everything.'

'Who are "they"? The authorities? No, they don't know anything. But even if they do, what's the problem? You've done nothing wrong,' he said.

'Do you remember the list you made with the American

professors after your first week here? The one we laughed at so much?'

'Yes. "One Hundred Things That Can Kill You in China." '

'You remember what was on it?'

'Yes. Let me see, it began with the air, if I remember right. Then the water. Then the food. The electrical system. The heating system. The open sewers. Missing manhole covers near broken streetlights. Loaded articulated buses with their lights and engines off freewheeling down hills at night. Slippery crap from kids pooping on the sidewalk.' He laughed under his breath as he remembered the list, trying to raise my spirits. 'Those who walk where the street's not lit, slip on little balls of shit!' he reminded me, smiling.

'You forgot something important I should have told you to add to your list.'

'What is it?'

'Words kill you here too.'

'Words,' he repeated. He didn't go on and I knew he was starting to appreciate my concern. 'Words,' he said again, and sighed. He paused and then asked, 'Is there anything I can do?'

I thought: Can you turn back the clock three months? Can you grow wings and fly me out of here tonight? Can you take me to Hong Kong? Or America? To some safe place? But I didn't say any of this.

'Yes, there is something I think you'll have to do,' I said.

'Anything. I'll do anything to help you out of whatever trouble you're in.'

'Make me a promise.'

'What is it?'

'When you leave this room today, I don't think we'll see each other again . . .'

'That's not going to happen!' he said, interrupting me.

'Listen to me! Please. Oh, God, for once, will you just listen?'

'All right. Go on.'

'If I am not here tomorrow I want you to promise that you won't ask about me and you won't try to find me. If you do, you will only cause more trouble for both of us. I want you to promise you won't ask questions about me. I want you to promise that you'll forget all about me.'

'That's not possible. You can't ask me that now.'

'Just promise me. That's all I ask. Someday you'll understand. Believe me! It is the only thing you can do to save yourself. Forget you ever met me. Forget everything we ever talked about. Deny everything. Get rid of my notes to you. Tear up my pictures. Don't ever think of me again.' I started to cry while I asked him these things.

'You're not making sense, Meihong.'

'If you do these things, it will help me. When someone asks if you knew me, tell them you didn't. Just tear me out of your memory. Never say my name again. Ever. That will help me. Then maybe I'll be safe.'

'This is crazy.'

'No. This is China. These things happen all the time. You just don't understand China.'

'Right after we met, you told me I understood China like no other American!'

'Sometimes I'm wrong. You don't understand. I don't think you can. People with round-trip tickets and blue passports can leave whenever they want to. They can escape. They live in another world. I made some mistakes – some bad mistakes. I'm sure I did. So you have to take my word for it now. I promise you, if you forget me, I will never forget you. It's the only way.'

'It makes no sense.'

'Promise me, I beg you. Promise me. If you care for me you'll promise.'

After a long pause he responded, 'OK, I promise.'

Neither of us spoke for several minutes. I was crying, and because our faces were touching and we were whispering into each other's ear, my tears ran down the side of his face.

He pulled away from me and wiped away my tears with the back of his hand. Then he fumbled with his wrist, unlocking the clasp on a slim silver bracelet he wore. As he removed it, he whispered, 'Now it's your turn. You promise me something.'

He carefully wrapped the bracelet around my left wrist and locked the clasp. 'My daughters gave this to me before I came here. They asked me to remember them every time I looked at it. They said it would bring me good luck. It did. I found you. Now you keep it and let it bring you good luck. You need it more than I do now.'

'I can't take this – it's from your daughters.'

'Yes, you can. They'd understand. They'd want you to have it. But there's more to it than that. This is only a loan. I want you to give it back to me someday. After everything turns out all right and you aren't worried anymore and we don't have to whisper and you feel safe, then you give it back to me! Will you promise me that?'

'You don't understand. I really don't think we'll be seeing each other again.'

'I think you're wrong.'

'I think I'm right.'

'Maybe you are. But I doubt it. This will all blow over. In a week we'll be laughing about it. Remember I told you that. But right now just promise me,' he said.

'OK,' I replied. 'I promise. Someday I'll return this to you.' I didn't believe my own words, but I said them anyway. That's what he needed to hear.

'I know I'll see you at breakfast tomorrow morning. But I don't want the bracelet back then.' He laughed.

'Tell me,' I asked, 'are all Americans like you? Are they all equally incapable of seeing reality?'

'Oh, God, I certainly hope so,' he said, and flashed one of his silly smiles that always made me smile back.

One of the things I loved about this man was his ability to dismiss the darker possibilities of almost any situation. He expected good things to happen. He'd seen too many happy endings in American movies and he'd started to believe them. In China we don't believe such nonsense. If something has a happy ending we're surprised.

I covered his hand with my own and whispered, 'You should go now. This won't look good if someone stops by.'

'OK,' he said. 'See you in the morning.' He stood, stepped to the door and turned the handle slowly to avoid making any sound, then pulled the door open, peeked out to see if anyone was in the hall. The coast was clear, he signaled, holding up his thumb. He turned and gave me a carefree wink and mouthed the words 'Bye-bye.' I mouthed the same words back and held up my wrist with the bracelet around it and forced a smile. He smiled back and nodded. Then he stepped into the hall, quietly closed the door and was gone.

I reopened my history book, read and reread the same page over and over again. Finally I gave up and dropped the book on the floor. I examined the bracelet, ran it back and forth through my fingers and said a silent prayer.

My prayer was interrupted by the loud ring of my telephone, which shattered the silence of the room like a fire alarm. I picked up the receiver and heard the voice of the gatekeeper calling from his post at the entrance to the Center. 'Miss Xu,' he said, 'you have someone here for you. Can you come down?'

My friend from Nanjing University, I thought. I almost forgot. 'I'll be right there,' I told him. We were required to meet guests at the gate and to sign them in, so a record might be kept for the authorities as to who entered and then left the building. Regular residents had passes, but everyone else was required to register.

I slipped into my sandals and decided, since this would only take a moment, not to put on a jacket.

I hurried down the stairs and across the lobby, past the telephone operator and receptionist. Two American students stood talking near the door. I waved as I passed them. When they realized I was going outside one cautioned me good-naturedly, 'Hey, Xu Meihong, what are you doing? It's freezing out there. You'd better put on a jacket or you'll catch your death.'

I laughed and shouted back, 'It's not time to die yet. I'll be back in a minute.'

As I pushed open the large doors, I passed two Chinese men entering the lobby from outside. Our eyes met only for a moment. I recognized neither of them. They wore matching gray overcoats. I thought it odd that they were coming into the Center unescorted by anyone – visitors needed a faculty member or student to sign them into the place. I glanced back at them for an instant and saw they had turned around just inside the door and were watching me and talking to each other. I could see their lips moving but couldn't hear their words through the glass.

I didn't stop to think about it. I wanted to get my friend and bring her inside as quickly as I could. I dashed across the concrete driveway separating the Center from the front gate. The elderly gatekeeper was standing inside his booth reading *The People's Daily*.

'Where's my friend?' I asked him.

He looked over my shoulder as if someone had been there and then disappeared. He seemed confused. 'I don't know,' he said. 'Your friend was here just a minute ago.'

'I'll wait here for her,' I told him. I wondered why she would leave so suddenly when she knew I was on my way down. 'For a few minutes, anyway,' I added, already feeling fingers of cold grasping my bare ankles, arms and legs.

I stood inside the booth with the guard for a minute without either of us speaking. He returned to his reading. I was shivering and impatient, so I stepped outside the gate and glanced up and down the sidewalk. A light dust of snow had started to fall again. My friend was nowhere in sight. Then I saw a military staff car parked at the curb only a few feet from the gate. I noticed the special license plate – it was from my military institute! The engine was purring and blue-gray exhaust fumes were floating into the frigid air. Dark curtains were pulled shut around the rear windows of the car. No sooner had I noticed the vehicle than a door on the passenger side opened and a fellow officer from my institute stepped out – Major Song. I was surprised to see him here.

'Major?' I called to him. 'What are you doing here?'

'I've come to bring you back to the Institute,' he said. 'There is a meeting you need to attend. It's very important. Very important.'

I studied his expression for a moment. He appeared both somber and uneasy.

'OK!' I assured him. 'But I need a minute. I have a friend I'm supposed to meet here. I want to leave a message for her with the gatekeeper and then let me get my coat.'

'We don't have any time,' he said, reaching out and lightly

grasping my arm. 'And there is a coat for you in the car.'

I suddenly felt sick. I knew he was lying to me. When I moved a bit I felt his grip on my arm tighten. I noticed his nervousness, and felt a pang of pity for him. I realized he had been given no choice. He was a personal friend as well as a fellow officer and this was his official assignment – to get me into the car and to take me somewhere. I'd seen this many times before – an officer ordered to betray a friend. Who better, after all, to help extricate someone calmly and without notice from a room or a building than a good friend? All of us in military intelligence had become practitioners of duplicity. It was standard operating procedure in our work – the art of betrayal. Now, as I realized what was happening and sensed the door of my trap closing, I felt sorry and ashamed for both of us.

Major Song quickly opened the back door to the car and motioned for me to get inside. I thought for a moment about breaking his grasp and running away – but it was too late for that. There was no place to run or hide. Not anymore.

Before crawling inside the car I glanced up one last time at the Center to see if anyone was watching from a window on the upper floors. I saw no one. There were no witnesses and no friendly faces. The gatekeeper remained inside his tiny post with his face buried in his newspaper.

Major Song got in and sat beside me, then closed and locked his door and signaled to the driver to go. The driver put the car in gear, the engine strained for an instant and we slowly glided away from the Center.

The driver glanced back at me several times and adjusted his rearview mirror so he could see me better. I recognized him. He had been my personal driver several times. We'd chatted as he drove me between the Institute and the Center. But that seemed long ago. When I looked up and saw him in the mirror I detected no friendliness or familiarity in his face, no sign of recognition. He seemed, instead, almost contemptuous of me. I stared back at him defiantly until he looked away.

The car proceeded for only half a block before pulling to the curb again where an alley intersected the main street. Two uniformed men trotted out from behind a wall to meet us. As they approached our car, I recognized them – I'd worked with them at the Institute on various occasions. The senior officer was Colonel Meng Fan Yan, who was in charge of security at the Institute. The other was his aide, a captain. Both men wore sidearms and despite the darkness of the late afternoon, the Colonel was wearing sunglasses. He pulled open the door and got into the car beside the driver. The captain ran to my side of the car, opened the door and got in next to me, so I was sitting between him and Major Song.

The driver pushed on the accelerator and I heard the wheels spin on the rain-slick pavement for a moment before we sped off again.

I knew precisely what was happening because I'd been privy to 'extractions' like this before. Someone under suspicion for a crime was seized. Usually at night without witnesses around. What was the old rule again? We plan in the day and act at night. But their innovative timing fooled me. They planned and acted in the day. That had thrown me off my guard. Now I realized that the two men I'd seen entering the Center when I was leaving were probably from the MSS. They'd merely flashed their identification cards to get past the gatekeeper and they were more than likely already searching my room. I'd been off my guard for three months. It was almost funny. I had been taken in a perfectly executed maneuver without a single eyewitness. The Americans in the Center had been correct. I'd gone outside without a jacket and I'd caught my death.

Suddenly the nervousness and anxiety I'd felt growing inside me for days started to wane and I felt as if a weight was being lifted from my back. The tightness in my chest eased.

At that moment I became like a patient who has just been informed by her doctor that she has cancer and only a short time to live. It was both terrifying and liberating. There were symptoms for weeks, but no actual diagnosis. I expected almost anything and was nearly paralyzed with anxiety about the unknown. Now, in a sense, the doctor had handed me his diagnosis. There was no longer an unknown to be imagined and feared – no mystery. What I felt instead was resignation and acceptance and a sudden clarity of vision. I knew exactly what was going to happen and I knew the meaning of all the past symptoms now. I felt strong and even a bit defiant.

I didn't try to initiate a conversation. I looked out the front window at the passing buildings and the people on the sidewalk trudging along through the snow or waiting stoically for a cold crowded bus.

I listened to the crunch and whir of the tires on the road as we drove through the city and the suburbs and out into the countryside. The others in the car were as mute as mindless robots.

I knew these men would remember everything that happened this day. Not only would each of them write a lengthy detailed report (and the reports would then be compared by higher authorities and the men would be questioned individually about what happened during the extraction) but they would also talk to their friends about it. I'd heard stories of how suspects were seized. I knew my captors would closely observe my behavior, remember every word I said, to relate it to others for their common enjoyment. I didn't want them to report that I was afraid or that I cowered. I didn't want them to laugh because they saw fear in my face or heard it in my voice. If I was going to die tonight – and that was a possibility, I realized – then I would make no plea for mercy or compassion. I'd heard stories and seen films and dramatizations of the pathetic behavior of sobbing condemned prisoners promising anything and everything to save their own skins – naming names of others who were guilty of worse crimes, pleading innocence and promising cooperation and slavish obedience in exchange for life. They slobbered and begged right up until the very moment that the sharp report of a pistol silenced them. Later people spit on them and laughed at their belated earnest protestations of regret and their last-minute conversions to support the Party policies they had violated. The loud and hilarious recollections of their last moments of life and their final words were made to sound almost obscene. Other prisoners went quietly without protest of apology to their deaths. In their silence and their final dignified acceptance of fate I found my example.

I had to remember that my life meant nothing at all to the men who held me now. If they were ordered to stop at any moment and shoot me, they would do it without hesitation. I was determined neither to apologize nor to beg. And I resolved not to cry no matter what they did to me. I had to find the strength to control my emotions. If I was asked to name a name to save myself, I would not do it. If I was asked to tell the truth to save myself, I would lie. If I was asked to lie to save myself, I would tell the truth. If I was condemned to death, I would go to that death holding final sweet memories of life.

Several times I saw the Colonel glance impatiently at his watch and then at the driver. 'You know where we are going?' he asked once. 'I think so,' the driver replied nervously.

But apparently he didn't. The driver missed a turn, uttered an expletive, made an awkward U-turn at the next intersection and got back on the right road. The Colonel looked at him with smoldering contempt. 'We have a schedule to maintain,' he said, with rising anger in his voice. The driver seemed to disregard the remark and kept his eyes and attention on the road.

I was unconcerned. There was no point in asking where we were going. Instead, I took pleasure in the Colonel's frustration and the driver's confusion.

We pulled onto a road that led to the gate of a military base. It was surrounded by a high wall topped with tangled barbed wire. Four armed sentries stood at a post outside the gate. They snapped to attention when they saw our car approach. Clearly, they had been expecting us. The Colonel rolled down his window and handed one of the sentries a document. He glanced at the document, looked back at me and then with the help of his comrades pushed the gate open. Moments after we'd pulled inside I heard the gate clatter shut behind us.

We drove slowly across an unlit parade ground and past a dozen darkened barracks before finally coming to one that had lights on inside. We pulled up to the front door and stopped. The men stepped out of the car. Major Song grasped my wrist to help me step from the car. 'This is it,' he said. 'We're here.'

I was escorted into the building. Several guards holding rifles were waiting inside, obviously relieved to see us. They surrounded me as we walked down a long dimly lit hallway to the far end of the building. The Colonel knocked on a door. It was unlocked and opened, and I was led inside.

A single bare lightbulb shone brightly from a ceiling fixture. The window was covered by newspapers. The only furnishings were four bare military beds.

Three female soldiers waiting in the room snapped to attention when we entered. Surprise registered on their faces when they saw me. We'd seen each other before. Two of the women I knew by name. The eldest of the three was named Li Xia. She was a major in her mid-thirties. We'd worked together on various assignments. Our eyes met for a moment. She seemed cold and unfriendly and didn't acknowledge my presence. She quickly turned to face the Colonel.

I also knew the youngest of the guards – a girl named Xiao Zhang, an enlisted soldier who served as a switchboard operator at the Institute. She was in her late teens and I'd known her since she came to the school to work. She stared at me in shock until she realized I was looking back at her and smiling weakly. She blushed and shifted her eyes to the Colonel.

He pointed to the bed farthest from the door and told me to sit down. Then he summoned Li Xia into the hall. After they'd stepped outside, I nodded to Xiao Zhang and the other guard, who stood beside her, fidgeting and obviously uncomfortable at being left alone with me. 'Do either of you have an extra jacket I could wear?' I asked. 'I'm freezing.' They looked at each other and then at me, shook their heads and stared nervously at the door again, awaiting the return of their senior officer. They seemed terrified.

Within a few minutes, the Colonel and Li Xia stepped back into the room. I was tired, cold and angry. I didn't stand up to acknowledge their presence. I simply slumped on the bed and looked up at them.

'This is where you will stay for now,' the Colonel informed me. 'Do not try to leave the room unaccompanied. Do not try to approach the door nor the windows. If you do' – he paused for a moment to pick his next words carefully – 'it will make things much worse than they already are. Just do as you're told. Li Xia is in charge in this room. If you have anything to say, address her. The more you cooperate, the sooner everyone goes home,' he concluded.

'Am I under arrest?' I asked.

'You will know in due time.'

'Wait,' I protested. 'If I am *not* under arrest, I have the right to move about. I have the right to leave this room or this post whenever I wish. I too am a PLA officer. Do I need to remind you of that, Colonel? You cannot detain me against my will unless I am officially under arrest.'

The Colonel studied me for a moment to determine my seriousness – or perhaps my sanity. He dismissed my questions and allegations with a word. 'Right,' he said. Then he continued with his instructions. 'You are in the Army. You must obey your senior officers. Stay here. Do what I tell you. Get some rest. You have things to do.'

He started to leave the room but suddenly turned to me again. This time he was angry and he made no effort to conceal it. 'And, if you don't mind, Xu Meihong,' he barked, intentionally omitting my rank, 'keep your mouth shut unless you are asked your opinion. It will save us all some time and it will save you considerable discomfort.'

The arrogance and contempt of his remark struck me. He was addressing me no longer as a fellow officer or an associate or friend but rather like a condemned prisoner. When he was finished he glared at me for a moment more, then he spun around smartly, marched out and closed the door behind him.

Li Xia turned the bolt lock on the door with a key fastened to her belt. She pulled the knob to test the lock, found it solid and stepped back to her bed, giving me a cautionary glance, as if to make sure I'd seen that the door was locked and tested.

The other women were dressed in trousers, blouses, sweaters, tunics and gloves. Their long winter underwear showed at the cuffs of their pants and tunics. I was trembling from the cold. I'm sure they could see it. Yet no one offered me a jacket or sweater.

Whatever discussion they might have been carrying on before I was consigned to the room had obviously come to an end. Li Xia read a newspaper, the other two women simply looked at me or stared into space lost in their own thoughts. My mind drifted. I wanted a jacket or a sweater, but I did not want to ask for one again.

It was all right. I'd been this cold before. I was from the countryside. I could suffer without protest. If this was going to be a test of wills, I wanted to win it.

I thought of the American. Would he remember to forget me? Had he destroyed my notes? I wondered what he might be doing at the moment. Was he looking for me, to see if I was feeling better? Did he still believe that nothing was wrong, that all of this would have a happy ending? Would he miss me at breakfast?

I felt the silver bracelet around my wrist and gently turned it back and forth between my fingers.

THREE

True Lies

Political language – and with variations this is
true of all political parties from Conservatives
to Anarchists – is designed to make lies sound
truthful and murder respectable, and to give an
appearance of solidity to pure wind.

— GEORGE ORWELL

i

I made up my mind to contest every allegation made against me. In defending myself I could not rely on an appeal to the truth. In China, the truth could neither save me nor set me free, because the truth is seldom true.

The Chinese Communist Party determines what is true and what is not in China. Party leaders may declare that they seek to discover truth from facts but they really mean they will find facts that fit the predetermined Party truth. When necessary, facts are invented.

When someone is accused of a crime in China he is assumed to be guilty until proven innocent. Therefore, to proclaim one's innocence following an arrest constitutes an insult as well as a challenge to the machinery of the Party and is more likely to compound the miseries of the accused than to result in exoneration.

When the system is working as expected, an arrest is a prelude to a confession. Someone who initially refuses to confess is likely to be coerced into making a confession and further cooperation with the authorities. This is done, it is said, for the good of the accused, who is finally forced to face the truth. A trial is just a showcase where charges are read and sentences pronounced to a cowed and contrite miscreant. Acknowledging one's errors, apologizing and naming one's accomplices are the recognized mandatory first steps on the road to rehabilitation.

I took a road less traveled by.

ii

I sat silently with my three guards for an hour before I became aware that my stomach was growling from hunger. I needed nourishment to maintain a clear head, I thought.

I turned to Li Xia and called out, 'Report!' – the formal equivalent of requesting permission to speak.

'I'm hungry,' I told her. 'I would like something to eat. And I'd like some hot water also. I'm thirsty.'

The three women looked at me for a moment, then carried on a frantic whispered conversation. Li Xia glanced at me several times during their talk as though there was something suspicious about my request.

Finally, she said, 'Not yet.' So I sat on the bed and tried to keep warm and ignore my hunger pangs.

About half an hour later there were footsteps in the hall and a sharp knock on the door. Li Xia unlocked and opened it.

The Colonel and his aides entered and the three female guards stood and saluted. I remained seated for a moment, then stood up slowly. I was freezing and hungry and feared that if I moved too rapidly I might lose my balance and fall.

I saluted and made a point of looking directly into the Colonel's eyes. When I lowered my hand, I felt a sudden dizziness, but steadied myself against the bed, stood straight again and kept my eyes fixed on the Colonel. Without any preliminaries, he began to read in a shrill, piercing voice from a document he held chest high. 'I am informing you, Lieutenant Xu Meihong, on behalf of the military headquarters of the People's Liberation Army in Beijing that, first, you are charged with endangering state security and, second, you are ordered to cooperate fully with us or to suffer the consequences. You know what those consequences are, don't you?'

I didn't reply.

Then, suddenly, his demeanor changed. He transformed himself in seconds from a stern accuser into an avuncular officer. He handed the official document to an aide and asked, 'Do you have any comments, Xu Meihong?'

I was taken aback by his sudden amiability. I thought for a moment this might be his real face and not a military mask and that he might be sympathetic to me in my plight. 'There has been a mistake, Colonel,' I told him. 'I don't know why I was brought here. The charge against me is absurd. You know I would never endanger state security. Someone has lied about me.'

Disappointed at my failure to respond in kind to his friendly words, he studied me for a few seconds and then replied in his more officious voice, 'This is not an exercise. There is no mistake. You have committed a serious crime. That's why we are all here tonight. We are here under orders from military headquarters. So let's do what must be done and let's do it as quickly as we can. We will require your complete cooperation.'

'It's a mistake, Colonel,' I insisted. 'And I believe if I am held here much longer, you will be putting yourself and these officers in a precarious situation.'

The Colonel's face crimsoned as he listened to my warning. I was not contrite and not in a cooperative mood and he was upset by this. 'The seriousness of the charge seems to have eluded you,' he said. 'That is unfortunate. But I'm not surprised. Let me repeat the charge so you can better appreciate its gravity: You have endangered state security. Do you know what that means? You have betrayed your country. You have committed treason.

'Now do you understand?' he asked. 'Now do you recall the consequences of such behavior?'

'Don't forget, it's only a charge,' I reminded him.

'Let's cooperate with each other,' he advised. 'Let's look for the truth tonight. There is, maybe, a chance that the charges against you are incorrect,' he lied. 'That's unlikely, but sometimes mistakes happen. You can help us uncover the mistake and correct it.' He flashed an almost reptilian smile.

Then his features softened once again as he reminded me, 'I watched you grow up. I saw you when you first came to the Institute. You were seventeen years old then. I know all about you – everything. You are a good girl and a good soldier and a patriot.'

His sentimental evocation of my background, his effusion of concern and of sympathy were, given the charges he'd just read against me, ironic, to say the least. But like most public officials in China, the Colonel was completely devoid of a sense of irony. He had no idea what the word might imply.

'Think about what you have done and later tonight you can tell me everything. Then, tomorrow, you may return to the Center and to your studies,' he promised.

He smiled again. Then he made a quick about-face and left the room, closely followed by his two aides. Li Xia accompanied the men and shut the door behind her. I overheard a hushed conversation in the hall, with the Colonel giving Li Xia instructions. I could only pick out a word here or there, usually a phrase that began with the word 'no.' Then they walked away. Less than an hour later Li Xia returned with several containers of food – four small bowls of rice with some fried vegetables and a large thermos of hot water. She had a military tunic and a thin coverlet slung over her shoulder. Without saying a word and without looking at me, she dropped the tunic and coverlet on the bed next to me.

The others ate eagerly – they were as hungry as I was. I picked up the lukewarm bowl of rice and ate some of it. But my appetite quickly diminished as my stomach turned to knots from listening to the Colonel's words. I placed the bowl and chopsticks on the floor, poured myself a cup of hot water and held it between my hands to warm them.

The guards finished eating and resumed whispering to each other. After a while, Xiao Zhang dozed off in a sitting position. Li Xia paged through a newspaper while the other guard lay on her back and stared at the ceiling.

I precipitated a crisis when I turned to Li Xia and announced, 'Report! I have to go to the toilet.'

Apparently no one had planned for such a contingency.

'What?' she asked, as though she couldn't believe what I'd said.

'I have to pee.'

She jumped up and made a quick circuit of the room looking for a chamber pot or a bucket. There was none. She gave me a hostile look, as if she suspected this was some secret strategy.

A command crisis ensued. Xiao Zhang was shaken awake and told I had to pee. She looked at me in awe, as though this was a strange and exotic practice. Li Xia left the room and ran to the end of the hall. I heard a door open and close and then open and close again and then more footsteps. She returned with the Colonel.

'You have to go to the toilet?' he asked me.

'Yes, badly,' I confirmed.

'There is no bucket in the room?' he asked Li Xia, glancing around.

She seemed frightened by this oversight. 'No, Colonel, I am very sorry,' she apologized.

'Then do what has to be done,' he said with resignation.

He summoned his aides. By their disheveled look, it appeared they'd been awakened just for this assignment. They were not happy about it. Then our squad of seven soldiers – four women and three men – walking in tight order – led me from the building. The Colonel, wielding his flashlight, led the way. We proceeded to a walled outside toilet a short distance from our building. All three women entered the enclosed area with me. Because of the darkness, I could not see more than one step in front of me, but as my eyes adjusted to the dark I found that the room consisted of four brick walls and a cement floor. Despite the fact that it was open to the outside air, it reeked. Slowly, we made our way across the room where I spied a long slab of concrete with a line of holes down the center. This was the common toilet for the base.

We stood for a moment in the dark without speaking. I expected to be left alone at that point, but the guards remained next to me and Li Xia impatiently ordered, 'Pee!'

'I need paper,' I told her. Fortunately, this had been arranged for, and Xiao Zhang handed me a napkin-size piece of newspaper.

'Could I have some privacy?' I asked.

Li Xia's response was immediate. 'Pee! We're freezing.' I did as she ordered.

Back in the room again I buttoned my tunic to the neck and wrapped myself in the thin cotton coverlet I'd been given. I leaned against the concrete wall and finally fell asleep for

71

several minutes. But I bolted upright at any sound – one of the women standing up or turning the pages of a newspaper or pacing the floor. My sleep was uneasy.

iii

Before dawn, there was a knock on the door. The Colonel's aide was allowed in by Li Xia and announced that the men were waiting for me. He escorted me to a room at the opposite end of the hall.

The interrogation room was small and lit by a single overhead light fixture. A small square table surrounded by four chairs was placed in the middle of the room directly under the fixture. Heavy curtains were drawn over the window. The Colonel was seated when I entered the room. The other officers sat on each side of the table and I was told to sit opposite the Colonel. A thick green folder stuffed with papers lay on the table. A portable tape recorder was placed at a corner of the table, its tiny red light flickered brighter and dimmer with the sounds in the room.

The captain picked up a notebook and prepared to transcribe everything that was said.

The Colonel looked across the table at me for a moment and initiated the session. 'Your name?'

'My name? You know my name, Colonel,' I reminded him. 'We're longtime associates. We're good friends,' I said loudly. I wanted this on the official record. 'You reminded me of that last night.'

He was thrown off guard for a second by my outburst of sarcasm. The atmosphere that he intended to create – that of the contrite prisoner and the capable and superior interrogator – was shattered.

'This is an official proceeding,' he shot back. 'You must answer the questions as I ask them.'

'Didn't you tell me you knew everything about me last night?' I asked. 'Let's not waste time with formalities, Colonel.'

Obviously annoyed at my response, he rephrased his question. 'Now, your name is Xu Meihong. Is that right?'

I inhaled deeply to calm my nerves, and then spoke softly as I exhaled. 'Yes. I am Lieutenant Xu Meihong of the People's Liberation Army of the People's Republic of China.'

'Where were you born and what are your parents' names and occupations?'

'What does that have to do with anything?'

'Damn you!' he shouted, and slapped his open hand on the table. 'Answer the questions as I ask them. I ask the questions, not you. I am in charge here. You had food last night. You drank hot water. You pissed in a toilet. That was all at my sufferance – my command. I can stop the food. I can stop the water. You can piss in your pants from now on for all I care. That is up to you. Can't you see I am trying to help you? Answer the questions as they are asked and spare yourself and your family unnecessary suffering.'

He thought it important to remind me that those charged with serious crimes never suffer alone. For centuries in China, punishment was meted out at many levels of one's family, household and friends. Crimes against the state are assumed to have a social dimension to them. The recognition of this serves as a deterrent. Just as everyone understands that there is no private life in China, there is no private punishment either.

'I was born in Jiangsu province,' I responded. 'In the village of Lishi near the city of Danyang.'

'Your date of birth?'

'December 6, 1963.' Then he again asked for the names and occupations of my parents and I told him.

'You are an officer in the PLA. I should expect that you always tell the truth, shouldn't I?' he asked.

I fell into the monotonous staccato rhythm of the session, answering each question as it was asked, waiting and watching for places where the Colonel tried to set his traps, trying to avoid them.

Every thirty minutes the tape recorder clicked and shut itself off. When that happened everyone in the room looked at it while the captain either turned the tape over or put in a new one. The click from the recorder was like a signal to be silent.

We were servants to the recorder as well as to the Party and its required procedure.

When I spoke, the men seemed fascinated, as if everything I said was information not included in my file.

When he was finished with these vital statistics, the Colonel closed his file and shifted the tone of his voice to something he must have believed sounded friendly. 'OK, Xu Meihong,' he began, 'now I want you to tell me everything about your life in the Center for Chinese and American Studies. Begin.'

'What could I possibly tell you about the Center that you don't already know? You read the incoming and outgoing mail, don't you? The telephone lines are tapped. You have people on the housekeeping and administrative staff reporting to you. You know everything that happens in the Center. What can I add that you don't already know?'

'That's what I am about to find out,' he said, fidgeting and struggling to maintain his composure. 'That's why we are here.'

'What do you want to know, specifically? A lot happens there. Where would you like to start? I have nothing to hide,' I answered.

'No,' he said. 'You tell me what you believe is important, in your own words. You tell me everything that happened there.'

'Everything? All right, Colonel, everything that happened. I came to the Center in early September 1988. I was assigned to room 213. I'm enrolled in three courses – two in American history and society and one in colloquial English.'

I droned on and on, providing him with every imaginable banal detail of life in the Center – classes, conversations, hot water, cold water, bad food, good food, parties, dances, music, movies, speakers, library rules, heating, leaking windows and walls, visiting delegations from the United States or from Beijing. I tried to miss nothing, no matter how irrelevant – laundry, housekeeping, kitchen staff, Ping-Pong contests and slippery floors.

Eventually, the recorder clicked off. I'd used up most of the sixty minutes on the cassette without really going anywhere.

My pedestrian tales of life at the Center bored even me. The captain leaned forward, fumbled with the recorder cassette, removed it, replaced it with a new one and turned the machine back on.

Suddenly the Colonel stood, drummed his fingertips impatiently on the table and barked, 'Stop it! I think you know what I want to hear from you. Tell me. Now.'

I did my best to appear genuinely confused by his assertion. 'Colonel, I do not know what you want to hear other than the story of my life at the Center, which I am telling you. If you are tired of listening to it, perhaps we should stop and return home now.'

He sat back in his chair, sighed and said, 'Go on.'

I continued: 'Sometimes, I leave the Center with friends and go to a Chinese noodle restaurant nearby. The owner changes money for the Americans. He also pays off the police for this illegal privilege. It's a very popular place – Zhou's, it's called. The noodles are good. We stay there and talk sometimes for hours – just like now – only friendlier. The police even eat there, but they don't have to pay, of course.'

As if in slow motion, the Colonel leaned forward and switched off the tape recorder. The captain stopped writing. 'Good noodles? Goddamnit, good noodles? Don't tell me about good noodles. And I am not interested in money.' Again he drummed his fingers nervously on the table.

'You know why you are here, don't you? Or are you the only one in this room who doesn't know the answer to that question? We are not here because of noodles. We are here because you let yourself get into trouble. We are here to talk about what went wrong. These dilatory tactics of yours won't work with me. Your mouth might have been your undoing. Now it may be your salvation. Do you know that? Are your ears clean? Can you hear me, Xu Meihong?'

I didn't interrupt his outburst. When he was finished we sat looking at each other across the table for a long time, as if taking a measure of each other's willpower and patience. He folded his arms across his chest as we stared into each other's eyes. There wasn't a sound in the room. At last, the Colonel leaned forward and switched on the recorder again. The captain held his pen over his notebook and prepared to resume writing.

'Tell me about the people at the Center.'

'Well, most of the people in the Center are nice except one,' I volunteered. 'That person is the administrative assistant to the Chinese co-director. He is always smiling, a very happy guy. But most people there pretty much hold him in contempt and distrust him. He headed the Red Guards during the Cultural Revolution and did terrible things. He snoops, still. I think he goes into the rooms of the Chinese students when they're in class. He has keys. He solicits sexual favors from the Chinese female students and staff. They have complained to the Americans and the Americans keep a file on him in their safe. You must have a copy of that file. Someday, when they feel bold enough, the Americans are going to ask that he be transferred. But I believe he'll stay because he works for the National Security Police. He might also work for you. Anything else?'

'Go on,' the Colonel directed, not even bothering to ask the individual's name. 'How do you know these things?'

'I have eyes and ears, Colonel.'

'OK. Continue,' he said.

I went down the list of names of Chinese students and faculty members at the Center. The Colonel interrupted. 'I am more interested in the Americans,' he said. 'Tell me about them. Not the students, the faculty. Tell me about the instructors. Who teaches the courses you take. What are their names?'

I named the language instructor. The Colonel was unmoved. Then I provided other names and at last said the name he had been waiting for. The Colonel immediately perked up. He smiled. I didn't smile back. I struggled to say the name in an even and dispassionate way.

Before I could move on, the Colonel withdrew a blank page from his folder and pushed it across the table to me, pulled a pen from his pocket and handed it to me and asked, 'Write his name down here, will you?'

I wrote the name of the American in both English and Chinese. Then I pushed the paper back to him.

The Colonel studied it carefully and grinned. He showed it to the others.

'Mr Larry Engelmann. Is that how you say it?'

'Yes, that's close enough.'

'A German name.'

'Originally, yes. The family was from Germany, three generations ago.'

'You know that? Family history? How familiar are you with this man?' he asked.

'He's a friend.'

'A friend?' the Colonel asked. 'A *good* friend, would you say?'

'A friend,' I answered.

The Colonel studied me closely for some indication that I was uncomfortable with this topic or that I was about to break down. It seemed that he expected me to burst into tears, confess, plead for my life, throw myself at his mercy and agree to say or do anything he asked. I sat up and continued to look straight into his eyes, controlling my emotion. My heart was pounding so hard I feared they might hear it. I did not want to say that name again. When I said it, the Colonel's look could only be described as something like a leer. Saying the name to him seemed a violation of trust, a breach of something I considered sacred.

We watched each other closely. It was like a childish game in which two individuals try to stare the other down. I refused to be the first to break off eye contact. This little test of wills seemed to last several minutes. Then the Colonel blinked. He smiled broadly as if he'd read some critical emotion, some sign of surrender in my eyes. I did not shift my stare, nor did I smile.

He looked away and asked his next question before again making eye contact with me. 'How well do you know Professor Chu?'

'She's a friend too. She's a *good* friend. She teaches courses in politics and diplomacy. She is Chinese too, as you know. Hong Kong-born. She speaks Mandarin and Cantonese fluently. Our talks, when we have them, are always in Mandarin.'

'What else do you know about her?'

77

'Her family is originally from Nanjing. That's all I know.'

'Who else do you know at the Center? The Americans.'

'I know every American faculty member there. That's not unusual. We live in the same building and eat meals in the same dining room. I know the American students too. Do you want to know about them?'

'No,' he said in a voice indicating both boredom and exhaustion. 'No, I don't.' He tilted forward, reached out and clicked off the tape recorder. Then he sat back in his chair, pushed himself away from the table and closed his eyes. He sat like that slowly rocking on the two back legs of the chair, considering his next words.

'That was a good start,' he said. 'You talked a bit this morning and it was helpful. I think we will make rapid progress.' I had no idea what he meant. Then he glanced down at his watch and added, 'You can return to your room now. Take a rest. You know these transcripts of these sessions will be typed and you will be required to sign each page of them to verify that they are true?'

'I understand,' I assured him.

He told the captain to summon the three women to escort me to the other room.

As I stood to leave, the Colonel smiled and shook his head. 'Xiao Xu, do you hear me? This is very important. You are accused of a serious crime. There is very convincing evidence. You can be sure of that. Perhaps there is some explanation we should hear. Then we might help you. After you tell us what happened at the Center, you may return there. Until then, consider this your new home.'

I told Li Xia I'd like to wash myself. She and the other two women escorted me to a tiny washroom next to our room. It had a single low-wattage bulb in a wall fixture, a cold-water spigot over a cement sink. I rinsed my face and hands and dried myself on a square of paper one of the women provided. Then I brushed my teeth with my finger, rinsed my mouth, and we returned to the room.

The sun was out but it was still cold. I could see the glow of daylight through the yellowing pages of newspaper pasted on the glass.

The women had slept in the room while I was questioned. Now they talked in hushed tones among themselves and agreed that one of them would go to a nearby building to get food. There appeared to be a standing order that at least two women had to be in the room with me at all times and that the door must always be locked from the inside.

My anxiety kept my adrenaline high. I wasn't in a mood to sleep, even though I was physically and emotionally drained.

Replaying the interrogation session in my mind, I wondered what the Colonel actually knew and what evidence he possessed to support his accusations.

If the charge against me was breaching state security and if the Colonel possessed what he considered to be proof of my crime, then I should have been executed within hours of my arrest. But I was still alive and that led me to believe that the Colonel did not have all the evidence and information he was seeking. He consequently needed me to provide the evidence of my guilt – through a confession – which I was absolutely determined never to give him. And he was probably seeking co-conspirators. He might tell me I was charged with a capital crime in order to terrify me into trading names or information for my life. I decided I would never do that.

I contemplated the character of the Colonel. He was merely another contemptible little man with power. He may at some early time in his life have been an idealistic young recruit into the PLA, the same as I had been. But that changed. When he had seen hypocrisy and corruption around him, his reaction was to join it rather than correct it. He had submerged whatever there might have been of his individuality and his personality and character deep in the sinkhole of PLA and Party politics. It paid off. He rose rapidly through the ranks. He represented everything I loathed about the PLA and the Party. For several years I was aware of what he did, what favoritism he showed, what back door he used for his friends for special privileges, which ones he used himself and which young female officers he pursued. As I listened to him attempt to convince me to cooperate with him, my contempt for him grew.

If, as Sun Tzu wrote, the first rules of warfare are to know your enemy and to know yourself, I had an enormous advantage in this confrontation. I knew the Colonel and I knew my own mind. He had power over me for the moment, absolute power as he reminded me. All he knew about me, however, was in what he read in the folder he held, and that was no longer me.

I didn't know how much time I had. The questioning might continue for days and weeks and the sessions would become much longer if my resolve to resist remained firm. At the Institute we'd studied China's wars and interrogation methods and even practiced them on each other in order to learn how to question and how to avoid answering one's questioner. It was axiomatic, however, that a prisoner could be made to confess to anything. In time, everyone has a breaking point far short of death. They only need to be convinced that death is imminent and that all that separates them from doom is confession and cooperation. The exceptions to this rule, we were told, were not worth discussing.

Allowing me time to sleep and reflect on my fate was therefore both a small favor and a tactic. The Colonel expected me to be consumed with guilt and fear and at the same time to repay his small favors by cooperation. Everything that was done to me was done in order to gain my confession.

I lay down on the bed, wrapped myself tightly in the coverlet. My mind was a jumble of questions and possible stratagems. I wanted to live. But there would be a price. What was it? Would I be willing – or able – to pay it? If I would not pay it today, would I pay it in a week? A month? Six months? How long could I keep my spirits up and resist? How long would it take before I would be willing to trade someone else's life for my own? And whose?

I prayed for timely help from my friends in the military. There were officers above me who now must be worried about my words. They might be in danger and so they must be working to find me, to free me before the danger spread to become a disaster. Either that or they might work for my quick elimination. That, too, would bring them a certain security. But things as they were at the moment – in a standoff – could not continue for long.

iv

Night came again. I walked to the window and studied the pages of *The PLA Daily* that covered it. Li Xia came to my side and put her hand on my shoulder – the first sisterly thing she had done since I was brought here. 'We want you to do us a favor,' she told me. 'We know you are cold. So are we. And we know you don't want to be here. Neither do we. We want to go home.

'My five-year-old daughter cries for me when I am not home. But I can't go home until this is resolved. I'm not even allowed to call her.'

'Li Xia, I'm sorry,' I said. 'But I am not here voluntarily. Why don't you tell these things to the Colonel? I have no power here, you know that.'

'Oh, but you do,' she responded. 'You do. Just don't be stubborn or sarcastic. Do what they ask. Cooperate. Please, tonight, just do what they ask and this will end. Tell them what they want to know and then we can *all* leave.'

Neither of us spoke for a time. I thought about what she'd said. I then reminded her of an oversight. 'Li Xia, I am accused of breaching state security. I am an Army officer. If I admitted that this accusation was true, what do you think they would do to me?'

She looked at me but didn't answer.

As we stood by the window, the other two women approached us. 'I agree with Li Xia,' the older of the two said. 'My son is in school, and every night I go over his lessons with him and cook for him. But now he doesn't even know where his mother is. He doesn't get along with his father. I need to get home too. Won't you do us all a favor? We know you are a good girl and that you are innocent of any crimes. Just tell them what happened to you at the Center, who gave you orders, and then all of us can go home – you too. This doesn't have to end unhappily, Xu Meihong.'

'No one gave me orders,' I told her. I knew that not a word I said was off the record. 'There is no one to blame. There was no crime. When they learn that, we can go home. But I don't think that will happen. They don't believe me. Tell the Colonel what you want, not me.'

The two older women signaled the youngest guard, Xiao Zhang, to speak to me.

'I remember you from the Institute,' she began.

Something in her voice was different, was more genuine and convincing than the other two women. I studied her face and said, 'I remember you, too, Xiao Zhang.'

'The cadets at the Institute envy you. They want to be like you. I have always watched you. I want you to know that I do not think you betrayed our country. There must be some miscommunication. Why don't you just tell them everything and clarify the misunderstanding so you can go back to your life and leave this room and this cold food and this stinky toilet behind?'

I wondered if her lines were scripted also. If she was saying what she had been ordered to say, I could forgive her, because when I was her age I might have been doing exactly what she was doing. I would have lied to help find a PLA traitor. Probably there was nothing I would not have said or done had I been told it was for the security of the state. And in that I was no different from any other cadet. But I had changed and they hadn't.

These three women were good soldiers. They would gladly shoot me for betraying the PLA. They had been trained to do that, to follow any order, to die for the country as well as to kill for the country. We are all soldiers, I thought, so we understand each other. Only too well.

V

The next morning, December 4, the Colonel arrived accompanied by his aides. I was escorted to the interrogation room again.

As I sat down in the chair facing the Colonel, I sensed a

wave of self-doubt and vulnerability sweep over me like an icy breeze. I wondered how long I might resist the blandishments and bullying of my interrogators. I wasn't sure anymore. The Colonel switched on the tape recorder and began tossing out questions.

'Did you sleep well?'

'No.'

'Did you eat?'

'Yes.'

'Did you speak with the other women?'

'No.'

'No?' he asked. He seemed genuinely surprised by my assertion.

'No.'

'Do you have anything to tell me now?'

'No.'

There was a very long pause. The Colonel looked at each of his aides and slowly shook his head.

Finally, he asked, 'Did you wash last night?'

'Yes.'

'Did you remember to wash your ears?'

'Yes.'

'I don't think so. I don't think you understand me. I don't think you hear me very clearly.'

Then suddenly, seething with anger, he leapt to his feet and kicked his chair away from the table. The chair flew backward across the room and made a loud clatter as it bounced off the wall. Then, bracing himself with his left hand, he leaned across the table and put his face only inches from mine. 'I don't think you heard me last night. I think you'd better clean your ears.' His face was scarlet, almost glowing. Before I could reply or react, he slapped my face hard with his open hand. There was a sharp crack and my head snapped to the side. I tasted blood in my mouth and my eyes teared. My ears were ringing. I immediately turned back to face him again. I said nothing. I glared straight into his eyes with as much contempt as I could convey. I felt tears running down my cheeks. For several seconds I thought I might faint or lose my balance and fall off the chair. But I steadied myself and maintained eye contact with him.

'Now can you hear me?' he bellowed. 'Can you hear me clearly? What were you thinking? Tell me!' He raised his hand again and straightened his arm. I neither cringed nor looked away. I kept my lips sealed tightly together so he could not see the blood in my mouth. I was tempted to spit in his face, but I decided to resist the temptation.

He had blundered. I felt a deep hatred for him bubbling up inside me mixing with the contempt I had felt previously. This was new, hot, determined hatred. It pushed aside the self-doubt standing in its way, along with my self-pity, sadness, melancholy, confusion, regret and sense of duty. Hatred gave me strength. I locked eyes with him and took comfort in my private thoughts. I swallowed the blood in my mouth. My face felt like it was on fire. I did not look away.

The Colonel slowly lowered his hand, composed himself, turned and picked up his chair and sat down again.

This tantrum intrigued me. I guessed that he was working under a deadline to get the information his superiors required. I suspected that my friends in the military must already be asking about me – perhaps someone at the Center had seen me being taken away. And if my friends and fellow officers were looking for me or demanding to see me, then the Colonel did not have unlimited time. If this was true, the more time I wasted by leading him down meaningless paths of inquiry to dead ends, the better it would be for me.

I listened to the Colonel breathing heavily. He looked at his aides again. They seemed astonished by his loss of control and his outburst. He muttered under his breath, 'God damn you!'

It was quiet for a while and then he reached out and clicked off the tape recorder. 'Take her back,' he told the aides, and they walked me back to the room. As we left the room, I turned and saw him start to rewind the tape in order to record over this session. He wanted no record of it and he was confident that no one could say it ever happened. The evidence was erased. It would be forgotten until, perhaps, some day in the future when his aides might be called upon to testify against him and tell about his abuse of fellow PLA officers.

There were no more questions that night.

vi

———◆◇◆———

Early the next morning, December 5, I was brought back to the interrogation room. As I sat down across from the Colonel, he smirked, clicked on the recorder and began the session.

'Do you recognize this man?' he asked, pushing a photograph of the American across the table so I could see it. I'd seen the photo before – it was taken by a commercial studio not far from the Center and was used on the ID issued to faculty members. The MSS office also had a copy. I wasn't sure if they'd acquired this from the Center or from the photographer. I was certain that when the Americans picked up their photos they were unaware that they paid for extra copies to be made and distributed to the authorities.

'Yes, that's Larry Engelmann,' I replied.

'How well do you know him?'

'As well as I know any of the teachers at the Center.'

'Did you ever write letters to him? Notes?'

'No.' As I answered, I saw the Colonel place a fat folder on the table. I could see, when he opened it, some of my handwritten notes.

'No?'

'No.'

'What are these, then?' he asked, laying several pages torn from a notebook on the table.

'I have no idea. Probably forgeries of my handwriting.'

He leafed through the notes and slipped them back into the folder, reinserted the photograph and laid the folder on the floor next to his chair.

'Did this foreigner – or should I say this *American* ever write to you?'

'No.'

'Are you absolutely sure? Think about what I've asked before you respond.'

'I'm sure.'

There was a long silence. The Colonel looked at his aides and smiled, then he looked back at me and shook his head slowly from side to side. 'There is no need to lie. We know the truth. We are here to listen to you confirm the truth. When you stop lying, we can leave. Don't you understand? Nobody forged your name to those notes. They were taken from the apartment of the American. They were torn from your notebook.'

'If you are absolutely sure, why do you need my confirmation? Why bother?'

His demeanor softened again and he spoke in a subdued and serious voice – like a forgiving father to a daughter who had strayed. 'I know you so well. All of us in this room are concerned about you.' He paused for an unusually long time between each sentence, as though he was giving a speech to an audience and was slowed by regular applause. 'We trusted you. Now we need your help. If you give us the truth, nothing will happen to you. I promise. Tell us what happened at the Center and we will release you. You know that we have your best interests at heart, don't you?'

It was hard to believe that this was the same man who had fulminated and spewed his hatred in my face the previous day.

'Please tell me more about this . . . *American.*'

I thought I should give him something at this point and use up time. I had no idea how extensive his information was or who his sources were. By listening and answering his questions, by providing some information and watching his response and hearing what he subsequently asked, I might determine what he knew. So I began. 'I don't know him well. I just knew him for three months. We met the first time in early September.'

'Well, tell us what you do know about him.'

'OK. I believe he used to work in California. He is a history professor. He has written two books and he is writing a third.'

'Have you read those books?'

'No.'

'Who told you about them?'

'He did.'

'And the book he is now writing. What is it about?'

'Vietnam.'

'Vietnam? Interesting,' the Colonel observed. There was a long silence again and he continued. 'You know something about Vietnam, don't you? Did you ever talk to him about Vietnam?'

'No.'

'No? Are you sure you've never told him anything about Vietnam?'

'No. I don't know anything about Vietnam.'

'I'm sure you remember something about Vietnam, Xu Meihong.' The Colonel stared at me to see if something in my expression might show I was lying. I relaxed. I didn't waver. I gave him no signals to read.

'Vietnam,' he repeated. 'Interesting. He writes letters to Vietnam. Did you know that? We have them. Letters to the Ministry of Defense. Isn't that interesting?'

'I wouldn't know.'

'Do you know about his family?'

'Not much. He once spoke of his daughters in Chicago.'

'Do you know their names?'

'No.'

'He is a writer?'

'Yes, he writes.'

'Do you know that he also writes letters?'

'Yes, I assumed that.'

The Colonel pulled out another folder, this one thicker than the first. 'He writes lots of letters,' he said, patting the folder. 'Not just to Vietnam. He sends them all over the world. Did you know that?'

'No.'

'What else does he do?'

'He helps Chinese students.'

'What do you mean?' the Colonel asked.

'He was upset when he found we had no textbooks in the library. He wrote to the American publisher and asked them to give free copies to the Chinese students. They were sent and

87

we all received free books thanks to him.'

'Anything else?'

'Yes. He promised to take us to the Jinling Hotel for hamburgers and french fries. He said, I remember, that we could never understand America until we ate hamburgers and french fries.'

'Hamburgers and french fries? How generous. And books! Your own books.' The Colonel feigned amazement. 'Why do you think he did these things? Did anyone else – any of the other Americans – do this or say this? Were you never suspicious of him?'

'No.'

'Is he a millionaire in disguise?' The three men chuckled at this sarcastic suggestion.

'Maybe he's just . . . different.'

The Colonel and his aides burst into laughter when I said that word. 'Yes,' the Colonel said. 'You noticed. Now we're getting somewhere. He is different, as you say. He is very different. Different. I like that description.'

Again, I didn't respond.

'How different do you think he is from the other Americans, Xu Meihong?'

'What do you mean?'

'Do you think he is just here to teach?'

'No. He also wants to learn about China.'

My words elicited a round of cold smiles from the three men.

'Yes, yes, yes. I am sure he wants to learn about China. Did he ask you to help him?'

'Yes. He asks questions all the time of the Chinese students.'

'But mostly he asks you, correct?'

'I don't know. I don't know why he would ask me more than others.'

'Perhaps . . . because of your position. Did you ever consider that?'

'He has no idea what my position is.'

The Colonel waited for further reaction from me. When there was none he riffled through the folder on the table and removed a photograph of me in my military uniform. I immediately recognized it. The American had taken it in mid-November. He'd promised he would return the film to me after he finished the entire roll.

'Let me get this straight. He doesn't know what your position is?'

I didn't go on. I stared at the photo and then at the Colonel again. There was nothing I could say. He would never believe my explanation.

'Xu Meihong, you know, you should have known for a long time that this American is, as you say, different. Of course he is *different*. His pose as a professor is his second occupation. He has been working for American intelligence for years. Teaching is just his cover. Didn't you ever suspect that? Weren't you told that?'

'You are wrong about the American. He is only a teacher. I never really suspected that he was anything else. If there was an American agent in the Center it could not be him. It could be almost anyone but him.'

'Anyone but him? Why would you say that?'

'He's open. He doesn't speak Chinese. He can't get around Nanjing on his own because of language difficulties. He couldn't possibly be anything other than what he appears to be. He's a teacher.'

'Can you be sure?'

'Yes.'

'Would it surprise you to learn that he speaks Mandarin fluently?'

Now it was my turn to laugh out loud. When I'd stopped, I asked, 'Colonel, who told you that? Someone is making a fool of you. It's a joke. He speaks no more than ten words of Mandarin. That's all. And he mispronounces those ten words constantly.'

'Think of him as an actor. He was acting. He was pretending. Didn't you ever think that?'

I was amazed at these allegations. They couldn't be true. The notion was absurd. Was this what they suspected? My crime was to befriend an American intelligence agent? If this was true, if this was their only charge, then the Colonel had to be depending on inept eyewitness accounts. His eyewitnesses were lying or exaggerating or stupid – probably all three.

'OK, let's not waste time today. First, we know that he works for the CIA. We know that he is here on an assignment. We know he replaced someone who worked for American intelligence under the cover of being a teacher at the Center. The truth of his occupation is beyond dispute.

'We think what might be interesting are his contacts. He sought you out. And through you he met others. We think he is here to establish productive relationships and to . . . how might I put it . . . recruit! We believe he recruited you. Maybe you aren't aware of it. Or maybe you are. We shall see. But we also think he recruited people who are using you, Xu Meihong. Other Chinese. That is why you are here.

'Think about it. You've known him for a short time. We have copies of his letters here. Did you know that he wrote to "a friend" and invited him to China? He told the friend he'd found "a good translator and guide." Were you aware of that? Would you be surprised to learn that you were named as the translator and guide?

'He invited an American named [the Colonel wrote out a name and showed it to me] to China. We think he works with this man. We believe he intended to introduce you to this man. We believe this man is his supervisor.'

'Excuse me, but this is crazy,' I interrupted. 'This is someone's wild imagination. Who put this together for you?'

'Crazy? Let me ask you this. Do you really believe he has two daughters?' he asked, smiling confidently.

'Yes, I do.'

'He has no children. The two people he writes to are co-workers. We looked into it. They don't even live in the state of California. Do you think [he paged through his file to find his notes], do you think "Kiki" is a real name? It's a code name.'

The story was getting loonier by the minute. I was surprised at how convinced the Colonel was of every word he said. His statements didn't seem to be only for effect – to elicit my reaction – but rather they were made in a straightforward, matter-of-fact way. I'd seen pictures of the daughters. I'd seen their letters. I'd been in his room when he'd received a telephone call from one of his daughters. Was that an act?

'We have evidence indicating you are involved with this man, how shall I say it, "intimately." Isn't that true?'

'If you know me as you insist that you do, Colonel, then you know that is not true. I hope that isn't why we are here.'

'But I do know you and I do know that this *is* true. You should know we know. Every one of us here knows. And your husband knows, Xu Meihong. Think about that. Your husband knows too.'

I felt myself redden with indignation and embarrassment. I glimpsed for a moment another path they were sure to follow in this ominous fantasy.

'Your husband is currently an officer in the PLA, correct?'

'You know that.'

'He is an aide to a general at the National Defense University in Beijing, correct?'

'Yes.'

The Colonel grinned. 'And your husband was in the United States last year. How convenient all of this seems. What a coincidence.'

'What are you implying, Colonel?'

He reached forward and clicked off the recorder. 'You've been to the NDU before. You know people there. You know what goes on. You know who the American is. You know how you met him, how you spent time with him. Why do you think that is? What do you think it means?' he asked.

When I refused to respond, he said, 'Think about all we've talked about today, Xu Meihong. Think about what you haven't told me. Think about the answers you know you should provide. We can talk later. You have an entire day to think about everything that was said here today. If you are honest we can finish this business tomorrow. Cooperate and you can leave. You have an opportunity to serve your nation and the Party.'

vii

There was no interrogation the next day. That evening, however, December 6, I was sitting on my bed when I heard the familiar sound of the approaching footsteps in the hall followed by a knock on the door. I assumed another interrogation session was about to commence. When Li Xia opened the door, there stood the Colonel and his aides holding a large cake. The Colonel entered the room and shouted, 'Happy Birthday, Meihong!'

I was dumbfounded. I was surrounded by six people singing 'Happy Birthday' to me – the same six people I'd expected only two days earlier to carry out my execution. They sang first in English and then in Chinese, then applauded, openly delighted at their success in surprising me.

The Colonel placed the cake on a small table one of the aides carried into the room. 'We know the dishes you like,' the Colonel said. 'And we've brought them for you tonight.' His aides brought in a dozen containers of food.

'No, please,' I protested, 'I really don't want anything like this for my birthday. I can't celebrate under these circumstances. Please forget it, will you?' He continued as though I had not spoken. This too was a scripted performance and he refused to deviate from the required lines.

Li Xia uncovered the containers of food. Cups were passed around and tea was poured for everyone. The Colonel toasted me and wished me a thousand years of life.

Plates, chopsticks and forks were distributed. The Colonel lit the twenty-five candles on the cake with his cigarette lighter and told me to make a wish before blowing them out. I did as he suggested. I closed my eyes, made my wish and blew out all the candles. But my wish didn't come true. When I opened my eyes I was still in that cold room and the Colonel was alive and standing beside me.

When we were almost finished eating the cake and the other

food, the Colonel announced, 'Meihong, congratulations. I hope you will always remember this birthday. And now I have a special gift for you.'

He handed me an unsealed envelope. I pulled out a letter and a card. I could see by the handwriting they were from my husband. On the card was a poem he'd composed for my birthday, telling me how he'd missed me and would always love me. In the brief letter he wrote, 'Nothing has changed between us. I arrived in Nanjing to celebrate your birthday and was told you won't be available for a while. I hope you will cooperate with these people and help clarify all of the misunderstandings that have arisen. I know you have done nothing wrong. Remember, I won't leave Nanjing until I see you again.'

I was both touched and stung by the letter. I at last had contact with someone who cared for me and was waiting for me. His confidence in my innocence no doubt led him to encourage me to cooperate with my interrogators. I wondered what they told him about me before they agreed to deliver his note. His words were sincere, of that I had no doubt. But like everyone else around me, he had been provided with just enough truth, blended with fantasy and conjecture, to ask me to cooperate with the very people who wished me, and anyone associated with me, harm.

My determination to show no weakness buckled. For the first and last time I allowed my guards to see my cry openly and without shame.

I placed the letter and poem back in the envelope and pressed it against my heart.

'We know that something unfortunate happened to you,' the Colonel said softly. 'We were ordered to help you. There were others in the military who immediately called for severe punishment for you – without delay. They looked into your activities and examined the charges and made their recommendations. But your friends intervened. They said there must be some explanation for your activities. We are waiting for that explanation.

'You are innocent,' the Colonel added. 'You are a twenty-five-year-old girl. When we were twenty-five we were innocent too. We made mistakes. Everyone does. If you admit that you made a mistake and tell us what it was, everything will be all right. We are not struggling against you. We are helping you and you have to allow us to help.'

Before the party ended, the Colonel summoned me into the darkened hallway. He closed the door behind us and stood close to me and spoke in a subdued and seemingly sincere voice. 'I should not have struck you. I want to apologize now. I lost my temper. I was out of line. I made a mistake. I'm sorry.' I knew, of course, that this too was just another act. Everything he said – every word – was predictable. I said nothing, neither accepting nor rejecting his apology. I did not thank him for the cake or the letter. When he had finished speaking there was an awkward prolonged silence as we faced each other in the dark. He expected some indication of my gratitude. I refused. I turned and went back into the room. As I opened the door, the other two men began gathering up the plates and remaining food. They left with the Colonel a few minutes later.

After they'd gone the three women laughed and chirped happily to each other and tried to strike up a conversation with me. Did I enjoy the food? Wasn't I surprised? Wasn't my husband's letter lovely?

'Remember,' Li Xia said to me, 'he is still waiting for you. He was permitted three days of vacation from his commanding officer. You're running out of time, Xu Meihong.'

'Can you get me some clean underwear?' I asked her. 'I've been here five days and I'm still wearing the same underwear.'

She was visibly shocked that I'd ignored her comments on my husband. Her sympathetic concern evaporated in a second. 'No,' she replied. 'This will be over soon. It's not necessary.'

Sometimes it seemed nobody in the building but me had a memory stretching back for more than an hour. Contrasting and contradictory personalities and attitudes were pulled on and off like sweaters and socks. Best wishes for a long life were forgotten before the very breath that carried them had completely left the lungs. Any hour might bring the threat of death, congratulations on past achievements, promises of a bright future, a slap on the face, a poem from my husband, statements of my innocence or a sharp rebuff if I asked for clean underwear. I thought this place might be an insane asylum. I had been kidnapped, I concluded, by inept uniformed red lunatics.

FOUR

First Love

Toward heaven
Which will judge me in the end
I lift my head.

Wind may sweep me away
But for my heart I reserve the right
To refuse to be counted among the lucky.

— SHU TING

i

The interrogation resumed shortly after dawn the next morning. As I seated myself at the table opposite the Colonel, he smiled broadly and nodded a greeting. He appeared more relaxed and he radiated confidence.

'Did you enjoy your birthday party?' he asked. I didn't respond. He didn't seem to mind my silence, and after several seconds he asked me once again, 'Did you enjoy your birthday party?'

'Yes, Colonel,' I replied. 'Thank you.'

'And the letter from your husband?'

'Yes, Colonel. Thank you.'

He began the formal session by suggesting that I had been merely a link in a chain that led to others. Perhaps I was truly innocent, he said. But that had to be proven. Others could have used me without my knowledge. That also was yet to be proven. He assumed there had been a conspiracy between an American agent and others. Even if I was innocent and ignorant of what really transpired around me, he needed me to tell him everything I'd seen and heard. Guilty parties could be identified and detained through my cooperation. Thus, he appealed to my patriotism and my loyalty to the PLA as well as my indignation at having been misled and misused by others.

After summarizing his suspicions – which he described as indisputable facts – and reminding me once again of the consequences of defiance on my part, the Colonel pulled a fat new folder from his briefcase and dropped it on the table. 'This is interesting,' he said. 'I have here three confessions, all signed. Two of them are true. But one is a lie.'

He studied me closely as he spoke, waiting for my response

when I realized what these documents were. 'Do you remember these confessions?' he asked. 'Do you recall your previous efforts to lie your way out of trouble? Your lies are part of your record, Xu Meihong. You should have known better. You wouldn't make that mistake of lying again, would you?'

ii

The Colonel was correct. I had lied for love in the past.

When I entered the Institute in 1981 all new cadets went through a lengthy orientation session during which we were warned of severe consequences of anything more than a professional and formal relationship with a member of the opposite sex. The discovery of an amorous attachment would lead to expulsion from the Institute and from the Army, we were assured. Female cadets were cautioned to remain above suspicion, avoiding one-on-one conversations with a male cadet and never meeting alone with a male either on or off campus.

For three years the twelve young women of my class obeyed the regulations and faithfully followed the rules. But when we returned home during the holidays and the summers and talked to friends who attended civilian schools, we discovered that many of them had become romantically involved. It was natural for men and women our age to fall in love, they said, and suggested that the cadets at the Institute were required to lead a stilted and unnatural existence. While we marched and trained and sublimated our amorous impulses, they dated and enjoyed themselves and sought out their future spouses. They didn't understand why we weren't allowed to do the same.

Things changed during our senior year. We were more mature, self-confident and reckless than we'd been as new cadets. In the first weeks of our final year, some of my female classmates revealed in the privacy of our barracks that they had found boyfriends during the summer. They boasted that they wrote letters to them and mailed them off campus. They also went to public telephones in Nanjing and called their boyfriends regularly and planned to visit them during the holidays. None of us were shocked by the revelations. The military admonition against boyfriends, we found, no longer intimidated us.

I fell in love the first time in my life during my senior year at the Institute. I knew this was a breach of military regulations, but I couldn't have cared less. The object of my affection was a fellow cadet named Lin Cheng. He was handsome, tall and slim, the brightest student in his class and a member of the Communist Party. He was expected to have a stellar future in the PLA and to rise rapidly through the ranks.

I first noticed him in my second year and immediately felt an attraction to him. But I resisted it for two more years. Since he was the class leader for the men and I for the women, we attended leadership meetings together but never spoke privately. I'd often listened to him make speeches and was impressed by his bearing and intelligence and by the respect the other cadets showed for him.

I found myself thinking about him often during the summer after my junior year. My feelings for him grew stronger and I dreamed about him and watched him closely. I sensed a quickening of my heart when I was in his presence.

Each morning the cadets jogged to the Yangtze River and back. I was usually the only woman to finish the entire distance. Lin Cheng led the men when they jogged. I jogged close behind him, listening to his breathing, hoping he might hear my footsteps and turn around to see me and recognize me and say something. Sometimes, as others dropped back, only the two of us remained far ahead of them. I'd put my feet where his had been and imagined that I touched the earth where he had touched it and thought there had to be some spiritual connection he could sense.

At other times, if I lost him in the crowd, I dropped out and then waited for him to return and fell in behind him without saying a word. Nobody seemed to notice my doing this. Not even him.

At night in my quarters I whispered to Tao Hui, my closest girlfriend, about him. She giggled and told me she thought I was losing my mind. 'You've got to be careful,' she advised. 'Somebody will notice what you're doing and you'll get into big trouble. And remember,' she said, 'he could be sent to Tibet or some other distant post after we graduate. What will you do then?'

'If he's sent far away,' I sighed, 'I'll wait for him.'

'Well, maybe you should talk to him about your feelings,' she suggested. 'But be careful!'

I agreed with her suggestion and decided, in my romantic desperation, to send him a letter. I carefully composed several lines telling him I had special feelings for him and that I wondered if perhaps he felt the same way about me. I wasn't sure how to get my message to him without anyone else discovering it. I carried it inside a book for several days awaiting an opportunity to slip it to him. One Saturday evening I went to a classroom to study and he was there alone. It took me several minutes to decide if I should leave or stay. Finally I entered the room and sat down. I didn't have the courage, however, to say 'hello' to him. I spent an hour staring at the same page without reading a single word. Finally, I rose, took the letter from my book, dropped it on his desk and left. He pushed it to the side of his desk, and continued reading.

My emotions were mixed as I hurried back to my barracks. On the one hand, I feared he might turn my letter over to a commanding officer and I'd be expelled from the Institute. On the other, he might read it and respond by revealing his own special feelings for me. So the fear I felt was tempered by elation and romantic expectation.

I couldn't sit still, nor could I sleep. Two hours later I returned to the classroom building. I was too self-conscious to enter, so I stood outside and watched Lin Cheng through the window. He was still alone in the room reading. I saw my unopened envelope on his desk. I returned to my quarters and asked Tao Hui to take a walk with me on campus. I told her what I'd done and what he'd done and all she said was that she hoped he wouldn't betray me.

The next evening I went to the same classroom. No one was there. I opened my assigned desk and took out my textbook. Inside the desk was an envelope. I slipped the envelope into my textbook and walked quickly to an isolated spot on campus where several benches were set in the middle of a grove of trees. I sat down, and looked around to make sure no one could see me. Then, for the first time in my life, I prayed. I hoped the envelope contained the key to my future happiness.

Lin Cheng began by thanking me for my letter. He said he had wondered about my intentions since he noticed me watching him and running behind him. 'But we are not supposed to carry on a romantic relationship, not now. I really wish you would concentrate less on me and more on your work and on gaining Communist Party membership,' he wrote. 'Don't let little things distract you from what is really important. Time is running out for all of us here. We should be busy preparing for the future.'

I read and reread the note, analyzing every character and trying to find something hopeful in it. I wondered what he meant by 'not now.' I showed the note to Tao Hui. She was disappointed and advised me to forget him. 'Do you know how many men are watching you when you walk on campus, enter a classroom or sit at the dining-room table?' she asked. 'Do you know how many men would die to have a chance to speak to you privately?' There were two thousand men and only twelve women in the Institute. Each of the women was aware of the attention of the male cadets every second of every day. But I only cared for one man and I was determined to do all I could to make sure that someday he'd be my husband.

The next morning I ran behind him to the river and back. He didn't acknowledge my presence. So in the afternoon I wrote to him again. I thanked him for his note and told him I would not bother him again, but I would wait for him forever.

The next day I received a reply from him. 'We need to talk,' he wrote.

That presented a challenge. If we were discovered speaking to each other in private in a classroom, we'd be questioned about it. To be safe, we'd have to meet far from campus. It took ten days and several more notes before we finally arranged a meeting. We prepared as meticulously for our encounter as if we were planning a military operation.

We took separate buses to a park in Nanjing far from the

Institute. I was so excited that I arrived an hour early. He arrived on time. We sat on a bench and talked nervously about the weather, the bus ride to the park, our commanders, our classes and our classmates. We were too shy and hesitant at first to say anything personal. Finally, after several hours, we became bold enough to talk about our families and ourselves.

I learned that he had always excelled in school and in politics. He had been first in his class in high school and at the Institute. He took his responsibilities and duties very seriously. He was a passionate believer in the Party and in the modernization policies of Deng Xiaoping. His words thrilled me. I found my faith in the future of the Party and the PLA bolstered by his selfless dedication to them. I thought if there were many other young officers and Party members like him, then the future of China was even brighter than I'd expected.

We talked all afternoon and into the evening, not noticing the passing hours. By the time we rose from the bench to leave, we discovered that the last bus to the Institute had already gone. We had to walk back. We were supposed to be in our barracks with lights out at 10 P.M. We were going to be late and we were worried about getting caught. So we walked as fast as we could toward the Institute. When I had difficulty keeping up with him, Lin Cheng reached out and took my hand. It was the first time in my life I'd held hands with a man.

We did not arrive at the Institute until 2 A.M. Lin Cheng pulled me to the side of the road when we were close enough to see the lights of the sentry post. He turned to whisper to me, leaned down and then, before saying a word, kissed me on the forehead. I blushed brightly.

If we tried to enter through the gate, he said, we'd be detained and held for questioning. But there was another way in. He'd heard that several nights earlier some senior cadets had sneaked out of the Institute and back in again through a gap in the wire on the wall. We walked along the wall until he spotted the place described by the cadets. Directly beneath the small gap in the wire, cadets had loosened some bricks and pulled them out to form steps up the wall. Lin Cheng helped me climb up first and boosted me as I neared the top. I crawled through the gap in the wire and then jumped down the other side. He followed close behind.

Before we parted he kissed me again and squeezed my hand. Then we ran in opposite directions to our barracks. Tao Hui was awake and waiting for me. We whispered about my big romantic adventure and she warned me again of the consequences of getting caught. 'You have to be much more careful after this,' she advised. 'You have to cool down your heart.' But I was in no mood to cool down. I was thinking only of the next time I'd see my love.

The following morning the student leaders among the seniors who were not yet Communist Party members were asked to fill out applications for membership. I was given a three-month probationary status while my behavior and my background were carefully examined. I began attending special study sessions for prospective Party members.

Meanwhile, Lin Cheng and I continued to meet outside the Institute whenever we felt it was safe. We even arranged to pass each other at night on campus and to reach out and touch hands when we did.

One afternoon we met in Nanjing. I wanted to buy some books, so after meeting at a prearranged place in the city we walked to an open-front bookstore. We were standing together paging through some new books. When I looked up I saw an officer from the Institute just outside the shop. He stared at us then hurried away.

I was worried, but Lin Cheng insisted that the officer might not have recognized us. Better not to worry about it, he said. The PLA had more important things to do than spy on senior cadets. But we'd have to be more careful in the future.

Early the next morning a guard appeared at my barracks and summoned me to a meeting with my political commissar. Without any preliminary questions, he asked me what I had been doing in Nanjing in the company of a male cadet. I denied it was me and told him that I had no idea what he was talking about.

Then he warned me that I'd made a second serious mistake. First I had been with a male cadet off campus and then I lied about it. 'You are in serious trouble,' he said. 'Why are you lying to me? What do you have to hide?' he hissed.

I told him I had nothing to hide and I'd done nothing wrong. After a pause he offered me a deal. He said he just wanted to know the truth. 'If you tell me the truth,' he said, 'there will be no serious consequences.' If I cooperated fully, he promised, I could get off with a simple warning since I was a class leader and a prospective Party member. I knew he had an eyewitness and I had to come up with a logical explanation of what had happened. So I told him that I ran into Lin Cheng in a bookstore in Nanjing by accident.

'Is that all?' he asked.

'Yes,' I responded.

'You've never met him anyplace else? Just at the bookstore in Nanjing?' he asked.

'Yes,' I affirmed.

'Are you in love with him?' he asked.

'No,' I lied.

'Are you sure?'

'I'm sure.' As I spoke, I felt my voice and my eyes contradicting me.

He asked me to write down what happened that day and then sign it. When I was finished he dismissed me.

I needed to tell Lin Cheng what I'd done. But I couldn't find him. I wasn't aware that other officers had summoned him to a separate interrogation while I was being questioned. They were friendly, reminding him of his stature on the campus and within the Party. They said they could never discipline him publicly and were willing to forgive almost any transgression should he tell them the truth. They chatted with him for two hours about life on campus and his future hopes and plans. They plied him with cigarettes and acted as though this was merely a friendly inquiry. In time, their assurances and deceptions worked. Lin Cheng told them he wanted to make an agreement with them. He would tell them everything that happened and take full responsibility for it only if they would leave me alone. They consented and said that was a reasonable and noble request. He then admitted that we had gone into Nanjing together and that we were in love.

They patted him on the back and assured him this was only natural and they understood. They asked him to write it all down – every meeting with me, every touch, every detail.

The next morning I spoke with him for a moment when we left class. I told him I'd lied in order to protect him. He told me he'd told the truth – told them he loved me – in order to protect me.

'What?' I asked. 'You told them you love me?' I was surprised that he'd told others about his feelings for me. He had never used the word 'love' in our conversations before. So my anxiety at his confession was tempered by my delight at his revelation of his feelings for me. 'How much trouble are we in?' I asked.

'None at all,' he assured me. 'I've taken care of everything. There will be no problem. Honesty is the best policy. You'll never hear anything about this again. I have their promise that they won't bother you. We have to trust the Party.'

'If they call me again,' I told him, 'I'll tell the truth only to confirm that you didn't lie to them.'

'My poor little girl,' he said. 'You worry too much.'

That afternoon I was again summoned to a meeting room. Several officers were present to question me. Their attitude was dramatically different from my interrogator on the previous day. They shouted, pounded on the table, shook their fists menacingly and waved my confession in my face. The word 'liar!' was thrown at me again and again. They demanded I write another confession or both Lin Cheng and I would be expelled from the PLA and sent home immediately. They wanted to know the details, they said, *all* the details. I panicked. I thought first of saving Lin Cheng's career. The whole thing had been my fault, I told them. I explained how I'd pursued him. They listened carefully and ordered me to write it all down. The only way to save his military career and my own, they said, was to do as they demanded and make a complete confession and apology.

I wasn't allowed to leave the small office until I wrote a lengthy confession telling them what I'd written in my first note to Lin Cheng, where we met and what we said, how we returned late from the park and climbed over the wall, how we arranged to meet in Nanjing and what we talked about when we met.

But the next day I was called back and told that my confession wasn't detailed enough. They demanded more. They suggested that we must have had sexual relations and told me that Lin Cheng had confessed it. I told them he could not have confessed to something that didn't happen.

'Are you accusing Lin Cheng of lying?' they asked.

'Lin Cheng is incapable of lying,' I told them. 'Please don't manipulate us and use us against each other,' I begged.

'How can we believe you?' they asked again, and waved my first confession in my face. 'You lied to us before. Are you lying to us again?'

Their accusations were so persistent and their demeanor so unwavering that I felt my resistance crumbling before their barrage of questions and contradictions of everything I said. I found myself wondering if I shouldn't just cooperate and tell them what they wanted to hear – even though it wasn't true. They promised forgiveness and understanding in exchange for full cooperation. But in the end I couldn't do it and I stuck with my truth.

When I got back to my quarters I was so demoralized and exhausted that I fell face-down on my bed and sobbed.

Lin Cheng was also questioned again. They showed him a copy of my original confession in which I'd said I was not in love with him. They teased him with it and suggested I had been playing a game with him. They said he should terminate our relationship and forget about me.

But Lin Cheng was angered by their words and resented the fact that trusted officers had broken their promise to him and had gone after me. He offered them no new information and insisted he loved me and he always would, no matter what they said.

The following day, I received official notification that I was suspended from my probationary period for Communist Party membership. I was also dismissed as class leader for the female cadets. Both of my confessions, I was told, had become part of my permanent record.

Suspending or expelling Lin Cheng from the Communist

Party would imply that they had made a mistake in admitting him and they were not prepared to go that far. But the officers wouldn't let him get off too easily. They decided to settle for a public self-criticism from him that could serve as a deterrent to other cadets.

I managed to meet Lin Cheng in an empty classroom. We tearfully confessed our love for each other and decided that no matter what punishment we'd be given for our romance, we would never be sorry for what we'd done. We even considered thanking the officers who'd questioned us because they had given us the opportunity to defend and protect each other and to proclaim our love before others. We embraced and vowed that we would be husband and wife someday no matter how hard others tried to pull us apart.

The next day the cadets were summoned to an evening assembly to hear the self-criticism of Lin Cheng. All the commanders and junior officers were present in the front rows of our assembly hall for his appearance.

When everyone was seated, Lin Cheng walked to the middle of the stage. He carried no papers – usually confessed wrong-doers read their confessions. He didn't even have note cards. I cringed as I waited to hear my name announced and to feel the eyes of everyone in the room on me.

'I am sorry,' Lin Cheng began. 'Two weeks ago I went to Nanjing for personal reasons and returned late. Please accept my apology.' He paused for a moment, looked around the audience, glanced at the officers, smiled weakly and returned to his seat.

His statement lasted less than ten seconds. Officers and cadets fidgeted and whispered when he'd finished. The political commissar was uncertain what to do next. A few minutes later he walked to the stage and dismissed us.

I heard several cadets snickering as they rose to leave. Lin Cheng had turned his confession into a triumph for himself and for me and the officers knew it. He had not demonstrated the anticipated contrition, nor had his words served as a deterrent to others. Yet he had done what had been required – made his public self-criticism. I knew at that moment why I loved him.

We were forbidden to speak to each other as long as we remained cadets in the Institute. But we defied our superiors and wrote to each other secretly on a daily basis. We invented our own special language and symbols to express our feelings for each other. There was a massive dictionary on the top floor of our library. It was so heavy that for years nobody bothered to move it from the shelf. It served as a perfect mailbox for us. I was happier than I'd ever been before in my life in those final weeks at the Institute. I knew that the most valuable thing I found in the PLA was love.

Lin Cheng paid for his defiant act. At the end of our senior year, while other class leaders were assigned to choice positions in Beijing, Shanghai and Guangzhou, he was sent to Taiyuan, the capital of Shanxi province, to teach English in a military school for submarine officers. It was not a prestigious institution and did not grant degrees. Lin Cheng's military future was no longer promising.

When I learned of his assignment I became physically ill. I felt responsible for damaging his career by pursuing him and confessing my love to him. I had no doubt he would have been given a prestigious assignment had it not been for me and my uncontrolled romantic impulses. Yet he never blamed me for what happened, never expressed doubt or regret about what we'd done.

None of the female cadets were sent to hardship posts. I was assigned to stay in Nanjing and work at the Institute. My new duty was to serve as an administrative aide on the staff of a one-star general.

Lin Cheng and I dreaded the approaching separation. Each time we met we talked of marriage. But the PLA had its rules – women had to be twenty-four and men twenty-five before they could marry. I was twenty-two at the time and he was twenty-three. We vowed to marry in two years.

Before the final banquet of our senior year, each of the graduates bought a special 'Memory Book' and we wrote notes to each other in it. On the cover of the book was a quotation from Chairman Mao: 'A thousand years is too long. Seize the moment.' Inside we signed our names, wrote down our addresses and birth dates and then added a personal note.

I asked Lin Cheng to sign my book and he wrote on the first page, 'If you are real gold, do not be afraid of being buried beneath dirt.'

iii

After his departure for Taiyuan we wrote to each other two or three times a day. On October 1, 1985, China's National Day, Lin Cheng was granted a brief leave of absence from his school and came to visit me in Nanjing – a thirty-eight-hour train journey from Taiyuan. We decided then that our separation was too painful and that we'd do everything – even sacrifice our military careers – to be nearer to each other.

In early December 1987 we reached the age required by the PLA for marriage. When I told my commanding general of my plan to marry he was unusually pleased. As a wedding gift to us, he said, he would use his connections to get Lin Cheng transferred to an important post in Beijing. He added that he expected to be transferred to the capital himself within a year and that he would keep me as his aide, so Lin Cheng and I could finally be united.

We made our application for marriage and the required background checks were initiated. Two weeks later we were given official approval to marry.

A day after we received the good news I traveled to Taiyuan to prepare for our wedding ceremony. But before plans could be finalized, the General sent us a telegram summoning us to Beijing. He notified us that he had secured early approval for Lin Cheng's transfer and he wanted us to meet him in the capital immediately. We postponed our wedding and caught the train to Beijing on the following day.

When the General told us what he'd accomplished, we realized how influential he was and how extensive his contacts were in Beijing. He'd succeeded in getting Lin Cheng assigned as the foreign affairs assistant to General Zhang Zhen, president of the National Defense University (NDU). I learned a short time later that the General had been working with others for several years to put promising young officers in influential positions where they could effectively work with him and other high-ranking officers in promoting reform in the PLA.

We were impressed by the beautiful campus of the NDU, which was near the Summer Palace. In the evening we took long walks through the campus and out along the shore of Kunming Lake. We were both excited by the prospect of living together in Beijing in the near future. All of our dreams seemed to be coming true, despite the difficulties we'd experienced during the early days of our courtship.

I returned to my post in Nanjing and Lin Cheng assumed his new position at the NDU. One of his first assignments was to take a delegation of American military officers around Beijing. He served as their host, escort, translator and tour guide for several days. The head of the delegation was so impressed by Lin Cheng's work that he extended an official invitation to him to visit Washington, D.C. His commander approved the trip and Lin Cheng hastily made preparations for his first journey abroad. He was provided with a generous bonus by the PLA to purchase a new wardrobe for his trip and his superiors advised him to buy only the best clothing and shoes available, since they wanted him to impress his American hosts.

We decided to marry before he departed for the United States. In early 1988, General Zhou Erjun hosted a beautiful reception for us that was attended by many of the top staff officers from the NDU and by representatives of several foreign delegations studying at the school. We had ten uninterrupted days together for our honeymoon before Lin Cheng departed for America.

I went back to Nanjing after seeing my husband off at the Beijing airport. When he returned two weeks later he phoned me and excitedly told me about America. 'It's incredible,' he said. 'It is the most beautiful place I've ever seen.'

His stories of the United States contrasted dramatically with everything we'd been told about it. He was impressed by the cleanliness of the country – the clean streets and the clear air and water. I could hardly believe his words. 'What is the condition of the peasants and of the workers?' I asked him. He told me there were no peasants in America and the workers were rich by Chinese standards. I was disappointed by his remarks and thought he must be exaggerating.

America was a revelation for him and he said so in his official report. His commanding officer, who had been to America six months earlier and favored closer ties with the United States, read his report and approved it.

But a high-ranking political commissar read it and took issue with my husband's observations. He summoned Lin Cheng to his office and cautioned him about his lack of criticism of the United States. 'You have to be more careful in what you write,' he warned. 'The Americans are good at deception. You didn't see the real America. You only met rich Americans. They have millions of homeless and unemployed and they conceal them from visitors. Remember that. The real America, the one they hide from us, is ugly.'

iv

The Colonel seemed to know almost everything about my husband and me. He held the confessions we'd made and he was aware of my husband's journey to America, his reports on that journey and the comments on the report by Lin Cheng's commanding officer, the people he associated with at the NDU, the man who'd hosted our wedding reception and the names of all those who attended. Any of those people could be suspects for the moment. But I was the key to unlocking the puzzle of a conspiracy, he said. Thus, it was important, he said, that I cooperate fully or face the consequences.

'I'd like to talk now about your husband and his friends. I'd like to talk about his trip to America and what he told you about it and whom he met there. I'd like to talk to you about his trip to Nanjing to meet your American friend.'

I stared at the folder and didn't respond immediately to his question. I didn't want to undergo prolonged questioning about my husband and his associates and friends. I feared that something I might say could, in some way, cause him trouble and, as in our last year at the Institute, jeopardize his career. He remained a good officer and Party member. He dismissed troubling events in the past and hoped to improve the PLA, the Party and the country. I didn't want to frustrate his dreams again. There was but one way to free him from suspicion.

When the Colonel leaned forward to switch on the tape recorder I asked him to wait for a moment. He paused and I asked, 'May I write a letter to my husband?'

'No, Xu Meihong,' he replied with a tone of something like compassion in his voice. 'You are not allowed to communicate with anyone outside.'

'Not even a brief phone conversation?' I asked.

He thought about it for a moment and sensed that this might be a point on which he could bargain with me and perhaps induce me to provide him with information he needed. 'What is it you wish to tell him?'

'I want to tell my husband to leave me alone and never to bother me again.'

'Why?'

'Because I don't love him anymore.'

'But I saw you crying last night when you read his letter. What made you change your mind overnight?' He turned on the tape recorder as he spoke.

'I no longer love him, Colonel.'

'Why is that? Has he done something to make you feel this way, Xu Meihong?'

'I just want to leave my husband out of this. I don't want to talk about him.'

'I don't think we can do that, Xu Meihong.'

'He's done nothing wrong.'

'I don't know that.'

'He's done nothing wrong, Colonel. I swear. It's a waste of time to talk about him.'

'I am the one who decides what's a waste of time,' the Colonel snapped. 'Let's just clear up a few things, then we can move on. All right?'

I stared blankly at the tabletop, avoiding the Colonel's stare.

'Who sent your husband – Lin Cheng – to the United States soon after his transfer to the NDU?'

I stared into space and pretended to be trying to remember who it was. Then, slowly, I said, 'I believe the NDU sent him, Colonel.'

'But who was it in the school – which officer gave him the assignment?'

'I don't think any single officer was responsible for it, Colonel. I think the entire staff approved his trip.'

'But he was invited by American military officers, wasn't he?'

'Yes. They were impressed by him and wanted to repay his hospitality.'

'He visited Washington, D.C.?'

'Yes, his hosts lived there.'

'And he visited the Pentagon?'

'I'm not sure, Colonel. I don't remember that.'

'Did he make any sightseeing trips to Virginia?'

'Yes.'

'Whom did he visit there? Do you remember any names?'

'Yes. He said he visited the home of George and Martha Washington.' The Colonel and his aide were about to write down the names, then they realized I was mocking them.

'You aren't very helpful, Xu Meihong.'

'I'm trying to remember, Colonel. I'm doing my best.'

'He visited New York, didn't he?'

'Yes.'

'And San Francisco?'

'Yes.'

'Do you know the location of San Jose, California?'

'No.'

'Not far from San Francisco. What a coincidence.'

'I don't know anything about that, Colonel.'

'Didn't Larry Engelmann drive to San Francisco to meet with your husband?'

'No.'

'This is important, Xu Meihong. Are you absolutely sure – *absolutely* – that Larry Engelmann did not meet your husband in San Francisco?'

I thought about the question for several seconds before asserting, 'Yes, I'm absolutely sure. My husband would have told me if they'd met.'

'Does your husband ever lie to you or keep information from you?'

'How would I know if he kept information from me, Colonel? I can't answer that.'

'How many times did your husband visit you in the Center?' he asked.

'One time. During the National Holiday vacation.'

'The week of October 1?'

'Yes.'

'Did he meet alone with Larry Engelmann at that time?' the Colonel asked.

'No, not alone.'

'But they met?'

'Yes, they met for a moment. They exchanged greetings in the hall. That was all.'

'How long did they speak?'

'Perhaps ten seconds.'

'Did the American give him anything? A book, perhaps, or a video-tape?'

'No. They said hello and that was all. Colonel, I said I wanted to leave my husband out of this.'

'In a few minutes, Xu Meihong. Did he meet other Americans in the Center?'

'It's difficult not to since Americans are everywhere in the Center.'

'Did he talk to any other Americans?'

'Certainly.'

'Did he meet alone with any of them?'

'No, of course not.'

'And in Beijing – you are sure he never met alone with Larry Engelmann there?'

'Yes. I am sure.'

A sudden look of triumph came across the Colonel's face. He pulled out another folder and said, 'I think you're lying to me again, Xu Meihong,' he said. 'We have pictures of them together with no one else present. Remember what will happen if you lie to me! My patience is limited.'

'Colonel, they never met privately in Beijing.'

'But we have pictures. They don't lie. Would you like to see them?'

'Yes, I want to see them. I don't believe you.'

He lifted a photograph from his folder and slid it across the table to me. It showed my husband and Larry sitting together at the same table in what I recognized as the Greenery Restaurant in the Jianguo Hotel in Beijing, where Larry stayed for a week. 'They were not alone together, Colonel. I'm sure of it. I've seen this picture before. I can even identify the photographer,' I said.

'Really. Who is it?'

'Me. I took this photograph with Larry's camera. That's why I'm not in it. I was there. If you look carefully you can see three settings on the table. So, you have an arrangement with the photo shops in Nanjing to turn over copies of his pictures, right?'

'I don't think so. We have far better sources,' he grumbled.

'If you have good sources, then you should know that they were never together without me. I'm telling you the truth, Colonel. The next time you show me any evidence, you'd better question your sources thoroughly in terms of how they obtain evidence.'

'Did the American ever meet with your husband's friends?'

'Of course not.'

'Are you certain? We noticed that you had a *distinguished* visitor from Beijing shortly after your husband departed in early October.'

I thought for a moment and then remembered the visitor. 'Yes,' I said. 'That's true. A general from the National Defense University visited me.'

'A *general* from the National Defense University. And not just any general, was it? Tell me more about this visitor. Two visitors from the NDU to the Center in two weeks. Interesting.'

'Yes, he did visit me, briefly.'

'Why? Whom did he see there?' The Colonel suddenly became highly animated and his eyes opened wide, as if he was about to bag a big prize.

117

'He came to attend a military meeting in PLA regional headquarters in Nanjing a week after the National Holiday. My husband had left his room keys in my apartment. He asked this general to pick them up for him. That's why he visited me – to pick up the keys.'

'You expect me to believe you?'

'If you believe the truth, yes.'

'Keys?'

'Keys.'

'And he met with no one but you?'

'Just me.'

'You're lying.'

'Just me, Colonel. Just me.'

'He met with the American, didn't he?'

'No. He met with me and I gave him keys.'

'The nephew of Zhou Enlai met with you in Nanjing to pick up keys?'

'Yes.'

'A two-star general came to see you rather than sending an aide?'

'Yes.'

'Did you know he has a daughter in the United States?'

'So does Deng Xiaoping. So do many other leaders of our country.'

'But Deng Xiaoping didn't come to your room in Nanjing to pick up your husband's keys, did he?'

The Colonel suddenly started to page through the remaining papers in his file, pausing to peruse a page carefully now and then. After several minutes he stood, closed his file, placed it in his briefcase and left without looking at me again. I stared silently at the wall for several minutes before the captain escorted me back to the room I occupied with my female guards.

That night I reviewed in my mind the questions the Colonel had asked in order to determine where he might go next. I still wondered what group was behind him. Whom did he meet with when he left this base? Who was providing him with files and questions? Who was it, really, who was toying with my life, deciding if I should live or die?

The Colonel didn't show up during the next five days. During that time, with the exception of a walk to the bathroom each morning, I remained confined to the room with my guards. I was not allowed to read newspapers or books. My conversations with my guards were brief. Most of the time I lay on my bed and stared at the ceiling, trying to anticipate what line of questioning the Colonel might pursue next. When I stood and paced back and forth in the small room, one of the guards always positioned herself between me and the locked door.

On the sixth day I was summoned to the interrogation room before breakfast. After I was seated, the Colonel opened a new line of questioning. Someone had decided not to pursue my husband's connection with this any longer. There was another target now – higher up and more vulnerable. The Colonel turned to my relationship with the General, my commander at the Institute, whom he referred to disdainfully as 'the Coffee General.'

'Your husband was given his position at the NDU because your commanding officer interceded on his behalf, isn't that correct?'

'My husband is eminently qualified for his position.'

'He had a patron. He didn't move from Taiyuan to Beijing without someone's help.'

'Yes, someone noticed his talent and helped promote him.'

'And this was your commanding officer – the General.'

'He was helpful.'

'Yes,' the Colonel said. 'He's an ambitious man with an interesting past. Let's talk about the General. He sent you to the Center to meet your American friend, didn't he?'

'I was sent to the Center by the Institute and not by any individual,' I said.

'We know the General visited you often at the Center,' he continued, pretending that he hadn't heard me. 'The General,' the Colonel began his new line of questioning. 'The *Coffee* General. Let's talk about him now, Xu Meihong.' Thus he set out in a new direction in his interrogation. He seemed confident and convinced that the General would be an easier target and I could be used to undercut the officer he hated more than any other in the PLA.

FIVE

The General

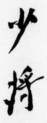

Our forefathers, however dumb, managed after
a few thousand years of reflection to elaborate
a subtle recipe to control people: crush all
those whom you can crush; as for the others,
put them on a pedestal. By putting them on a
pedestal, you can also control them – you
merely need to whisper constantly in their
ears, 'Do as I tell you, otherwise I shall bring
you down.'

— LU XUN

i

I gradually saw how the Colonel, in his zealous resolve to expose disloyalty in the upper ranks of the PLA, carefully arranged disparate people and events to create a convincing vision of conspiracy. When he shifted from asking me about my husband and his colleagues and started to question me about the General, it became clear that he imagined a nefarious U.S.-Nanjing-Beijing-Shanghai intelligence conspiracy and that I was in some way central to communication between the various conspirators. He wanted desperately to use me and my relationship with the American to unmask, discredit and purge a clique of PLA officers who had been working quietly for broad reforms in the military. The General, a prominent leader of the reformist group, had worked for years for closer ties with the United States and for rapid modernization of politics, economics and the military. Class struggle and correct political thought, he said, had to make way for pragmatic approaches to the problems that faced China.

The Colonel and his superiors, on the other hand, comprised part of a powerful, entrenched conservative clique of PLA officers – many of them elderly – who felt threatened by the ambitious young reformers ever since Deng Xiaoping assumed power and began to ease the aging Maoist ideologues out of positions of power in the Party and the Army. This old guard constantly searched for a way to discredit the reformers. In early 1987 they'd forced the resignation of the most outspoken reformer in the government, Party General Secretary Hu Yaobang. They awaited their next chance to silence their outspoken critics within the military. When they thought they could link leading reformists with a foreign intelligence agent, they seized their chance. All they required for a swift and fatal blow to the reformers was my cooperation and confession.

The General was a tempting target. Over the years he'd made powerful friends within the Party and the PLA. But he also had many powerful enemies. During his crusade for closer ties to the United States and for more military and cultural exchanges with the West he'd actively recruited young officers from around the country to his banner. The conservatives were frightened by his program and his success and they watched and waited for the chance to bring him down.

He was not unaware of the dangers of endeavoring to change China. He'd warned me to be vigilant and to expect his detractors to make a move against him at any time. He had me swear I'd never betray his trust and I'd assured him I never would.

For years he confided in me and shared extensive information on the membership and the operations of his cabal of officers and their broad-ranging reform agenda. But the General's clandestine group was only one of many PLA factions jockeying to position themselves for a power grab. As he and his associates worked and planned, the General constantly watched over his shoulder for a sign that he'd been betrayed. He had good cause to worry. He'd been purged from the PLA once already, imprisoned, sentenced to death and then miraculously exonerated and restored to power. He knew he was taking an enormous risk once again. But he and his friends were willing to make the necessary sacrifices in order to achieve their goals and, as they saw, save China.

The General assumed that when his rivals sought to rein him in they would first solicit the cooperation of his aides and close associates and turn them against him. Power struggles in China customarily involved cutting the small roots from under the tall trees first. Once the roots were severed, the tree toppled easily. The defection of those around an ambitious or powerful man left him isolated, vulnerable and weak. And so the General chose members of his inner circle carefully and coached them on how to behave and what to say or not to say should we ever be detained and questioned about him. 'Never sign a confession,' he told me several times. 'No matter what they promise you, don't sign it. Your signed confession can be your death warrant. Even if it's not, it will remain with you for the rest of your life. You can never escape and you can be sure that when the political winds shift, someone will bring it out and punish you for it.' He also cautioned me never to leave a paper trail. 'Destroy all your letters. Never keep a diary. Burn your notebooks when you're finished with them. In that way, when you must create a past for yourself, you can do it from your imagination and none of your words will resurface on papers from the past to contradict what you say in the present. And if you are arrested, always remember that your friends will be working for your release, no matter what your interrogators tell you.'

So when the Colonel asked about my relationship with the General and my knowledge of his activities, I knew what to expect and I was prepared to protect my friends.

ii

In the summer of 1985, following my graduation from the Nanjing Institute I was assigned as an aide to the Institute's executive officer. I moved my belongings from student quarters into a small apartment in an officer's facility.

The pay and privileges of a PLA officer at that time, compared with other professions, were generous. Starting salaries for military academy graduates were twice as much as those for graduates of civilian schools. Room, board and uniforms were provided without charge and transportation by chauffeur-driven military car was also available.

Yet I was not happy. My final year at the Institute had disillusioned me. I saw firsthand how the Party and the PLA used deception and lies to confound its own and to turn friend against friend and lover against lover. At the same time, the man I loved had been assigned to a faraway post as punishment for his transgressions and I too was therefore punished by our forced separation. I thought about leaving the military, but when I'd been inducted into the PLA in 1981 I'd promised them fifteen years of service in exchange for my education. I was not prepared to desert and I knew of no other way at that time to escape my military obligation and my unhappy existence. Friends took note of my pay and privileges and couldn't understand my complaints about military life.

My commander, the Institute's executive officer, was charged with supervising every aspect of the education and training of the cadets who would become the future military leaders and intelligence agents of the PLA. The young male and female graduates from the Institute received their initial assignments from him. He continued to support them and promote their careers in the PLA in the following years. When they succeeded and rose within the officer corps, they not only added prestige to the Institute but also to their commander back at the Institute. Just as he commended them he expected in turn for them to remain steadfast in their loyalty to him, no matter where their assignments took them.

Military headquarters in Beijing also sought the support of the executive officer so they could send promising young recruits to him (often family members) and receive the finest young graduates from the Institute to serve on their own staff. It was therefore possible over time for an ambitious and talented executive officer to put together a powerful network of officers in influential positions around the country who worked together to further specific military personnel and programs.

Three months after I assumed my new position at the Institute the elderly executive officer retired and a new one was assigned. The new executive officer – the man the Colonel referred to as 'the Coffee General' – we learned, had been appointed to the post by the Central Military Commission in Beijing and was a rising star in the PLA. The Institute was considered his stepping-stone to a higher position within the PLA, so he was not expected to remain long in Nanjing.

On the morning of his arrival, we put everything in order and lined up in front of our office building to welcome him. The new executive officer was in his mid-forties, tall, handsome and very distinguished-looking. He wore stylish aviator sunglasses and moved with uncommon grace and composure as he inspected us.

During his first day on the job he addressed his staff. He told us we should expect dramatic changes in his office. He let us know he would tolerate no favoritism or incompetence. A new era was about to begin for us, he said, an era of strict professionalism. Much would be expected of each of us. But in the end, he said, both the Institute and the PLA would be vastly improved by our efforts.

He quickly demonstrated uncommon enthusiasm and ability as he pursued his duties and he inspired his staff by his example. Within days he'd visited every class on campus and spoken with the instructors and students about the curriculum. He invited comments from students and faculty alike and carefully weighed each of their complaints and suggestions.

A few weeks after his arrival, the General soon disclosed his innovative master plan for the Institute. He was determined to modernize military intelligence training, he said, to raise the quality of instruction on campus. To do that, he'd need financing and support from Beijing and connections with influential military leaders in the regional headquarters of the PLA as well as other military academics and schools. He also energetically courted high Party officials and sought their support for his plan.

I got along well with him from the start and he soon entrusted me with broader duties and named me his operational officer. I was sent to monitor and evaluate classroom instruction and the competency of our teaching staff. He asked me to provide detailed reports on everything I saw and heard and then he discussed my reports with me at length. The bureaucratic torpor I'd first found in the executive office gave way to a dynamism and determination.

The General gradually took a select corps of junior officers at the Institute into his confidence. I was among them and I became part of his privileged inner circle. Over the course of many months he became increasingly candid with us, sharing his complaints and plans during private lunches and dinners at his home and asking us detailed questions about our own dissatisfaction with the PLA and our ideas for improving and strengthening it. He flattered us often and told us he preferred to work with young officers who were still idealists. The older officers, he observed, were often cynical and suspicious of change and bound to outdated ideologies. Rapid modernization and reform were absolutely necessary in the PLA, he told us. Without it our military was becoming increasingly ineffective and inefficient. The people who could bring about the necessary changes were the idealists and the dreamers, he said. But they had to be prepared to confront and overcome the resistance of entrenched hard-line conservatives who preferred to leave things as they had been and to preserve power they already held.

Those of us who listened to his discourses on change smiled and nodded at one another when he spoke. We agreed with everything he said. We were moved by his determination to modernize the PLA through the rapid adoption of new technology, cooperation with foreign experts, advanced training for our officers and an end to corruption, favoritism and the emphasis upon correct political thinking. The General was a pragmatist. If China was ever to see herself truly among the great nations of the world, it must adopt an ideology that brought all Chinese together to work efficiently and effectively. All of the young officers were convinced that change was imperative and that we could make it happen if we worked together. We became, in time, more acolytes than aides to the General.

One afternoon when I was alone with him in the office I told him that I supported his reform efforts but I had doubts about its chances for success because of the entrenched conservatism and favoritism in the PLA. I told him how I'd become frustrated and disillusioned with the Army and admitted to him that I thought about leaving the PLA because of my unhappy experience as a cadet. He listened quietly and expressed his concern for what I'd been through. He then assured me that if I was resolute I could transform the PLA and rid it of the people who utilised it for petty personal advantage. If I left the PLA, he said, I'd be surrendering to the very individuals who'd misused their power and influence within the organization. Rather than leaving the Army, he told me, I should work within the PLA with others like myself. There were still enough good people in the Army, he said, to restore it to the status it was meant to achieve.

The General's words and his faith in me and in other younger officers tempted me to reclaim the ideals I'd lost since entering the Institute. There were many times when, after listening to him, I thought he must be reading my mind. Here was a capable, compassionate and incorruptible idealist, I concluded – the kind of senior officer I'd doubted still existed in the PLA. He repeated often that he needed our help to set things right. There were others like us in the PLA, he assured the junior officers. As competent and honest officers moved up and onto the staffs of the Central Military Commission (CMC), the National Defense University (NDU) and a thousand other positions of power and influence, change would inevitably take place. As the old guard – the Maoists within the military – passed on, the young reformers would gradually come into their own and a new age would dawn for the PLA and for China.

I wondered what motivated him. I asked him many times about his background and, at first, he deflected my questions and changed the subject. But one afternoon, three months after he'd taken his position at the Institute, he invited me into his office for coffee, and while I was seated with him, he closed the door and told me the story of his life.

His father was from Sichuan province, he said, and he'd joined the Nationalist (KMT) Army when he was a young man and traveled to Japan with scores of other young officers to study in a military academy there. He met Chiang Kai-shek, who was also studying in Japan at the time. The Chinese sought to learn from the Japanese, who were modernizing rapidly while expanding their influence and power throughout East Asia.

His father returned to China with Chiang Kai-shek. Over the years he worked his way up and became a two-star general in the Nationalist Army. When he was in his late forties, he met and married a young woman from an influential and wealthy family in Shanghai. The marriage produced one child – a boy. The family settled into a mansion along the shore of Xuan Wu

Lake, the most picturesque site in Nanjing.

His father became disillusioned with Chiang Kai-shek, who was more concerned, he found, with remaining in power than improving the lives of the people of China or expelling the Japanese.

In 1948 he split with Chiang and took his army with him to the Communist side. After the Communist victory in 1949 he was honored as a People's Hero. His reward was a top position in the municipal government of Shanghai. But before he could assume the position, he suddenly died, leaving behind his young wife and his ten-year-old son.

The General recalled that his mother, with the help of her family, was able to provide well for him. He followed the path of his father. He attended the best schools in Shanghai and was admitted to a military academy in Beijing. He became one of the top cadets in his class and following graduation he was kept as an officer at the academy. He met and married a young woman from Shanghai.

The General expected to rise to a top rank in a modern and powerful military force. But his expectations were shattered by the Cultural Revolution, which was launched in 1966. Then, he said, he saw China suddenly go insane. His mentors and his most beloved generals were jailed and tortured. Some of them were beaten to death or publicly executed. His vision of a powerful and incorruptible Party and PLA vanished. His military academy ceased to function, so he remained at home more and more. Finally, he left the PLA and moved back to Shanghai.

In Shanghai he formed a secret group to work against the policies of the local leaders of the Cultural Revolution. But the group was betrayed by someone and the General and his friends were arrested. He was incarcerated with condemned prisoners in a prison in Shanghai. Every day, he said, the names of several men were called and they were dragged from their cells in the prison and taken out and shot. But his name was never called.

Following the death of Mao and the arrest of the Gang of Four, political prisoners were released. But the wheels of justice turned slowly for the General. When his former co-conspirators were released from other prisons, they appealed to Deng Xiaoping to release the General. A special committee was selected to investigate his case and in mid-1978 a delegation of Party officials came to the prison, shook the General's hand and announced that he had been wrongfully accused and imprisoned. He'd spent three years in the same cell. Now he was released and exonerated. His Communist Party membership was restored and his opposition to the leaders of the Cultural Revolution was termed heroic. Party newspapers praised him and he was hailed at Party rallies.

When he came home his wife hardly recognized him. He weighed only ninety pounds, his hair was thin and gray. His health was broken but he was vindicated, alive and free.

As a reward for his service to China, the General was named vice-mayor of Shanghai. But he turned down the honor and the office. He wanted only to return to the PLA. His wish was granted. He was reactivated in the PLA. Within a few years he was promoted to general.

When he finished his story, the General told me, 'I am ambitious and impatient. But I am not ambitious for myself. I am ambitious for my country. I love China. After I was released from prison, I met with my Shanghai group again. All of us are in the PLA once more. We all went through hell. We want to make sure that what happened to us and what happened to millions of others in China in our lifetime will never happen again. We want to make sure that good capable men lead the PLA and the Party. When that happens, all of our dreams will come true and everything we've suffered and everything we've sacrificed will be worthwhile.

'I want you to work with me – and with my group. But you should be aware that such an undertaking involves risk. There are pitfalls everywhere. There are powerful people – old and young, some of them right here in Nanjing – who are terrified of any change. They live in the past. They know change will throw them on the trash heap of history and so they will stop at nothing to destroy anyone who threatens their power and position and privilege.

'The political climate in China changes often,' he continued. 'I know that from experience. There are beautiful days and there are stormy days. I was caught in a storm in 1976 and barely survived.

'When the storm comes we use a rod to attract the lightning and to protect the house from burning down,' the General continued. 'Sometimes, for the sake of a cause, we have to ask someone to serve as the lightning rod to prevent fire from consuming what we build and to ground the shock. If it ever came to that, could you be that lightning rod? Could you catch the bolt and ground it, prevent it from going further, from burning down our house?'

Without hesitation I answered, 'Yes, I could.'

'And remember, even if we win, we will never be rich. That is not the reward we should seek. We may not even receive recognition. But we will change this country. And if we succeed you could be a hero . . . just as you'd dreamed. But if we fail, you could be denounced and imprisoned and your name erased from history. You must be prepared for the worst.'

'I am,' I assured him.

'Good,' he said. 'Then let's get to work.'

I realized at that moment that the red dream of my youth had indeed followed me around like a stubborn puppy. Every time I thought I'd lost it for good it came racing around the corner again and I couldn't resist bending down to pick it up once more and embrace it and promise never to let it go.

When the General told me about his suffering, his restoration to power and his renewed faith in himself and in his country, my own dreams and my faith were revived. He was able to touch a part of my heart that told me things could be different and people in China would respond to what was good and just and true. I wanted to believe that socialism could truly create a world where all men and women treated each other kindly and where people prospered and were happy and children were healthy and strong. And I wanted to believe that the People's Liberation Army was a band of incorruptible brothers and sisters standing tall and leading the march of China to a brighter future.

I wanted desperately to believe.

iii

Within days of our talk the General expanded my responsibilities again. I was introduced to two senior colonels
who were also part of the General's inner circle, and the three
of us coordinated our efforts in drawing up detailed plans for a
graduate program at the Institute to attract the best junior
officers in the country. The General arranged for a telephone to
be installed in my apartment, a privilege that was normally
extended only to ranks of major and above.

Our early work was successful. After the General lobbied in
Beijing for our new program we were given the green light and
the required funding to proceed. A good deal of political
give-and-take had been involved, the General said, and connections and obligations and favors played their part. The
presidents of prestigious universities in Shanghai, Beijing,
Tianjin and Guangzhou came to visit us and were wined and
dined and provided with special treatment and gifts to help
win support for our undertaking. Especially critical, the General told me, was the backing of the families whose sons and
daughters were admitted to the school for study and then
given choice assignments following their graduation. Such
favors resulted in critical alliances and obligations that could be
utilized to promote our reform agenda.

This constant use of favoritism bothered me. We never
seemed to succeed on merit alone. We never seemed to try.
Connections (*guanxi*) and favoritism produced rewards. I began
to wonder about the genuine dedication of some of the people
involved in the reform movement – when the promotion of
their personal interests and the enhancement of their power
was the reward for their cooperation. There was not as much
selfless idealism among the reformers as I'd expected. I saw the
General and his fellow officers using the very methods they
eschewed in their informal talks to win support for their new
program. I couldn't help but question the wisdom of using

connections and considerations and gifts in order to put together a system of eradicating such practices. The General suggested that ends justified means and that once we were successful we could eliminate the favoritism and nepotism. But I had my doubts.

iv

Serious problems concerning the behavior of one of our officers surfaced at this time, indicating how pervasive corruption within the PLA had become. One of the highly visible and ambitious political commissars at the Institute, Colonel Zhu Long, was accused of gross moral impropriety. The manager of a hotel in Hangzhou reported that the colonel had spent a weekend in his establishment with a pair of very young prostitutes.

A special military board of inquiry was convened to examine the charges against Colonel Zhu. Much to our surprise, Colonel Zhu confessed that the charges were true.

Then, however, instead of appealing for mercy, he became defiant and arrogant. After admitting his guilt, he shouted at his interrogators indignantly, 'Why are you telling me what I did was wrong? Do you have any idea what officers above me do every day? I can tell you that what I did in Hangzhou was nothing compared to what goes on every day in the PLA. NOTHING! NOTHING!' He insisted that corruption and 'so-called immoral behavior' were pervasive in the officer corps of the PLA and in the Party.

None of his interrogators pressed him on his scandalous allegations and no one challenged or contradicted him. His arrogance and certitude stunned me, as did the timidity of his accusers.

Zhu was kicked out of the military, but the PLA made sure he landed comfortably on his feet. Within days of leaving the Army he was named supervisor of a labor camp (Laogai) for political prisoners. In his camp the prisoners worked from dawn till dusk making manufactured goods for export and sale on the international market. The profits from the labor of the prisoners went directly to Zhu and his associates. Within a few years he became a very wealthy man.

Colonel Zhu was the officer who interrogated me in 1984 and was responsible for blocking the career of Lin Cheng and humiliating us for falling in love. But, as a married man with a child, he himself conducted an infinitely greater breach of morality. I saw now what a charlatan he was, what wickedness he embodied and what misery he had gleefully inflicted on others. And I knew he was not alone.

V

The General intensified his efforts to improve the performance and training of students in the Institute and in acquiring important assignments or advanced training for them. He worked tirelessly to further the careers of talented young officers who were loyal to him. The opening in Nanjing of a joint educational venture with the Johns Hopkins University and Nanjing University, the Center for Chinese and American Studies, presented an opportunity for officers from our school to study with American teachers and to make contacts that might facilitate further study in America. In fact, the General and other high-ranking officers from the Institute worked quietly behind the scenes promoting the venture, seeing what an advantage it might provide for our cadets, graduates and staff. There, near our school, they could improve their language and academic skills, make important contacts with American students and faculty and perhaps befriend them and gain sponsorship abroad.

The General's successful efforts to upgrade and modernize the curriculum and training at the Institute along with the connections he cultivated resulted in an important honor for him in 1987. He was elected by the PLA headquarters in Beijing to study for a year at the National Defense University

(NDU). High-ranking officers from around the country came to the NDU for study and networking. Although the General said he hated to leave Nanjing for a year, it was important that he go to the NDU because it was sure to lead to promotion to a more powerful position.

He returned to Nanjing in the spring of 1988 with a revolutionary new plan for the Institute. He told his aides that his year in Beijing convinced him that the Nanjing Institute needed to make some rapid and dramatic changes in order to upgrade the training of our officers and overseas agents. He'd held lengthy discussions in Beijing with officers who'd been to the United States and he'd heard some American guest lecturers at the NDU and from that experience he concluded that our English-language training was not good enough and that the understanding of American society given our graduates was completely inadequate. The language we taught our graduates was too formal, he said. He wanted the cadets to learn colloquial English and to be comfortable with all current American idioms. The English our graduates spoke made them seem like bumpkins in the United States. Their awkward phrasing and pronunciation along with their discomfort and unfamiliarity with the customs of America made them stand out when they were supposed to fit in. Their ability to make contacts, blend in with the crowd and gather information without attracting any attention was compromised. When they arrived in America, he said, they might as well have been handed a large sign indicating to everyone around them that they were from China. We had overlooked training our people in some of the most essential practices of blending into the population of the United States. They didn't know how to drive a car or pump gas, they were confused by American banking, checks and credit cards, how and what to order in restaurants from an American-style menu, and they didn't understand computers – a major and essential new tool for acquiring and transferring information. We were, he lamented, out of date and we were becoming more antiquated with each passing day.

He'd thought about the problem and come up with his own solution. He wanted to construct a small American city near the Institute. He said the KGB had constructed such an installation in the Soviet Union and it proved to be useful. Officers from around the country could be assigned to our secret installation for final training before being sent to America and thus be better prepared to carry out their duties the moment they arrived in the United States. Trainees could live in our American city and ride the buses, drive cars, shop in the supermarket, buy movie tickets, write checks, use credit cards and computers. The only language spoken in the city would be English.

Although there was some enthusiasm for the General's plan and members of the reform group of officers applauded the scheme, there was also outspoken resistance to it from conservatives in the Institute and in Beijing. They were wary of those who wanted to immerse our cadets in an analysis of the values, ideas and organization of capitalist societies which might at the same time undermine Marxist values. They implied that too much exposure to America could be a dangerous thing and they wanted to teach no more about Western democracies to our recruits than was necessary. They feared 'peaceful evolution,' as they termed it, or the steady erosion of Marxism and its replacement by liberal Western values.

There were also officers who were envious of the General and saw him as a threat to their position. If he went ahead with the project and achieved support, the best recruits from around the country would come to our installation. Those officers would be bound closer to him personally and would become part of his circle of friends and loyalists. The reformers could make a great leap forward with a success like this. So the conservatives were determined to see it fail.

I watched the General cultivate connections aimed at promoting his scheme. He arranged for a select group of young men and women to be admitted to the Institute for special English-language training in preparation for taking entrance examinations for American universities. These youngsters were not members of the military, but were from influential families in the military and the Party. The General provided special treatment for these people and made arrangements for their accommodations and tutoring on campus and made sure that the visiting parents were entertained with lavish banquets at the Jinling Hotel.

The General gave me the important additional task of drawing up more specific plans for the American city. But I begged off and told him I thought I needed a rest from the constant pressures of my work. He was surprised at my assertion, but after thinking about it for a few days, he said he agreed with me. He thought if I could get away from the Institute for a short time, I might return with new ideas and enthusiasm and the school would benefit.

Late that spring of 1988 he told me he'd arranged for me to have a year's leave to enroll in a graduate program at the Shanghai Foreign Languages Institute.

I was delighted by the prospect. But before I could enroll in the school the General changed his mind. 'I want you to study at the Nanjing University joint venture with Johns Hopkins University,' he informed me. 'It's more expensive than Shanghai, but we will pay for it.' He said he'd arrange for my admission, even though the deadline for applications had passed.

The reason for the change, he explained, was that the Center was organized and operated in the American way and the instructors were all Americans. He felt that in Nanjing I could better learn colloquial English as well as study American history and society and observe firsthand the teaching methods and styles of the Americans. When I returned from the Center I could incorporate what I'd learned into the curriculum of the Institute and use it in putting together the plans for our new American city. He also entertained the idea of bringing one or two American instructors to the Institute – a highly unusual step, we knew – and to have them lecture to the students about American culture and society. He wanted to familiarize our students not only with the content of lectures by Americans but with the style of teaching and sources used. Therefore, he reminded me, it was important that I make as many friends and contacts as possible at the Center. In time, he said, my contacts could be exploited in the United States – for travel, entertainment, and information. It was important to learn about America and Americans and to win their friendship and trust, he suggested, while at the same time making sure I revealed as little as possible about my own background. 'You'll probably meet some interesting characters in the Center,' he said as I departed. 'Keep your eyes and ears open.'

He was so intrigued by my descriptions of life and study in the Center that he came to visit me on three occasions that fall. He dressed in civilian clothes and was accompanied by his wife. He wanted to see all parts of the facility, to examine the dormitory rooms and the library, the auditorium, classrooms, kitchen facilities and offices. He asked numerous questions about the day-to-day operation of the Center and the division of responsibility between the American and Chinese administrators and the procedures for enrollment and funding. He asked me to introduce him to some of my teachers – but as a friend rather than as a military officer – so he could talk to them about their teaching methods, their research and resources. When he learned that the American brought scores of books and recent American feature films with him to China, he asked me to borrow some for him and his associates.

Seeing how the Center operated heightened the General's determination to establish his American city. When I returned to the Institute each weekend he spoke with me at length about his dream city and how he would staff it with the best scholars in China – men and women who had studied with American teachers and knew all there was to know about contemporary American culture, society and history. He would bring the very best students from throughout the country to his city and the Institute, he said, and prepare them to represent China abroad and to usher China into the twenty-first century.

vi

The Colonel withdrew a fat folder from his briefcase filled with materials on the General. 'How many times did the General ask you to introduce him to the American?' he began.

'Never.'

'Did he ever visit the Center?'

'No.'

'No? You are lying again. Why? Are you trying to conceal something? We have photographs!' They are thrown on the table.

I recognized a picture of the General, his wife and me sitting in the dining room of the Center. 'Oh, yes, he did visit the Center, with his wife. I remember now. But he wasn't in uniform, as you can see. I forgot. It wasn't important. Just a social call.'

'Did he ask to meet the American?'

'No, he didn't.'

'Did the American ask to meet the General?'

'Why would he? He wasn't even aware of the General's existence.'

'I don't think that's true, Xu Meihong. I think he was aware of the General's existence and that he wanted to meet the General.'

'I don't know why,' I said.

'Of course you do. He wanted to meet the General to deliver messages to him. You know how he communicated with the General, don't you?'

'I have no idea, Colonel.'

'The General's wife met the American, correct?'

'Briefly, in the hallway, we passed each other and I introduced her to him.'

'Tell me more.'

'We passed in the hall and I introduced them to each other. He didn't know she was the wife of a general. It was a chance meeting.'

'There is no such thing as a chance meeting, Xu Meihong. You should know that. Did she ask to borrow anything from the American?'

'No,' I said.

'Didn't she ask to borrow videotapes from him?'

I paused and thought about my answer for a moment, then I volunteered, 'Oh, that. I asked him for videotapes.'

'Did he give her one?'

140

'He loaned me one, and later I loaned it to her.'

'Did you view it?'

'No. But I know it was a feature film.'

'How can you be sure?'

'I read the title on the tape.'

'But you never actually saw what was on the tape, correct?'

'Later, I did see the tape, Colonel.'

'And?'

'And it was a feature film about a large shark.'

The Colonel smiled when I told him about the videotape. I could tell he didn't believe me. There was a long pause as he shuffled through his papers trying to find another document. Finally he asked, 'And how many times did the General ask you to bring the American to the Institute?'

'Twice, I think.'

'You never wondered why?'

'I knew why. The General wanted him to lecture to our cadets on American culture and society.'

'And did the American go to the Institute?'

'No.'

'Why didn't he? Do you know the reason?'

'Yes. He said he was too busy.'

'Or . . . perhaps he was awaiting instructions from America? Could that be possible?'

'I don't know what you're talking about.'

Despite my denials, the Colonel pressed on, going back and forth over the same materials hour after hour and day after day, checking to see if my answers were consistent.

'Did the General give you any money to entertain the Americans from the Center?'

'No.'

'You never saw large amounts of money in his office?'

'No.'

'I don't understand. Why would Americans come to the Institute to lecture if they were not paid for their services?'

'They didn't come, Colonel.'

'Why did the General think they would come if there was no money involved?'

'It was meant merely as a scholarly exchange. The cadets

141

might be given the opportunity to hear an American lecture on his own country, and the visiting scholar could spend an evening with us and gain more firsthand experience with Chinese students. The idea was that we would be intellectually enriched by the experience.'

The Colonel and his two aides laughed at my answer. 'Intellectually enriched? You think the General asked to meet the American for intellectual enrichment alone?'

'Yes, I do, Colonel. The General is a scholar as well as a military officer.'

'Did you know the General has relatives in the United States?'

'No, I don't know anything about that.'

'So, to the best of your knowledge, the General and the American did not discuss common acquaintances in America?'

'To the best of my knowledge, they had no discussions at all. They never met.'

The Colonel suddenly switched to the General's friends in the NDU and I insisted I knew nothing about them.

'Can you give me the names of the General's close friends in the PLA in Beijing?'

'I know none of them.'

'Your husband's commanding officer is his friend. You know him, don't you?'

'Only professionally, Colonel.'

'Can you name his friends in Guangzhou?'

'No, I don't know them.'

'Then let me read the names to you.' The Colonel slowly read from a list of names. Some I recognized. Some I'd met at the Institute when they came to visit the General. The Colonel's extensive lists included more than a hundred names – many of them, I realized, were members of the General's reform group within the PLA. I denied knowledge of any of them.

He asked about the dinners the General hosted with the junior officers. What was said? Who was there? What did the young officers say after leaving the General's house? I said I didn't know.

He questioned me about speeches the General had given and

reports he'd written and details of his travels. I told him I couldn't recall any of that. He asked about the American city the General planned to build. I said I knew little about it. At times I lost track of the line of questioning. I rambled in my answers. During some of the Colonel's lengthy and convoluted explanations of events I watched his lips move and listened to his voice but my mind drifted off. Then he'd suddenly shout, 'Are you listening to me?'

'Yes, I hear you, Colonel,' I responded. 'What did you want to know again?' Then a slap on the table, a shout, a warning, reminders of how important this was and again a litany of facts and fantasy, a break for the men, who smoked and watched my every move. The tape recorder continued to run and stop and run and stop and the captain continued to fill a notebook with his meticulous notes and the Colonel stopped to allow him to rest and then we went on. I made sure the Colonel extracted nothing from me that could be used against the General.

'Have you seen the General shred or burn documents?'

'No.'

'Have you or anyone else on his staff ever destroyed documents for him?'

'No.'

'You're lying. We know documents were destroyed. We have an eyewitness.'

'Then go ask your eyewitness. I know nothing about that, Colonel.'

After questioning me for seven straight days about the General, the Colonel suddenly indicated that I might not have been the only officer arrested on December 2.

'Did you ever hear the General make telephone calls to the United States?' he asked.

'No, I didn't.'

'Did you ever hear him speak of plans to go abroad? Did you hear him speaking to a representative from an airline perhaps?'

'No.'

'Has the General ever told you he had been sentenced to death in 1976?'

'No, I've never heard of that,' I lied.

'He was, you know. And now he'd do anything – anything – to stay out of prison again. He'd even cultivate American friends in order to get his family to America if he got into trouble again.'

'I don't know, Colonel. I don't know why he'd get in trouble. And I don't know anything about his arrest and imprisonment. My impression has been that he has always been a model officer.'

'He never told you his life story – his father's career and his arrest? Do you know his father was a general with the Nationalist Army?'

'No, our association was entirely professional. He never told me anything about his private life.'

I started to wonder if the General had been arrested on December 2 also. And if he had not been arrested yet, then perhaps he was about to be toppled. Since I was one of his protégées, his fall from power would mean I was finished also. I wanted desperately to ask if the General had been arrested or had fled to another country, but I dared not. I tried to decipher the General's fate from the questions I was asked. At the same time I wondered if those questions were merely another ploy, an attempt to undermine my confidence by making me believe that my friends and supporters were gone.

He asked about the graduates from the Institute, where they'd been sent, how many wrote to the General, what the General said about them, their visits back to the Institute. Again and again I denied any knowledge of these associations and friendships. The Colonel persisted for several hours, repeating the same questions and, in the end, paging through his papers, leaving the room – I assumed to make a phone call to superiors – and then returning to dismiss me or continue my interrogation.

'Do you know anything about the existence of a "peaceful evolution" group within the PLA?' he asked.

'No, I don't.'

'You know nothing about the General's Shanghai associates?'

'No.'

144

'You've never heard talk of a clique of reformist officers in Beijing, Shanghai, Guangzhou and Nanjing?'

'No.'

'I hope you are telling me the truth, Xu Meihong. I hope you are not concealing anything from me, because the General and his friends are trying to divide the PLA when they should be trying to unite it. If he is left to his own devices he will weaken the Army and the nation. The General is a very ambitious man – an individualist. But we know all about him. So, if I were you, I would not rely on his help.'

'I rely on the truth, Colonel.'

He studied me closely as I answered. Then he turned back to his files. 'Hmm,' he mumbled to himself as he stared down at the files he'd scattered on the table. He tried to think of a new line of questioning to pursue, but appeared to have arrived at a dead end.

Sometimes there was a lapse of several days between sessions and I had nothing to do but lie in bed and stare at the ceiling or walk around the room and read the old copies of *The PLA Daily* pasted over the windows. Then the sessions began again. But after three weeks, the Colonel apparently concluded my information on the General was limited and wasn't taking him where he wanted to go. So in mid-January he returned to my relationship with the American.

He was convinced he was close to uncovering a serious breach of security. He might not be able to pin it on other officers in the PLA – not yet. In the meantime, he still had the American and me to fall back on. His evidence of my transgressions, he believed, was quite convincing, even though he'd not yet tied me to a conspiracy with higher-ups in the PLA. He could always punish me, he was sure, and there would be no objections.

SIX

The American

The line between the actually very serious and
the actually very funny is actually very thin.

— JOHN LE CARRÉ

i

In early September 1988, I packed some of my books and belongings in two bags and arranged to be driven to the Center in a military car. The driver helped me carry my bags inside. As I passed through the large glass doors into the lobby, I was unaware that I was not merely moving into another educational institution. I was entering a new world that would change me and my life in ways I'd never dreamed.

It was suggested that each Chinese student select an English name and American students select a Chinese name to be used at the Center. I chose the name Rose, which was a loose interpretation of my Chinese name.

I was assigned a small room on the third floor of the dormitory building. My room had a private telephone and private bathroom. The facility was luxurious compared with those provided students in any Chinese university.

I was in my room for only a few minutes when the telephone rang. 'Welcome to the Center,' the voice at the other end said. It was vaguely familiar.

'Who is this?' I asked. 'How did you know I was here?'

'Guess, Xu Meihong,' he said.

'I have no idea. Don't play games with me.'

'You don't remember?' he asked. 'I'm disappointed. This is Li Yan.'

He had been a top student at the Institute, graduating in 1982. I'd heard he had been demobilized in the past year. 'God, where are you?' I asked. 'I haven't seen you in years. What are you doing?'

'Can we meet?' he asked. 'I can answer your questions then.'

149

'Of course. When? Where?'

He wanted to see me that afternoon. I asked if he'd like to see the Center and he said he'd already been there a number of times. He preferred to meet me somewhere nearby. An hour later we met on a main street near the Center.

I was waiting for him on a corner when a car pulled up and he jumped out. He was dressed in civilian clothes and wore dark glasses. But there was something I recognized in the way he carried himself, the way he looked at the people around us, and even in his self-confidence.

'Are you working for the Ministry of State Security now?'

'Is it that obvious?' he asked, smiling.

'A guess,' I said. 'Congratulations. Do they pay well?'

He ignored my question and responded. 'You've done well for yourself also, *Lieutenant* Xu Meihong. Long time no see. How are things at the Institute? How is the General?'

'You know the General?'

'Who doesn't? He's making a name for himself,' he said, smiling. 'He's ambitious. He's going places. Are you going with him?'

'No,' I said. 'I'm just going to the Center. And I'm going to have tea with you.' We both laughed at my feeble attempt at humor.

We walked to a small restaurant and ordered tea. We talked about the Institute and about our classmates and friends. Some had risen high in the ranks of the PLA. Some worked for the new military-related companies like Norinco and Poly Technologies and were getting rich. Still others – some of the top graduates – worked abroad under cover as journalists, businessmen and graduate students, and had become part of the PLA's international intelligence apparatus.

He told me he was aware of my admission to the Center and he'd been awaiting my arrival. 'You must have studied everybody's personnel files at the Center,' I told him in a matter-of-fact tone of voice. 'And don't tell me you are not supervising some of the staff of the Center who keep you abreast of everything that happens there.'

'It's standard operating procedure,' he said.

'I understand, but it sounds like a waste of your time and talent.'

'I'm doing what I'm asked to do.'

'I suppose the phones are tapped.'

'Being from where you are, you know how everything works, don't you?' he replied. I knew he'd avoid straightforward answers. I tried to read his expression, his eyes, to see if there might be something important he was not telling me. I was bothered by the fact that I couldn't. When I'd first met him at the Institute, I was a freshman and he was a senior cadet. Our contact was limited but I remembered him as a bright, energetic and very capable young man.

As we talked, I realized something in him had changed. There was none of the youthful jocularity in his expressions that I remembered. Everything he said and did, even when tinged with humor, had the familiar odor of officiousness to it.

I had the strange feeling also that we were like two old acquaintances playing word games. We talked around every subject. Each of us was curious to know what the other knew without revealing much about ourselves. At the same time we pretended that we weren't aware of what we were doing. We were wearing masks.

'Why did you contact me?' I asked. 'Is the MSS monitoring the PLA now?'

'Of course we're not,' he said. 'It's the Americans. We want to know about the activities of certain Americans, their real reasons for coming here and staying in the Center. You know how it works.'

'Yes,' I said, 'I know how it works. But why the Center? It's an educational institution. Why would an agent be sent there?'

'It's not our fault. The Americans do these things. We are forced to respond because of their actions. If they insert someone into China – even into a place like the Center – we have to identify him, watch him and get rid of him or neutralize him.'

'Where do I fit into your agenda?' I asked. 'Are you recruiting?'

'Not really,' he said. 'But you are the best person to help us on this operation.'

'What do you want from me, then?'

'I'd appreciate your help and I'd understand if you said no. But if you say yes, I'll make it worth your time,' he said.

'What if I say no?'

'Don't burn your bridges, my dear friend. Who knows where I'll be next year – or where you'll be. This can be a great opportunity for each of us.'

'I'm not working,' I told him. 'I'm not here on an assignment. I'm a student.'

'What do you mean you're not here on an assignment? Didn't the General send you here? You were initially going to Shanghai and then were sent here. Why was that?'

'My God, you know everything about me. You must have friends in the Institute. Who are they?'

'You know we're all in the same family, Xu Meihong,' he replied, smiling again.

There was a disingenuous quality to our conversation because both of us knew that I could not refuse to cooperate with the MSS if they asked for my help. The only point to be negotiated was how much I must help. 'What is it specifically that you want me to do?' I asked.

'Watch someone – an American.'

'Isn't that something the housekeeping staff does for you?'

'I need someone trained for this – like you.'

I told him I'd do what I could for him but that I really wanted to devote myself to study. He assured me that my tasks would consume only a minimal amount of time and effort.

When we'd finished our tea he said he'd like to show me something at his office. It was a nice afternoon. We walked several blocks to the local MSS headquarters. In his office he removed a large brown envelope from his safe and placed it on his desk. Then he laid out some photos and copies of documents, most of which looked like official applications or medical reports. The photos were of an American – alone in some pictures and in a group in others. One of the photographs looked like a passport picture. 'Take a look at this man,' he said.

'Look at his blue eyes!' I said. 'Who is he?'

'His name is Engelmann. He is from California, he says.'

152

'He says?'

'That's what he says. Maybe he is from somewhere else. Maybe from Washington.'

'Tell me more about him,' I said.

'He arrived yesterday and was assigned an apartment on the fifth floor of the Center. He will be teaching two classes – American history and American culture and society. Help me find out if this man is really who he claims to be.'

'Who does he claim to be?'

'A professor.'

I slowly went through the photographs. 'Where was this one taken?' I asked, holding up a picture. It showed the American standing on the street at night with two other people. His shirt was soaked with sweat and he was wiping his brow with a handkerchief.

'It was taken in Hong Kong. One week ago.'

'How did you get it?' I asked. He pretended not to hear my question, indicating I should know he could not tell me.

'This sounds like something important, Li Yan. What exactly do you want to find out?'

'I'm not entirely sure what to look for,' he said. 'Just watch him for anything unusual. But don't tell anyone about this meeting or our conversation. Not a single soul should know what you're doing for me. Agreed?'

'Agreed. But what do I get for my extracurricular activity?' I asked jokingly.

'Dinner? Once a week?' he replied.

'Is that all?'

'We'll see,' he said, and smiled.

As I walked back to the Center, I worried about what Li Yan had asked me to do. This was an unwelcome intrusion in my life. I decided to do as he requested and not to tell anyone – not even the General – about the favor I was doing for him. I hoped his suspicions would be unfounded and that my work with him would be brief.

ii

The first week at the Center was referred to as 'shopping week.' During that time students attended as many classes as possible (on a variety of subjects, including international relations, economics, political science, history, culture and literature), met the professors, listened to their introductory lectures and then decided which two elective classes to take.

The General asked me to concentrate on American political history and social studies so I could use what I learned to help him with his American city. Keeping both his and Li Yan's requests in mind, I chose two classes taught by Larry Engelmann – American political history and American culture and society. My third class was an intensive English-language course.

Curious about the alleged American agent, I arrived in class early and sat to one side of the front row. About twenty students were in attendance for his initial class session. I was surprised when I first saw him. He was tall and slender, had curly brown hair and the bluest eyes I'd ever seen. He didn't dress like any professor I'd ever known. He wore blue jeans, a white dress shirt open at the neck and a sport coat. Before he began speaking he removed his coat, draped it over a chair and then sat on the edge of a table in front of the room. He then began talking – not lecturing, as we were accustomed to – but speaking simply in a low, normal, conversational tone. He seemed confident and eager to make us laugh. He punctuated his lecture with humorous anecdotes.

'I am going to tell you how I got here,' he began. 'You may find it an enjoyable and instructive story.' I saw several students writing rapidly while others grimaced, realizing that what was about to be said probably would not be covered in an examination and was therefore going to be a waste of time.

He asked the students to put down their pens. Apprehensively, they did as he requested. Then he said he would prefer that they not take notes during the period. This is all 'introductory,' he said. 'Mine is an unusual story,' he began. 'Strange in a funny way. Funny strange, we say. Parts of it, though, are funny sad and parts are funny ha-ha. Or funny funny.'

'What language is this man speaking?' I wondered. 'Is this some arcane American dialect?' None of us was prepared for this.

After several minutes he noticed our concern and confusion at his language. 'If you think I am speaking too fast, please put up your hand,' he asked. Immediately, all but a few hands went into the air. He laughed and said he would speak more slowly. The hands went down.

'If you understand what I just said, then raise your hand.' No hands went up. He explained carefully the various qualifiers for the word 'funny' and most of us finally grasped what he had been saying. We were amused by the ways in which English could be 'twisted,' as he put it. Through the remainder of the semester he was constantly pausing to explain English language structure and contemporary idioms to us.

He told us he thought the man most responsible for his presence in Nanjing was Nikita Khrushchev. In 1957, he said, the Soviet Union put up the first Earth satellite – Sputnik – and the American Congress was so alarmed by the technological feat that, among other things, it passed a massive student loan program that allowed qualified students from low-income families to borrow money to attend a university. He secured a student loan and that made it possible for him to attend the University of Minnesota. 'God bless Nikita Khrushchev!' he proclaimed. He later earned his graduate degrees (MA and PhD) at the University of Michigan and then moved to California and started teaching at San Jose State University. 'In 1975, because of the collapse of South Vietnam, 130,000 South Vietnamese fled from their country to the United States,' he explained. 'Several hundred ended up in my university. Many were in my classes – last year twenty-five percent of my students were Asian-born, mostly Vietnamese. They convinced me to write about Vietnam.'

While writing about Vietnam, Engelmann met a *New York Times* correspondent, Fox Butterfield. The *Times* correspondent had been in Saigon in 1975 and later headed the *Times* office in Beijing. When he visited California he stayed in Engelmann's home. He told of his experiences in China and encouraged Larry to apply for a teaching job at the Nanjing University–Johns Hopkins University Center for Chinese and American Studies in Nanjing. Larry followed Butterfield's advice, applied for the position, was interviewed for the job and was hired.

'So you see,' he said, 'without a Communist victory in Vietnam, there would have been no Vietnamese students in my class, no visiting *New York Times* correspondent in my home and no American from California standing before you right now. If you have problems with my class or my teaching methods, complain to the Russians, OK? Or blame your own government for helping North Vietnam. It's all their fault.'

He laughed loudly at his own joke, but the students remained silent.

When he'd completed his introductory lecture, he announced, 'I've told you personal things because I think you can learn about America from my experience. I have as much to learn from you as you do from me. I think that's why we're here. Let's make this a memorable experience.'

I went to his office to get his approval and signature to enroll in both of his classes. His door was open and when he saw me he invited me in and asked me to sit down. The office was crowded with books – scores of them – on the floor and in boxes and on the shelves. And then there were stacks of videotapes and audiotapes and a half dozen large boxes of documents.

I asked why he'd brought all of the books and papers with him to China and how he could afford the shipping charges.

He was in a talkative mood. 'It's not as expensive as it looks. Most of it I put in the mail at the beginning of the summer. It came here by ship, not air. I want to stay here for two years at least. And I want to continue my research. So I brought everything I thought I'd need.'

'How many books did you bring?' I asked in amazement.

'I think around two hundred,' he said. 'Maybe fifteen or twenty boxes.'

'And how many videotapes?'

'Only about fifty. But there are three movies on each tape. So, maybe a hundred fifty movies. I love movies. I thought I'd have trouble with customs, but they let them all through.' (He didn't realize that customs regularly duplicated the new movies foreigners brought in and then sold them on the black market. Thus, a wait of one to two weeks could be expected before movies were 'cleared' and copied.) 'Now, I find there's an auditorium here with a VCR and a big screen and I can show them to everybody – I hope – with approval. It'll be nice. You can all learn a lot about America from our movies. And you can get some good laughs from them. Someone told me I'd need something to keep my spirits up while I was here.'

It sounded wonderful to me because I loved American movies too. And as I read the titles on the cassettes I realized I'd never heard of any of the films he brought.

I was surprised to see the papers he'd piled along one wall. They were typed documents marked 'Classified' and 'CIA'. 'What are these?' I asked. 'Are you allowed to tell me?'

'Oh,' he said, laughing. 'They're for my next book. These are from Saigon and Washington in April 1975. It's declassified. Field reports from Americans monitoring North and South Vietnamese military units. The black line through the word 'classified' means the stuff is available to researchers.'

'They let anyone see these in the United States?'

'If you're doing research.'

'And they let you bring them here?'

'Yeah,' he said. 'I guess they didn't think I'd sell them to the Chinese government. There must be millions of people here with money who want to learn about the fall of Saigon thirteen years ago, right?'

I wasn't sure how to respond, but I believed that this was one of the reasons the MSS singled him out. I had no context for understanding the American concept of declassifying sensitive materials. Documents that had been declassified in America would still be very interesting to the intelligence services in China. They would at least indicate which kinds of materials have been kept secret even if the content is no longer important.

'How do I say your name?' he asked, looking at my enrollment form.

'Meihong,' I told him. 'But you may call me Rose – that's my English name.'

'That's nice. Beautiful. I'm learning Chinese, however, so let me use Meihong,' he said, mispronouncing my name. 'Would that be all right with you?'

'That's fine with me. What should I call you?' I asked. 'Don't you have a Chinese name?'

'I have one, but it's silly. It's La Li. They tried to make it sound like Larry.'

'It has no meaning,' I told him.

'That's what they tell me. I've also been told in Shang-hainese it means Zipper. And in other Chinese dialects it means Diarrhea or Bald. I don't think any of those names is exactly flattering. So you'd better just call me Larry.'

'But you are a professor,' I said.

'So . . .,' he said, and gave me a puzzled look.

'I . . . we . . . should call you Professor Engelmann or Dr Engelmann.'

'No, please,' he said. 'Please call me Larry. Some of the students are nearly my age. I'd like to keep things as informal as possible while I'm here. Make it Larry, OK?'

His openness and candor were disarming. I enjoyed talking with him and he seemed sincerely interested in everything I had to say.

He'd shipped a computer to the Center and had reassembled it on his desk. When I asked about it he showed me how the word-processing functions worked and let me type words and commands on the keyboard and showed me how to print what I'd written. At that moment Carol Chu, his American colleague and my academic advisor, joined us. She'd been working in her office next to his and heard us talking. Larry suggested the three of us have lunch together – outside the Center. We walked to a nearby noodle restaurant, Zhou's, which served also as a black-market money-changing office for foreigners. I noticed how Larry loved to make jokes about almost every-thing and everyone and he laughed out loud at his own jokes as if he'd never heard them before. After lunch the three of us walked through the campus of Nanjing University talking and laughing as if we'd always been close friends.

Late that night while I sat reading at my desk I turned for a moment to look out the window. I noticed a light in a window across the way in another wing of the Center complex. The light came from Larry's office. I turned out my light and pulled the curtains open farther so I could see in the dark without being seen. Larry was sitting in his office in front of his computer, slowly paging through a stack of papers and then pausing occasionally to type something. As I watched him, I thought about some of the things he'd said and recalled the allegations of my friend at the MSS and wondered if he could possibly be anything other than what he said he was – a professor. Was it possible he was lying about his background and his life and work? He seemed completely ingenuous and open. I assumed the MSS had made a mistake in their estimation of him. Someone else in the Center had to be their man – or woman – if the American government had really put an agent in the place.

On my third morning at the Center, I received a call from my friend at the MSS. I went to his office and described in detail everything I'd learned about Larry. I suggested strongly that he was not the agent the MSS was looking for.

iii

During our first class sessions, Larry encouraged students to take notes in the margins of their textbooks and to underline critical parts of the narrative. He suggested this would provide a useful study guide. But the Center had purchased only four copies of the textbooks for the entire class. We had to check books out of the library and they were examined by the librarians carefully when they were returned. When we pointed this out to him, he thought about it for a moment and said he'd see that we each got our own copies of the books. We found this hard to believe.

That afternoon he composed a letter to the publisher of the textbook. He wrote that he'd assigned their books for years in

America and then described his work in China and asked the publisher to consider sending free books to his students.

He gave the note to an administrative secretary and asked that it be telexed to the United States. He heard nothing about it for two days. Then his letter was returned to him with a note from the American and Chinese co-directors stating tersely that it was not the policy of the Center to provide textbooks for every student.

The next afternoon he walked to the Jinling Hotel and telexed the message to the publisher himself. One week later a truck arrived at the Center and unloaded the textbooks. When the Chinese co-director discovered the gift he was furious. The issue was never who was right and who was wrong, but rather who had authority and power and who did not. The Chinese co-director would never forgive Larry for ignoring his directive. Despite the fact that every student benefited from the gift of books, the Chinese co-director branded Larry a troublemaker and from that day on watched for a way to humble him.

The arrival of the books aroused apprehension in the students as well. Surely, they suspected, an obligation accompanied the generous gift. They wanted to know why an American publisher gave away books of such value to students in China they'd never met and probably never would meet.

Larry tried to explain. 'I guess they did it because it was the right thing to do. It was a generous selfless gesture. Sometimes that happens, even in a capitalist society.'

The idea of a substantial gift with no strings attached, or unsolicited kindness or generosity, for that matter – of a random act of kindness – was something alien to the thought processes of most of the students. A gift created an obligation and implied influence and the cultivation of connections and therefore opened doors. When my friend in the MSS asked me what favors I thought Larry might expect from the students in exchange for the gift, I confessed that I could see none.

The Chinese students at the Center were primarily mid-career professionals like myself. We had graduated from universities several years earlier and had worked in our

professional careers. The students included Chinese professors, teachers, administrators, editors, journalists and military
officers ranging in age from their mid-twenties to their
mid-forties who were returning to the classroom to refresh
their education and to learn how and what Americans
taught. We each belonged to a 'work unit' – where we
practiced our profession. That unit maintained a permanent
personal file on us. If we moved from one city or assignment
to another, our file followed us all of our lives. When we
completed our year at the Center, the Chinese co-director
was required to write a report on our activities for the year.
His letter became part of our permanent file.

In the classroom, Larry never fully appreciated the pressures
under which his students labored. Any politically incorrect
remark made casually or humorously might be reported to the
Chinese co-director and find its way into our personal file and
stain our record for the rest of our lives. So, when Larry
repeatedly asked our opinions of various subjects and then
tried to relate them to the contemporary world and compare
them with political policies in China, or when he asked us
about the importance of some concept – individualism, conformity, privacy or liberty – in our daily lives, we were
reluctant to answer in anything but the most general terms.
This disappointed him, and when he pried, the students
commonly backed away. The most common answer to his
questions was 'I don't know.'

Most of the Center's Chinese students had gotten where
they were by not challenging authority. In China, getting
ahead meant getting along, and getting along meant never
challenging authority and memorizing a distinct, finite set of
principles laid down by an authority figure.

Students enjoyed their class most when Larry spent the
entire period talking about American writers and philosophers
and reading from their works. Outside the classroom, in small
groups in the privacy of our rooms, we discussed the questions
he'd asked in the classroom – questions that had gone unan-
swered. And we talked about the books he'd assigned and the
ideas they presented. We were delighted at how Larry made
writers like Melville, Hawthorne, Thoreau, Whitman and

161

Emerson relevant to our experience when he spoke of fanaticism and the burdens of history and witch hunts and scarlet letters and the examples of great men. I am sure he was disappointed at our answers to his questions, and I know he wasn't aware that by his recitations he was throwing open the windows and doors of our minds and letting in fresh new thoughts. Our thoughts and our feelings were kept private. The fact that we did not – could not – express them did not mean we did not have them. The fact that we could not stand and speak our minds did not mean that our minds were not working feverishly and that our imaginations were not operating. He thought that what he could not see and could not hear wasn't there. But that is a mistake most foreigners make in China.

As the weeks passed, I busied myself in the Center with study and also with the social life of the place. In addition to classes there were parties, dances, movies and informal discussions every week. One of the American women started afternoon aerobics classes and I enrolled. I had papers to write and examinations. I also had to spend several hours every week in the language lab listening to tapes in English. What little free time I had I spent in the library poring over books. But every minute of life in the Center was enjoyable. I lost myself in it and I loved it.

I told the General about my experiences in the Center and he decided to visit me to see the place for himself. One morning, he and his wife came to the Center, attired in civilian clothing, and dined with me in the cafeteria. At that time he encouraged me to seek out a professor to invite to the Institute to lecture the students on contemporary American life and culture. I asked Larry if he'd consider lecturing at the Institute, but he declined, saying he was too busy with teaching and writing. What little spare time he had, he said, he chose to enjoy rather than in giving guest lectures. 'Maybe next semester,' he said.

On another occasion the General's wife visited me in the Center and we passed Larry in the hall. I introduced my guest as my mother. Larry was gracious and commented on how much I looked like my mother. I requested several videos for 'my parents to watch' at that time. Larry got them for me. The General and a few of his colleagues watched the films during the following week. One week later I returned them to Larry and thanked him and said my parents enjoyed them very much.

iv

One afternoon I was taking a walk by myself and I saw Larry emerge from the front gate of the Center and start walking down Beijing Lu. He was very happy when he saw me. 'I need to mail these,' he said, holding up a fistful of postcards and letters. 'How would you like to come with me and translate for me at the post office?'

'You must have many friends in the United States,' I said upon seeing the number of items he planned to mail.

'Most of these aren't going to the United States,' he said. 'They're going to Vietnam.' Larry had spent a month in Vietnam before he came to China. He explained that he'd gone there to interview and do research for his next book, *Tears Before the Rain*. 'Look at this,' he said, and showed me one of the envelopes. I recognized the name on it – Colonel Bui Tin, the man who had taken the surrender of South Vietnam in 1975. Tin's address was the Ministry of Defense in Hanoi.

'Is this man your friend?' I asked.

'No, but I interviewed him. I plan to see him again in Hanoi in January. This is a thank-you note and some information on my next visit to Vietnam. He was very helpful and hospitable when I was there in August.'

I felt uneasy when Larry attached stamps to the letters and dropped them into the mailbox. I knew that the letters would be sorted out and copied and placed in the folder my friend at the MSS kept in his safe.

On the way back to the Center, Larry waved to a Chinese girl, about fifteen, who sat on a small stool on the sidewalk just across from the old Drum Tower (Gulou) near the post office.

Pieces of automobile tires were stacked around her, and beside her was a small box filled with nails and razor blades. She replaced worn-out shoe soles.

'I'd like to talk to her,' Larry said. 'Will you translate?'

'Of course,' I told him, though I could not imagine what an American professor would have to say to a street shoe-repair girl or she to him. I was touched, however, by his care and concern for this little girl's well-being. I translated their conversation. He asked about her school, her hours of work and her family. I wasn't sure why he was so curious about her and wondered if he intended to help her in some way. I asked him later about his questions and he said he was just curious. He said he wanted to know how people lived – the people most of the tourists never met or talked to or cared about. Again I asked why. And again he insisted it was merely curiosity – nothing more.

I accompanied him to the post office again several days later. We sat down in the park across from the Drum Tower to watch people passing by and he asked me, 'How do you like the Center?'

'It's luxurious,' I said.

He looked at me in astonishment. 'You're kidding, aren't you?'

'No, I'm not. Hot water – sometimes – private showers, telephones. That's unusual for students here. Very nice.'

'They've cut corners,' he said. 'It's supposed to be nicer.'

'What do you mean?'

'They put fifteen-watt bulbs in our apartments. When I bought new bulbs and tried to change them, the sockets fell out of the ceiling. They were held in with toothpicks. Someone had stolen the screws. And when I tried to replace the socket I found there were no junction boxes.'

I'd learned to live with dim lightbulbs and couldn't appreciate his concern. 'I didn't realize that,' I told him.

'Every time one of the maintenance workers needs to change a lightbulb, he wisely pulls the main lever on the main fuse box and all the electricity in the building dies. Then he does his work. It's safe for him, but for those of us working on computers – well, every time a lightbulb is changed we lose our work. I have to program my computer to save my documents every minute. It's funny in a pathetic way.'

'But this place was built by the Americans.'

'No, this place was *paid for* by the Americans. This place was built by the Chinese, I believe. It's called "cooperation" by the Americans, but some of us refer to it as "complicity." I've never seen a building in America like this one. I want to get out of it when the first big storm comes along. Have you seen the van?' he continued. The Center owned a van that was used to transport the faculty around Nanjing on official business or to take them to or from the airport or train station.

'No, I haven't. Students don't use the van.'

'Someone – our "driver," most likely – liberated everything from it but the seats and the steering wheel and the gearshift. All the dials are gone. There are just holes in the dashboard.'

'Why would he do that?'

'He said he was "fixing" them. And you know, of course, there is a second van, don't you?'

'No, I've never seen it. Where is it?'

'That's a good story. Apparently, the second van was given to the president of Nanjing University for his personal use. On the books it is for the use of the Center and for the staff and the students here. We were advised not to make a big deal out of it. It's one of the "little" things that go on here – one of the considerations given the Chinese in positions of power – that the Americans do to keep the Center running. Complicity again. Putting up with petty theft is their idea of cultural sensitivity. Every time we complain to the administrators at Johns Hopkins they respond, "But this is China! What did you expect?" '

'That is how things work here sometimes. People get things done by giving and receiving personal favors.'

'In America people go to jail for it,' he said, 'unless you're in Chicago.' Then he laughed at his own joke. 'The budget for food is way out of line with the quality of the food served. For what we're paying here, I really don't appreciate the bean sprouts with dental floss they serve every other night. And I know of no American who likes the specialty of the day – rice with pebbles. One of the American students broke a tooth on the rice. And when they served chicken soup the other night, Carol found a chicken head in her soup – beak, eyes, feathers and all. I might add that the only overweight Chinese staff member is the kitchen manager. Early one morning, one of the students pointed out how the kitchen manager leaves each day on his bicycle with a large load of food and returns later without it. Do you think he sells it? Where is the food that the American money buys?

'And the water,' he continued. 'Have you seen it?' The water piped into the Center was 'colorful,' as he put it. It changed hue from day to day. Some days it had a gray cast to it, sometimes a copper cast and sometimes it turned yellow or gold. This was the water that we bathed in. And, of course, despite the promise of 'hot water twenty-four hours a day beginning at 7 A.M.' (Larry called the phrase 'Communist logic'), hot water was a precious commodity. It was seldom available in the morning or in the evening when people customarily need it. Most often it appeared in the late morning and word passed among the faculty members and students that there was hot water, in the same way someone might announce they'd discovered gold. People hurried to their rooms to shower. But it quickly ran out. Larry asked me why in Communist countries the water was provided in only two temperatures – 33 degrees or 211 degrees. It never quite settled at anything between the two. Showering in Vietnam as well as in China, he said, seemed some sort of exotic Oriental torture system.

Americans were advised to purchase and clean their own chopsticks. Those who used the chopsticks provided by the Center washed them thoroughly in hot tea or vinegar before use. No napkins were available, so students and faculty alike had to provide their own or, as some did, wipe their hands on the tablecloths, when available. All of this, they were told, were necessary cost-saving practices. But if this was so, some of the Americans wondered, why was there money for the expensive banquets served each time a visiting delegation showed up from the United States? Who paid for the flights of the numerous delegations (and their spouses) to the Center, when there weren't funds for books and supplies and napkins in the Center?

'All the computer software is pirated. Nobody from the United States – because of "cultural sensitivity" – tells the Chinese administrators that it's against the law to pirate our software and then sell it.'

'Do all Americans complain like this?'

'No, I'm sorry. I know this must seem tiresome to you. I apologize. I'm not used to this. Everything is so different from what I'd expected. Not just exotic and colorful but also crooked. Everything that's not tied down is stolen. They say there is little crime here but, as anyone can see, petty crime is rampant. Everyone with a little power is on the take, it seems to me. And the Americans who should know better just smile and look the other way.'

'Larry, things are getting better here. Just try to be positive.'

'You're awfully tolerant. Are all Chinese like you?'

'Some things can't be changed very easily. Complaining about it does no good. It wastes time. You'll only end up a cynic. This is China, Larry. You have a lot to learn, I think, and the first thing you have to learn is patience.'

He was quiet for several minutes and then he conceded, 'You're probably right, Meihong. I'm impatient. I had no idea things were like this. I should have known better. I'm sorry if I offended you. There are a lot of good people here. I like the people working on the street – the shoe-repair girl, the tailors, the fortune tellers and the noodle makers. They all work hard.'

I could tell by his tone of voice and his expression he was serious. 'Nobody here is blind,' I said. 'We see what you see. But we can't change the situation overnight. So we do the best we can. We don't complain. We make adjustments. We do what we must to survive.'

'Why don't you help me then,' he said. 'I'll teach you all I know about America and you teach me what you can about China. Help me see what you think I should see and help me avoid making mistakes here.'

'OK,' I said. I realized how easy it was going to be to watch this man, to discover if he really was who he claimed to be, and to provide that information to my friend at the MSS.

V

And so on the following afternoon when Larry called my room and asked if I was available for another walk, I said I was and I agreed to meet him outside the Center. He said he wanted to wander around the area and perhaps talk to people and take pictures. It was a beautiful day. After dropping off postcards and letters at the post office we walked to the Jinling Hotel, where we had coffee. Then we took a long circuitous route back to the Center. He stopped and spoke for some time to a man who had his own noodle stand on the street. The man remembered the Japanese occupation of Nanjing, and Larry listened to him and asked questions for nearly half an hour. People gathered and listened. The man seemed flattered that a foreigner was interested in his memories. Then Larry spoke to a little girl who stood on the corner with a scale and a measuring device. For three fen she would let you weigh yourself and measure your height. For another three fen she could give you a card telling your IQ. He was fascinated by the fact that she spent all day there and wasn't in school.

He began practicing Chinese. He asked me the word for nearly everything as we walked along and seemed tone deaf to the language itself. He became frustrated, laughed at himself and couldn't make people on the street understand a word he said. I helped him adjust and change his tone and eventually, after a struggle, people figured out what he was trying to say. 'May I take your picture?' or 'Your child is beautiful' or 'We would like some tea, please.' All of it was difficult for him and he forgot words almost as quickly as he heard them but insisted that through repetition he would someday speak fluent Mandarin. I had my doubts – he had no talent for languages, I thought – but I didn't discourage him. He also taught me American idioms along with words that were unfamiliar to me – like 'hassled' and 'frazzled' and 'cool' – as we walked along the streets and through the city.

He genuinely enjoyed listening to the people he met, I found, and I enjoyed my walks and conversations with him.

'I've never met anyone with as much curiosity as you,' I told him. 'What do you learn when you listen to all these people? What is it you're looking for?'

'I guess I learned a long time ago that everyone has a good story to tell. Academics and writers don't have a monopoly on what's happening in the world, you know. In fact, I think academics as a class are the most boring people in the world. They talk about life rather than live it. Sometimes – I would say almost all the time, in fact – people on the street are better at analyzing what's going on than people in ivory towers or in government offices.'

I agreed with him. 'If you talk to people like these every day, you'll get a picture of this country that most foreigners miss,' I said. 'The reason some of these people are surprised when you ask them a question is that nobody else is interested in their lives – not the government, not the scholars, not the tourists, not anybody but the police. They are naturally suspicious of you – and of me – at first. But if they see you out here on the street often, I think they may open up to you more and more.'

'And what about you? If we take walks every day, will you open up to me more and more? You must have a good story about your life too, don't you? Tell me about yourself. Where are you from and how did you get here? I'll bet there's something interesting in your background.'

'Not really,' I replied. 'My life has been like that of anyone else you know here. I studied in a university before I came to the Center. And I'm married.'

'Are you? Where is your husband and what does he do?'

I thought it unwise to disclose my military background. My reluctance to provide details might arouse his curiosity or his suspicion. So I lied. 'He's a businessman in Beijing. We met when we were both university students.'

I watched his reaction when I spoke and he appeared to believe every word I said.

He nearly caught me in the lie one week later when he came to visit me in my room. On the previous weekend I returned to the Institute and received my commission as first lieutenant at a special ceremony. My new officer's uniform was ready for me at that time. I wanted to see myself in it standing before a full-length mirror, so I brought the uniform with me to the Center in a wardrobe bag. While I stood looking at myself in the mirror there was a knock on the door. Without thinking, I unlocked the door and stood behind it as I opened it a few inches. It was Larry. Through the open door he could see me in the mirror – I'd overlooked that. He was nearly dumbstruck when he saw the uniform. 'What's that?' he asked. I wanted to provide him with an innocent explanation he'd believe. I opened the door and invited him in and then closed it and locked it behind him. 'Do you like it?' I asked.

'I've never seen one like that before,' he said. 'Where'd you get it?'

'It belongs to a girlfriend,' I said. 'I'm keeping it here for her. She just had it cleaned in Nanjing and she's picking it up later this week.'

Larry was carrying a pocket camera and he suddenly said, 'Smile!' and snapped a picture.

'I'd like that picture,' I told him immediately. 'Can you give me the film?'

'There are more exposures on the roll. I'll give you a print when I develop it,' he said.

'No,' I said, trying not to sound anxious. 'It's against military regulations for me to be seen or photographed in this uniform – because I'm not in the Army. Please give me the film, Larry.'

He told me not to worry and promised he'd give me the film after he'd finished the entire roll. I had to believe him. But for the next several days he took no more pictures and by the time the roll was used, he'd forgotten his promise to me.

vi

I began meeting with Larry every day. I helped him practice his Chinese and I translated for him on the street and walked around the city with him. When the weather was bad or Larry was tired he'd invite me to his apartment and we'd talk there. Sometimes we'd watch one of his videos and he'd explain the context of a film to me. When I asked if I might use his computer in order to write some of my papers, he said I could use it anytime he wasn't writing. When I complained that sometimes there was too much noise on the student floor for me to study, he let me read in his apartment while he worked in his office.

Often, when I was reading in his apartment or working on his computer in his office he left me alone to attend a meeting or to do some work in the library. Thus I gained access to the files in his office as well as his apartment. I read through his papers, letters and diary looking for anything that might indicate he was secretly communicating with someone in China or sending reports back to the United States. I found nothing like that. But I found my name in the letters from his friends in the United States. They seemed to know about our walks and conversations. When I worked on his computer I figured out how to bring up the letters he'd written to friends in America. Again, I found lengthy passages about me. I felt uneasy when I discovered what he'd written because he kept repeating how much he valued me and my friendship and said he had developed 'a special affection' for me. He said I was one of the few people to whom he could speak openly and candidly and that sometimes he poured out his heart to me. He wrote that I listened patiently and was perhaps the most honest and sympathetic woman he'd met in years. Some of his friends wrote and even asked if he was falling in love with me. 'She's right out of a dream,' he wrote to a friend. 'Or should I say she's right out of a Chinese silk-screen painting, the most lovely creature God has ever seen fit to place in my path.'

As I read his words I felt ashamed because he had no idea that I was repeating our conversations to the security people. I thought for a long time about him and about what I was doing and I didn't like it. He was a complete innocent when it came to comprehending the complexities and the dynamics of the politics of China. He laughed too much. There were so many things around him that were not funny and he didn't seem to see them. I wanted to shield him and prevent him from being hurt. I felt drawn to him when I read what he thought of me, felt a strange attraction, a compunction to protect him. I also felt a stirring in my heart. I knew that any sympathy I felt for him could be dangerous for me. But, like him, I couldn't help it.

I decided not to tell my friend at the MSS that I'd read what he wrote privately. I believed that would have been a further violation of his trust and I decided not to cross that line.

As we spent more and more time together, I found Larry trusted me completely, but I was untrustworthy. I enjoyed our time together – looked forward to it – and I found I cared for Larry's well-being. I wanted to tell him about the suspicions of the MSS. But I couldn't warn him without revealing my role in watching him. And I couldn't convince the MSS to stop their surveillance. I was not sure what to do.

One evening I decided to go to his office to see if there was a way I might caution him about his writing and to warn him that he was being watched. It was late and the halls were empty at that time and my footsteps echoed up and down the corridors as I approached his office. His door was slightly ajar and he was writing at his computer, apparently oblivious to the time. I said hello and entered the office and sat down in a chair beside the desk and asked him how he could work so late.

For the first time since I'd known him he looked at me and I saw weariness in his expression and detected an uncharacteristic sadness in his voice. He said he worked hard to escape from thinking about things that made him unhappy. I asked him if he wasn't happy with China and he said he wasn't happy with his life. China had nothing to do with it.

He stared out the window as he spoke and told me he'd been lonely for a long time. He'd been lonely since his divorce, eleven years earlier. He'd lived alone since then, he said, and he hated it. Yet it seemed to be his fate. He didn't think it would ever end. He told me he joked primarily to try to make himself happy by pretending to be happy. But it didn't work.

I listened silently, almost hypnotized by his admission of vulnerability and inner gloom. He said that in America he'd had nearly everything he wanted but he still felt that something was missing from his life. He felt dead inside.

'What did you expect when you decided to come to China?' I asked him.

He'd come to China, he said, to try to find a new life for himself, but the old emptiness and sadness traveled with him. There was no escaping it. He said if he were a Buddhist he'd conclude that he was paying for something terrible he must have done in a past life.

When he was finished neither of us spoke. As he stood and stared out the window at the black starless sky, I wanted to stand beside him and to put my hand on his shoulder and to tell him everything would turn out all right. That fate changes unexpectedly and unhappiness ends and we can never tell what the future holds for us. But I did not.

Finally he turned and looked at me and forced himself to smile and said, 'I'm sorry to burden you with this. The last thing I want to do is share my personal problems with you.' He sat down at his computer and with a few keystrokes saved his work and then turned the machine off. The light on the screen quickly imploded to a tiny green dot and then the dot faded and disappeared. He pulled the door open and switched off the light and we stepped into the hall. As I stood to leave he turned and brushed his fingertips against my hair and lightly touched my face and said, 'You know, you are so beautiful. You'd probably better stay away from me from now on. I'll make you unhappy or I'll get in trouble or I'll make you hate me. I'm good at that.'

I didn't respond to his statement. At the stairwell where we parted I reached out and took his hand and asked, 'Are you going to be all right?' He seemed to recover from his sadness and told me he would be fine after some sleep. He patted me on the shoulder and wished me good night and I let go of his hand and he turned and slowly climbed the stairs to his apartment.

I returned to my room and sat in my chair and thought about his words for a long time. I wondered how he'd feel if he knew I read his mail and his diary and reported our conversations to the MSS. How could I betray and violate such a trusting soul? 'I have to stop this,' I told myself. 'I can't do this any longer.'

I took out some paper and wrote a brief letter to my husband saying I missed him and asking him to visit me soon.

vii

I was absolutely convinced that Larry had nothing to do with an American intelligence agency. He was a complete innocent in China.

But no matter how adamant I became in my assertions, my friend in the MSS insisted I was naive. He provided more evidence in his case against Larry. He pointed out that the first American co-director of the Center was not an academic. He was a diplomat from the embassy in Washington – a Mr Leon Sloane. Sloane, he said, was a *political officer* at the American Embassy – and the way he said the words *'political officer'* indicated there was more to the position than simply analyzing the politics of China. Sloane was handpicked for his position and remained at the Center for two years. When he left, the MSS believed he would be replaced. The MSS examined the files of the American teachers and students and became convinced Larry was their man. His connections to the American media (journalists were believed generally to double as spies) and his visit to Vietnam along with his correspondence with high-ranking officers in Vietnam and his possession of declassified CIA documents all indicated he was involved in intelligence gathering.

At this stage I realized that it was pointless to try to convince Li Yan of Larry's innocence. I also knew if I persisted in my disagreement I might arouse suspicion against myself. I concluded that the best way out of the matter was to warn Larry to be careful and not to fall into any political trap set for him. I also needed to remind him not to mention my name in his letters to America since I sensed that his political innocence might compromise my career and my future.

One afternoon I went to his office and asked him to take a walk with me. 'Is anything wrong?' he asked as soon as we stepped outside the Center's main gate.

I didn't say anything until we sat on a bench in a nearby park. Then I asked him, 'Have you finished your roll of film? The one with me in uniform? You promised to give it to me when you were finished.'

'Why are you so cold today?' he asked. 'What's happening with you?'

'Larry, I want that roll of film. I need it.'

'I finished it,' he said. 'I just sent it to the local developer. I'll give you the prints when I get them back tomorrow.'

I couldn't believe what he was telling me. 'You know,' I told him, 'you're going to get me into a lot of trouble with those pictures. You really are a professor, aren't you?'

'First, I don't know how I can get you into any trouble, and second, yes, I am a professor,' he asserted with solemnness. 'Are my lectures that bad?' and he laughed at his own joke.

'I know you want to learn about China. And I'm trying to help you. But there is an invisible world here and you don't know about it. I want you to be aware of it because if you aren't you can get yourself into a lot of trouble,' I said. 'I want to warn you to be careful and not to trust others so easily.'

'You've lost me,' he said.

'OK, let me make it very straight. When you write letters to your friends in America, please stop mentioning my name.'

'How do you know what I write to my friends in America?' he asked.

'Larry, all foreigners are under suspicion here. That includes you. You have to be aware of that and be very careful.'

'And how do you fit into all of this? Are you watching me?'

I could not answer his question directly. All I could tell him was that it was routine for agents of the government to read the mail of foreigners. 'You have to remember that here in China you don't have a private life,' I cautioned him. 'Don't trust anybody and don't mention my name in your letters, please.'

He was quiet for several seconds and then asked, 'OK, Meihong,' he said. 'If you say so.'

'And that film?'

'I'll get the prints to you tomorrow,' he promised.

'I need the negatives too,' I told him.

'The negatives too? My God,' he exclaimed, 'you are thorough. What are you anyway? A spy?'

'I'm not a spy,' I told him. 'I'm just a friend who's very concerned about your welfare.' I was convinced that he believed me and that he'd do as I asked. But he didn't. We returned to the Center and he went straight to Carol's room and repeated our conversation. He asked her if she thought I was telling tall tales. Carol called two other American professors to her room and the group talked about what I'd said. That night Larry wrote letters to his friends and described our conversation and the paranoia he felt all around him in China. He was frustrated and confused, he said, and he found my warnings to be half-humorous cloak-and-dagger material.

Every word that was spoken in Carol's room that afternoon was recorded by the MSS and his letters were copied and placed in his MSS file.

viii

In the next weeks I thought Larry had accepted my warning and changed his behavior. He didn't refer to my revelation again and when we spoke it was usually about classwork or the impending trip to Beijing. I assumed he would be more cautious in what he wrote and said and as a result the MSS would gradually lose interest in him.

On November 1 the students and faculty from the Center took a field trip to Beijing for a weeklong stay at the capital. I promised Larry and Carol I'd serve as their tour guide in Beijing. On their first day in the city I took them to the Forbidden City, Tiananmen Square, Mao's Tomb and the Temple of Heaven. That evening when we returned to the Jianguo Hotel, where Larry and Carol were staying, they invited me to have dinner with them. They wanted to thank me for showing them around Beijing by taking me to Justine's – an elegant continental-style restaurant in the hotel.

Each table in Justine's was beautifully decorated with a centerpiece of candles and flowers. The waiters were unusually deferential. Larry and Carol said they wanted to splurge, 'in honor of the best tour guide in China.' They ordered French wine and dinner for me since I had no idea what might be good and I'd never ordered from a Western-style menu in a hotel before. We had a wonderful time that evening.

On his last night in Beijing, Larry invited me to a nightclub. We sat and talked about the remainder of the semester, the sites we'd visited in Beijing, and we listened to the music and watched the dancers. When a slow song played Larry asked me if I'd like to dance. We walked through the crowd to the center of the dance floor. He held out his arms in a very formal way. I took his hand, he pulled me close to him and we danced. The lights were low, the room was warm, the music was very romantic – Larry softly sang the words for me in English while we danced – and I felt confused and lost. When the music stopped I said we should leave but he asked me for one more dance and I said yes and we danced again and then one more time again. Each time, it seemed, he held me closer, and each time, it seemed, I felt myself lost in his embrace as we moved across the dance floor. I found I wasn't anxious to leave anymore but finally he said it was time to go. He took me to a taxi and paid the driver to take me back to where I was staying. Before we parted he kissed me on the forehead and took my hand and held it for a moment and thanked me for the days in Beijing. He said he'd never forget them, ever.

When I returned to Nanjing, most of my time was taken up by studying for examinations. Sometimes, in the evening, before launching a marathon study session, I took a short walk to get fresh air. Larry joined me a few blocks from the Center and we walked on a regular route around Nanjing University and back. Sometimes, in the darkness, he reached out and took my hand and helped guide me through the dark streets. But I noticed that when we approached a streetlight he continued grasping my hand and I continued to let him. I knew at those moments that we had crossed another line in our friendship. But neither of us dared to give voice to what we were thinking or feeling. Each of us knew, I believe, that it was wonderful and it was warm and it was wrong and we didn't care – at least for the moment.

One night we sat on a bench near Gulou where we'd gone on our first walk in September and we looked up at the stars. I asked him if he still felt sad and had moments of regret and gloom. He told me he didn't and that he'd found a cure for his blues – me.

When I asked him if he thought he'd miss me after he left China, he said, 'Meihong, I think in a different place, under different circumstances, in a perfect world, I'd fall madly in love with you. I'd love to take you to all the places you want to go and see the world with you.'

That night I sat at my desk in the dark and stared out the window. My mind was filled with dreams. I saw Larry working in his office in front of the computer. I watched until he stood and turned off the light and closed the door and the room went black. He was unaware that I had been watching him. And both of us were unaware that there were others in the dark that night watching us with the confidence of men who already knew how this story would end.

ix

In mid-November I went to visit Li Yan at the MSS. I wanted to make a report on everything that had happened on the Beijing trip and again to emphasize that I believed that Larry was not a foreign agent. I was surprised to learn this time that Li Yan agreed with me. 'You were right and we were wrong,' he confessed.

'You mean you believe he is what he says he is? A professor?'

'Yes. Nothing else.'

I breathed a sigh of relief. We then turned to other topics. I asked him about his wife and family and his plans for the future. He asked me how I thought I'd do on my exams at the Center. I felt as if a heavy burden had been lifted from my shoulders. At last, I concluded, I am a full-time student. I was unaware that I'd just made one of the biggest mistakes of my life.

X

⸺◆⸺

'You liked this American, didn't you?' the Colonel asked me when he resumed my interrogation in mid-January. 'In fact you liked him very much, didn't you?'

'Yes.'

'How much?'

'As you say, Colonel, very much.'

'Would you say you *loved* him?'

Almost reflexively, perhaps because I was exhausted, I answered, 'Yes, I suppose.'

I could tell in a moment by the way he sat forward and glanced at the tape recorder that I'd made a mistake, that I had carelessly agreed with the word he interjected – 'love.' It was meant to hurt me and it did.

Words were weapons. The Colonel supplied the word and I, perhaps out of exhaustion, repeated it. It was a self-inflicted wound. Now the word was on tape and in the notebook and there was no taking it back. It was part of the Colonel's case.

There were knowing glances from the Colonel to the others and he smiled broadly. 'We knew this a long time ago.'

I was exhausted and I didn't want to argue the meaning of the word we'd used. Love alone was not a capital crime, I reminded myself. 'That is my only mistake, Colonel,' I said. 'Is it really that important to you? Is that why I am here? Yes, I loved an American. I am innocent of anything other than that.'

The Colonel reached forward and switched off the tape, ending the session. I concluded he'd report my admission to his superior and new questions would follow. I was right. In the afternoon session the Colonel asked if I ever thought I'd been blinded by love. I said I had not. Had I been seduced by the American? I said I had not.

'Why didn't you tell us you loved this man from the start?' he asked. 'You could have saved all of us so much time.'

'I am a married woman,' I said. 'I didn't want what was left of my life destroyed, Colonel. I wanted to keep my life, my career, my marriage, my dignity. Now you know my mistake. Is that what you have been looking for?'

'We want to understand something,' the Colonel responded. 'We know you love your husband, and it's impossible that you'd fall in love with this foreigner. You are a good girl,' he said, with pretended paternal pride. 'We now see things more clearly. He took advantage of your youth and your innocence. He seduced you and made you tell him many things you should not have told him.'

I shook my head from side to side as the Colonel spoke but he ignored my silent disavowal of his insertions. What he wanted now – what he demanded – was my cooperation in exchange for my future. He proceeded to lay out the tale he wanted me to repeat in my own words. When I did that, the story would be recorded and written and become part of the official record of the case. The Colonel assured me he had cleared this tale with a 'friend of China' – an American would act as the go-between in what was arranged. Everything was fixed.

'First, I want to know how this American operated,' the Colonel began. 'How did he win your trust? What was his method? His words? You knew him for three months. Look what he did to your mind in that short time. What happened to you? We think he has used some device, some special manipulation, to deceive you. Your brain was washed by him and we want to know how. How did he weaken you? Did he drug you perhaps, Meihong, before forcing himself on you? Did you ever feel drowsy or dizzy after drinking with him? He might even have put something in your tea before . . . *raping* you.'

'Colonel, this is only your filthy fantasy.'

'Did he offer you money, Xu Meihong? Did he buy things for you or promise you anything?' the Colonel asked.

'You don't understand, Colonel. You probably can't under-stand. We are friends. We spent time together. We talked. We shared ideas. We danced. We had dinner together. That's all. He didn't seduce me. He didn't make me do anything. He didn't expect anything. There was no deception. I've told you all there is to say about him. There is nothing to which we can backtrack. I am the only one guilty of wrongdoing because I am a married woman and as an officer I am not supposed to have any emotional feelings toward a foreigner.'

'Meihong, this American forced himself on you. We can finish all of this with a simple document from you. I want you to compose a statement. After you write and sign it, you may leave. This is the last thing I will ask of you.'

'What do you want me to write?' I asked warily.

'For the sake of the PLA and the Party, for the security of the country, we want this man to leave our country. This man took advantage of his position – your trust – coerced you into revealing your position and rank and lured you into providing him with information that should never have been entrusted to a foreigner.'

'I never told him my rank and position.'

'But look at this picture,' the Colonel said, and pushed a photograph of me in my new uniform across the table.

'Colonel, you wouldn't believe me if I told you the true story of that photo.'

'You're right,' he said. 'I wouldn't believe you. But there is a way to make things right. We have a statement prepared for you that says the American raped you. And it says you came to us because the American abused his power over you. You were confused at first and you were ashamed of what happened. You demanded justice for yourself and for your husband and for China. You want the Chinese authorities to drive him away in order to protect you and all other Chinese women. I want you to copy this statement in your own handwriting and then sign it.'

Someone had to pay. The Colonel could not report that he'd spent all this time and come up with nothing but a little love story. He needed something more scandalous. A tale of rape and revelations of national secrets would serve that purpose nicely.

I struggled to hold back my tears. I didn't pick up the pen. I stared at the blank piece of paper.

'Lieutenant, this is important. For God's sake, this man is just an American,' the Colonel reminded me.

'But I know him. How can you ask me to destroy an innocent person? Do you think the American administrators will believe this? I'll look foolish and so will you.'

'On the contrary. The Americans will accept this. This is not your problem. Don't worry about it. This is all that is required. All we are trying to do is to get rid of a dangerous foreigner with a minimum of publicity and embarrassment.'

I had no energy left to raise my voice and give added emphasis to my determination. 'You can do anything you want to me, Colonel. You may threaten me however you wish. But I can't write this. I am not going to help you dispose of him with this lie.

'From the moment you brought me here you told me you wanted only the truth. When I told you the truth, you threw it away. We wasted so much time. This statement is not the truth, it was not what you were looking for and it is based on no evidence and not a single word that was spoken here,' I said.

'The truth? The truth, Xu Meihong, in case you have forgotten, is what we say it is. It is not for you to decide or to judge,' the Colonel proclaimed. 'We know this is the best way out of a problem that *you* created for us. Can't you see that? This is to protect you. We have done so much for you for so many years, and this is the only time we have asked you to do something for us in return. If you think this is a sacrifice, that is as it should be. Make this sacrifice for your country, Xu Meihong. This man is not Chinese. He is not one of us. Whose side are you on now?'

'This American did nothing wrong. Nothing. I know the truth and so do you. Even if I disliked this American, I would not write this lie for you. Colonel, I would not sign this even if you were the man falsely accused of rape.'

He pulled the paper back and then said, 'OK, I understand. You don't have to write a thing.'

'Thank you,' I said.

He smiled as if he had the perfect solution. 'Why don't you

just sign your name at the bottom of the document? I'll take care of the rest,' he said.

I laughed. I hadn't laughed in weeks. It felt good. I held my arms across my stomach and bent over with laughter. Tears were coming from my eyes, but they were tears from my recognition of the absurdity of all this. 'I'll never do that, Colonel. And if you dare to forge my name to the document I will tell people the truth about it.'

'You will tell people the truth? The truth is too big for you. I offer you your only doorway out of here and you refuse to walk through it. This bastard has destroyed you and you don't know it yet. This man is the one who put you here. If he did not exist you would have a good life and a bright future and a good marriage. Now you will have none of those. They have been poisoned. Your life is finished. Don't you see that? If we reveal that he raped you – repeatedly, like an animal – then you are the victim and you have no responsibility for anything that happened. There will be no need for you to explain. Instead of condemnation, you will receive praise for coming forward and revealing this secret crime.'

The Colonel paused for nearly a minute before concluding his appeal. Then he said, 'Think about it, Meihong. We have a little more time. Think about it for a few hours.' He motioned to his aides to return me to my room.

xi

My female guards had prepared a surprise for me. Over the many weeks of my incarceration I had spoken often with Xiao Zhang, the youngest guard. I was sure she was given permission to talk to me at length in the expectation that I might reveal things to a woman that I wouldn't reveal to the Colonel and his aides.

She often asked me about my life in the Center and at the Institute. I told her all the good things and all the humorous things I could remember. I could tell, by the way she asked for clarification that she was writing reports. But at other times, she seemed to lose herself in our talks. She was genuinely curious about my life and my close relationship with a foreigner. She'd never met a single foreigner.

I had worn the same clothing for eight weeks. My requests for clean underwear had been denied. One afternoon I asked Xiao Zhang if she could bring me clean underwear during one of her home visits. I said I didn't want this favor without repaying her and asked what I could do. She said she knew that I was one of the best dancers among the female officers at the Institute. She lamented the fact that she had never learned to dance. She would bring me underwear, she said, and I could, as a return favor, teach her to dance. I agreed.

When I returned to the room after hearing the Colonel's persistent pleas for me to charge Larry with rape, I found a small blue paper bag on my bed. Inside were two new pairs of underwear. When I saw them, I smiled at Xiao Zhang, who beamed back at me.

'Do you want to learn to dance now?' I asked her. She looked at Li Xia, who nodded approval. The other women stopped reading and watched us as we prepared to dance. 'This is easy,' I told her. 'Just follow me. I'll take the man's part.'

As we practiced, I hummed a song Larry taught me during our walks – 'Somewhere Out There.'

'Now let's do it for real,' I said. I stood in front of her, put my right arm around her waist, took her right hand in my left and pulled her gently against me. 'Don't be so stiff,' I told her. 'This isn't like marching. You're supposed to have fun. Follow me.'

I hummed the music and counted out the steps as we moved in a tight circle around the floor again and again, past the other two women, who sat on their beds gaping at us. 'Don't look at your feet! Look at me,' I told her. She looked at me and smiled. I held her tightly and said, 'Here's a secret: sometimes you can rest your head on the man's shoulder, if you aren't afraid. Try it.' She rested her head gently on my shoulder. I closed my eyes and we whirled around in our little space while I sang the count as if it were words to the song. I remembered dancing to the song with Larry in Beijing. 'Close your eyes,' I told Xiao Zhang. 'Think romantic thoughts and you can fly away to some other world.'

After we'd danced for several minutes she whispered to me, 'We're leaving tomorrow. Did you know that? We're going home.'

I felt a sudden chill. 'Really?' I said. 'How nice.'

'What was he like?' she asked after a pause. She had an expression of ingenuous curiosity. Would she report everything I said? Was she really going home tomorrow? How cautious should I be?

'He was . . . an American. It's difficult to describe him. He liked to dance. He laughed at almost everything. He laughs loudest at himself. He makes everyone laugh. But he has a sadness inside. A darkness he's always fighting. His biggest mistake is that he is too trusting and too innocent. He trusts the wrong people. Always the wrong people. He wants to be happy,' I said. 'But he doesn't know how.' I knew as I spoke those words that Xiao Zhang could not possibly understand the man I was describing.

We circled the room a few more times and then I stopped humming and released her. 'End of lesson number one,' I announced. She wanted to continue, I could tell. She looked disappointed but didn't object. We pushed the beds back to their original positions. I lay down and closed my eyes and tried to sleep.

xii

We were awakened just before daybreak when the Colonel came to the door and told us to prepare to leave. The women had already packed their personal belongings and were ready.

'Am I leaving too?' I asked him.

'We are all leaving,' he said, and closed the door again. I heard two cars pull up to the building. The door was opened again and, as if on command, the three women walked out.

Xiao Zhang turned and waved to me before leaving the room. I heard car doors outside open and close and listened as a car drove away.

I was alone for less than a minute when the Colonel came into the room and ordered me to leave with him. We walked to the waiting car. I was guided into the back seat and the door was locked and the curtains drawn. No one spoke.

We passed quickly through the gate and out onto the main road. Dawn was breaking. Nobody told me where we were heading. I didn't bother to ask. I wondered if I was on my way to a military jail or if I was on my way to freedom. I knew that in the next several hours anything could happen to me.

Two hours later the driver stopped in front of a large brick apartment building. The outside was filthy and in disrepair. Here and there bricks had fallen out of the walls or been chiseled out and stolen. Many of the windows were broken. After several minutes I realized that I was not far from my military institute. I'd walked past this place on my way to the bus in the past.

I was led to a small dark room. The only furnishings in the room were two military beds. A small washroom was adjacent to it.

'You will stay here,' the Colonel told me before he left. 'Since this is your new home, you may want to clean it up.'

I poured water in a bucket and scrubbed the floor and walls of the room. A guard who was stationed outside the door brought me food twice each day.

I had no visitors for three days. My time was filled with daydreaming. On the fourth day the Colonel and his aides returned. The Colonel told me things were not so bad after all. 'Everything is clear,' he said. 'We just need you to write a document telling them why you left the Johns Hopkins–Nanjing Center. We want you to write that you left because of your fear of the American, Larry Engelmann.'

'I have a better solution,' I said. 'Take me to the Center and let me stand before the Chinese and American students and faculty and tell them in my own words why I was taken from the Center and why I cannot return. Let's give them real Chinese drama!'

'What we need is an official notice of withdrawal signed by you. It is in everyone's best interest.'

'Everyone's? Mine? My husband's? Larry Engelmann's?' I said in a near-shout.

'I should have told you that the American is gone for good,' the Colonel said. 'The document is for the record alone. It's a formality.'

'What has happened to him?' I asked, my voice shaking. 'What did you do to him?'

'He's gone,' the Colonel said. 'He won't be coming back. He left of his own accord, perhaps because of his guilt. He said he didn't like living in China and he asked to be allowed not to return. The American administrators granted his request. Everything has been taken care of in a satisfactory way. This document will help you get back your position at the military institute.'

The Colonel was remarkably patient. For the first time I harbored hope that this was going to end less tragically than I initially expected.

'This is the only request we can make. When you sign this document, it will clear your record.'

He handed me a writing pad, a sheet of paper and a pen. I sat down on the bed and prepared to write. 'I'll dictate it to you,' the Colonel directed.

'While I was studying at the Center for Chinese and American Studies, I had an affair with my American professor, Larry Engelmann, and now I regret what happened and I feel that I do not want to return to the Center again. I am ashamed of what I have done.' I stopped writing after the first phrase.

'If you want to stay here in this room the rest of your life,' he responded, 'then by all means persist in your arrogance. You control your own fate now. If I leave this room without the document, I swear to you when I come back I will nail that door shut and never let you out of here again.'

'I have to think about this,' I told him. 'Come back later.'

Surprisingly, he agreed to my request rather than continuing to berate me. He left with his aides and returned two hours later. He offered me another option.

'We've thought about it and we can change the wording,' he

announced. 'You do not have to say you had an affair with the American.'

'Then what is there to write?' I asked. 'Our business is finished.'

But the Colonel handed me the paper and pen again and said, 'Write this, Meihong. Say you do not want to return to the Center, so you are withdrawing of your own free will. Write this: "Due to some personal difficulties (*sheng huo wenti*) I have decided to withdraw from the Center." The specific words he asked me to use could be construed in several different ways – not having enough money or not being able to take the pressure of life there or having family problems – life problems.

Despite the ambiguity of the words, I wrote the statement and signed it. The Colonel gave a sigh of relief when he read what I'd written, and without saying another word departed.

Three days later six military officers came to the room. Three of them were from the Second Bureau, the other three were from the Institute. One of them was the General. This was the first time I had seen him since he'd summoned me to his home in November and asked me not to betray him. I was true to my word and he knew it.

I could tell by their expressions this was going to be a somber ceremony. I knew once again that the Colonel's promises were lies.

One of the senior officers announced, 'We have been investigating your case, Xu Meihong, for some time. Now we have come to a judgment.' He said the General would read the decision of the board of inquiry.

I knew why this confrontation had been choreographed the way it was. The General's enemies still wanted to provide me with a final chance to save myself by betraying my commander. As he read my punishment, they expected me to break down and blame him for everything. My confession, they hoped, would mean his condemnation.

The General stepped forward. In a formal, flat voice he read the decision. The PLA had concluded, first, that I had made a serious error in forming a personal relationship with a foreigner, he read. Second, it was suspected that if the relationship had been allowed to continue I might have been induced to compromise confidential information concerning state security. Third, by my actions and my obvious intentions I had seriously damaged the image of the PLA and of the People's Republic of China. I had also damaged the image of all good Chinese women.

He droned on and on. I felt myself blushing and thought I was becoming sick to my stomach. Still, I stood at attention and listened to the list of charges.

The PLA headquarters had weighed them against my stellar record in the military prior to September 1988. There would be leniency, therefore, in my sentence.

First, I was discharged from the Communist Youth League. Second, I was stripped of my military rank and was discharged from the PLA. Third, I was to return to my home village to work as a peasant for the rest of my life.

Finally, there was a warning. I was forbidden to contact any foreigner. If I attempted to do so, 'the most severe punishment' awaited me.

As the General read, I turned the silver bracelet Larry had given me at our last meeting back and forth between my fingers, trying to calm myself. When I touched it, I felt stronger.

After reading the statement the General asked if there was anything I had to say regarding the charges and the decision.

I remained silent for several seconds. Then I said, calmly, 'Comrades, I would like to thank all of you. I am innocent of these crimes. But you have made what you consider to be an honest judgment, I know. I accept it like the good soldier I have always been. I appreciate your leniency as well as everything else you have done for me. I will never ever forget my years in the PLA. I will never forget this day and I promise I will never forget any of you men.'

When I'd finished there was a long moment of silence. My eyes met the General's for a second. I thought I detected relief and gratitude in his look. I had been true to my word. He was the only man in the room who knew I was exactly what I said I was – a good soldier.

That evening I asked the guard for a pen, paper and an

envelope and composed a short letter to my husband. I dated it at the top and wrote, 'I need to talk to you. Come to my parents' home to discuss my new situation, please. I will wait for you at the Danyang railway station. I'll be there for you for seven days. If you do not appear in that time, then you will never see me again. Thank you for everything you have done for me. You have always meant so much to me and I will never forget you. If I did anything to hurt you, I am sorry. That was never my intent. I cannot explain to you what happened because even I am not sure yet myself. Believe nothing about me that others may tell you. You know my heart. They don't. Please take good care of yourself.'

When I finished writing I lay down to sleep. But half an hour later the door was flung open and the light switched on. I sat up in bed, my heart racing. I feared they had come to take me away again and that the afternoon was merely a charade.

I was stunned and speechless when I saw the Colonel and, standing beside him, my husband. Lin Cheng was wearing his dress uniform and he looked so dashing and healthy and handsome.

He ran to me and embraced me and kissed the top of my head again and again. Then he whispered in my ear, 'Smile. Smile for this son of a bitch.'

I smiled through my tears. The letter I had written was on the floor. I picked it up and said, 'I meant to send this to you tomorrow. I didn't know if you would come back for me.'

'Didn't know if I would come for you?' he said in astonishment. 'What are you talking about, you silly girl? Of course I will always come back for you. You are my wife. I am here where I should be. I have been here for several days waiting for you. They refused to tell me where you were until tonight,' he said. 'I just needed to see if you were all right tonight. They said you cannot leave until the morning. So I'll be back then.'

He embraced me again and kissed me on the forehead and the nose and lips and then left with the Colonel.

When they were gone I switched off the light and went to bed again. I started to cry. I bit down on my hand so I would make no sound for the guard to hear.

It was over. I had survived. My old life was dead. Tomorrow morning I would start a new life.

Lying there, crying, I asked myself the same question over and over again, 'Xu Meihong, what have you done?'

SEVEN

Lost Girl

Lie still now
while I prepare for my future
certain hard days ahead,
when I'll need what I know so clearly at this
moment.

I am making use
of the one thing I learned
of all the things my father tried to teach me:
the art of memory

— LI-YOUNG LEE

i

My sleep that night was fitful and I was fully awake before dawn. I washed myself at the metal sink. The temperature in the room was below freezing and the water from the tap was piercingly cold. During my eight weeks of interrogation I had not been allowed to shower and I'd never been given a mirror in which to see my appearance. On this final morning of incarceration I wanted to appear clean and fresh in order to show my captors that although they had the power to hold me, they had been unable to destroy me.

Around eight o'clock, Lin Cheng appeared at the door with the Colonel and three armed soldiers. 'You look wonderful this morning,' he said, and embraced me tightly. Then he removed his military coat and helped me into it. The Colonel and the other soldiers were there to escort me back to my apartment at the Institute. A van awaited us outside. I was told I would be given half an hour to pack some of my daily necessities and then I was to be driven back to my village outside the town of Danyang.

The van let us out just inside the gate of the Institute and we walked the remaining distance to my apartment. We encountered several soldiers and cadets along the way. All of them stared at me as though I had just arrived from another planet. They'd been briefed on my case and told of my punishment. None of them dared be seen or heard greeting me.

One of the people we passed was the vice president of the Institute. She seemed to be in a hurry to get somewhere and was shuffling through a folder of papers. I knew her well. When she was within a few feet of our group, she glanced up and saw me. Instantly, she gave me a mean look, then turned back to her papers and stepped aside. There is an apt Chinese description for her expression – she looked as if she had just swallowed a fly – the look of someone who finds something so distasteful they need to vomit to be rid of it.

Before we arrived at my quarters, we met one of my former instructors. I had been one of his favorite students in an English composition class and we'd become friends over the years. When he saw our group, he fixed his eyes on my husband and exchanged pleasantries with him, but he acted as if I wasn't there. I'd become invisible.

ii

The General was waiting just inside the entrance to my building. He held the key to my apartment. He greeted us and instructed the Colonel and his guards to wait on the first floor while he accompanied me to my room. He asked my husband to wait with them.

We ascended the stairs without speaking. Once inside he closed the door behind us. I breathed more easily. I assumed he'd searched the apartment for microphones and that it was safe to speak candidly and we would not be overheard.

'Did they get any evidence? Did you confess anything?' he asked. He was so nervous he was actually trembling.

'What are you talking about? What evidence?' I asked him. I was confused.

'Did you tell them anything about me that might be used as evidence against me anytime in the future?' he asked.

'Didn't you read the transcripts?'

'I'm sure they were edited. I'd prefer to hear what was said from you. Did that son of a bitch downstairs ask about me?'

'Yes,' I said. 'He asked about you many times. He wanted something on you very much. But he knew nothing. He still knows nothing.'

'And what did you tell him when he asked about me?' the General asked nervously.

'Calm down, General. I kept my promise that I'd never betray you. I didn't betray anyone. You're safe. I'm the only one in trouble.' I went to my dresser and picked out some items of clothing to bring with me. The General didn't speak while my back was turned.

When I was finished I turned to him and said, 'And how are you, Xu Meihong?'

'What?' he asked.

I said, "And how are you, Xu Meihong?" Aren't you going to ask about me? I'm the one being punished, remember? What will happen to me now? Are you interested?'

'I'm sorry,' he said, obviously embarrassed by my statement. He'd begun to regain his composure. 'I'm sorry, Meihong. You know I am very concerned about you. My wife wanted to see you to say goodbye. But she could not take the day off. She asked me to say goodbye for her. She wishes you well. She will miss you, she said.'

These words warmed me. I still had friends who cared for me. I struggled to hold back tears when he told me. 'I'll miss her too,' I said. 'Please tell her that for me, will you?'

'There are some things you should know,' the General said. 'You should be aware of what happened while you were being questioned.'

'Yes, tell me,' I said. 'I'm curious, even though it will do me no good now.'

'It might help you,' he said. 'The Second Bureau [of the PLA] and the MSS still suspect you tried to work with a foreign agent and they believe you violated military regulations by carrying on a relationship with the American.'

'They're wrong,' I told him. 'But what difference does it make now?'

'I feared for your life,' he said. 'I really believed they would harm you. Your husband, your friends and I all defended you. We did what we could. But in trying to help you, we came under suspicion. We were limited in what we could do. If you had cooperated with them, everyone working to help you would have paid a high price.'

'I know,' I assured him. 'I didn't cooperate.'

'They underestimated your determination. They thought

you'd break down quickly and confess to whatever they asked.'

'What did they expect me to say?'

'They wanted you to say you were involved in corruption. They wanted you to say you were aware of stolen funds, of selling national secrets to an American agent and of helping him make productive contacts in China. They wanted you to be their convenient mouthpiece. They had bigger targets than you, of course. They wanted me – and they wanted my friends and associates. They wanted to wipe out a bloc of the reformist wing of the PLA in one big swipe. This was just the beginning, I am sure. It's going to get far worse.'

'What am I supposed to do now?' I asked.

'They think you'll become desperate and careless. They're not done with you. They're playing a waiting game now. They think you'll contact co-conspirators and seek their help and if they don't give it you'll turn on them. They also suspect that once you're in the countryside you'll be overwhelmed by the hardship and the harassment of the people around you and you'll eventually crack and make a deal with them. They fully expect you to lose your confidence and your trust in your friends and to side with them in the end. You have to remember they'll be watching you constantly. You may elude them for a time, but eventually they'll find you and stay on your trail. You can be sure of it.'

'I don't understand. Why am I still so important to them?' I asked.

'After your arrest, someone from Nanjing provided Party General Secretary Zhao Ziyang with an account of accusations against a junior military officer from Nanjing. That was you, Xu Meihong. Zhao took an immediate interest in it. He put his friends on the case. He even wanted to take over the interrogation. He seemed convinced this was the tip of an iceberg. That's when things got out of hand.'

'My God, what do I have to do with him? Why was he interested?'

'His political reforms aren't working,' the General explained. 'They're in shambles, in fact. And he badly wants a scapegoat. As you know, he has little support from the PLA. Zhao doesn't have real power because the Army doesn't back him. The real power in Beijing is still with Central Military Commission Chairman Deng Xiaoping and President Yang Shang Kun. Both are from the PLA. So there is a political struggle going on right now. Zhao believes the Army has been undercutting him and so he needs to discredit some of its ranking officers. When he was told of your case he saw an opportunity to taint the Army by exposing a group of disloyal officers. Zhao wanted to make it a big deal. Zhao wanted to demonstrate through the case that there is widespread corruption and disloyalty in the Army. It could have been a significant victory for him – to tie some of Yang's associates to a conspiracy within the PLA. So the moment Zhao Ziyang tried to step in, the men who arranged to have you arrested lost their support from the PLA headquarters. General Yang immediately saw the danger in what was happening and as soon as he did he informed the Second Bureau that he wanted the case disposed of as quickly as possible. So the men who arranged for your arrest were caught in their own trap. They weren't sure what to do next. They needed an out and they needed a valid explanation for their actions. It's almost funny to see how they shot themselves in the foot.'

'Who told Zhao Ziyang of my case?' I inquired. 'That's the person who saved me whether he meant it or not.'

'I can't give you a name, Meihong. But you've learned a lesson about politics now, haven't you?'

'I hate politics.'

'But politics now loves you and it will follow you the rest of your life.'

'What about you, General?'

'Politics isn't new to me. It's an endless struggle. I've been through this before and now I'm prepared to go through it again – and be arrested, probably. But don't worry about me. You should be thinking about yourself. You are hated by many people now. You caused the conservative old guard to lose face. Yet you are not welcome with the reformists anymore either because you were almost a weapon in their destruction. You are dangerous to them now and they want to distance themselves from you. Just remember there are people waiting for the opportune moment to arrest you and interrogate you again.'

'What shall I do?'

'You have to get out of China as soon as you can. But that may be very difficult – even impossible. Something will have to happen to divert the attention of those watching you. But it would have to be very big. A national catastrophe would serve your purposes very nicely, but I wouldn't count on it. Let's pray for a political upheaval soon. And when it happens, you should make your move.'

'And if I need help?'

'There will be help,' he assured me.

We returned down the stairs to the guards and to my husband. A van had been summoned to transport me to my village. I was directed to the rear bank of seats. A guard was seated on each side of me. My husband rode in front with the driver and the two remaining soldiers sat in the middle seat.

I stared out the window as we pulled away from my apartment. The General stood stiffly and watched me go. Neither of us waved. The van turned a corner and stopped at the gate. The driver handed some papers to the sentry. Outside the window I saw the soldiers walking by, going about their business. I was so familiar with this place – the trees, the lawns, the buildings, every path and road reminded me of something. I had been here for almost eight years – some of the best years of my youth were spent here. Now that was all gone. I started to cry quietly. My husband turned to look at me. He held up his hand and mouthed the words 'Be strong.'

The drive to Danyang took four hours. The longer we rode, the more despairing I became. I knew what shame I was bringing home to my family.

I was always a shining example in my village. My parents glowed with pride at my accomplishments. Everywhere I went people pointed me out and told their children they wanted them to grow up to be just like me. My return home, escorted by military guards, would be hard on my parents. It wouldn't take long for everyone in the village to know why and how I came home. I remembered what happened to my Aunt Lingdi when she returned to the village. I knew I would be treated like a leper.

To make matters worse, my brother's wedding had been scheduled for the week of the Chinese New Year. He was the only male child in the family, so my parents intended to make the wedding a particularly special celebration. Of course, my presence had been expected to add prestige. Now I could imagine people looking at me during my brother's wedding and whispering, 'She was convicted of a crime' or 'She slept with a foreigner. She betrayed her husband.'

Fifteen minutes from my village I started to cry again. My husband spoke to the Colonel and was permitted to sit next to me. 'I don't want to be escorted to my parents' front door by armed soldiers,' I told him. I knew this would be a nightmare for my parents and that they'd be humiliated by it in front of the other villagers. They'd be asked to sign a document that they'd received me from the PLA as if I was returned goods.

Lin Cheng snapped open his suitcase and pulled out five cartons of Marlboro cigarettes. He'd purchased them in Nanjing to bring to my parents as New Year's gifts. Now he had a better use for them. He handed each of the soldiers and the driver a carton of cigarettes. 'Listen,' he said to the Colonel, 'Meihong is my wife. I am her real family. It would be appropriate if you just turned her over to me, here, now. I am a Party member and a PLA officer. I'll sign for her and we can walk the rest of the way. You can save time and get back to Nanjing for the holiday. Just let us off here.'

The Colonel thought about it for a moment and then said, 'I understand your situation.' He told the driver to pull over and stop. Lin Cheng signed the required document and we got out with our bags. We stood silently and watched the van turn around and disappear down the long road.

I told my husband I needed to rest a moment. We sat on our bags at the side of the road. I tried to think of an excuse to give my parents but I couldn't find the right words. 'I don't want to go home,' I told my husband. 'Take me anywhere else, but not to my parents. I can't go back like this.'

'Quit being childish,' he said. 'Home is always home. Your

parents will understand. They will always love you. They've been told you're coming. They expect you today. If you don't show up, they'll start making inquiries. It will only be worse. There is no way out now, Meihong. You have to go back. Sooner or later you have to face this situation. You can't escape it. The only thing you can do is to cheer up, be as happy as you can to show your parents you can handle this.'

'You mean they know everything already?'

'Yes. Last week the Colonel visited your parents in the village. He told them.'

Standing there at the side of the road I cried quietly in my husband's arms until I had no more tears.

iii

When we arrived my mother was preparing lunch. I couldn't look into her eyes. Her smile was forced and unconvincing. My father greeted me and then left the room. I went to the bedroom to be alone. My mother served lunch a short time later, but I had no appetite. I sat silently at the table without eating.

After lunch my husband asked me if I'd like to go outside for a walk. We put on our coats and walked through the frozen, snow-covered fields.

'You can see what will happen here,' I told him. 'I can't stay. I can't face up to my mother's pain. I can't live here with the realization that I've brought so much humiliation to my family. Help me get away from here. If I don't get away, I know I will die here.'

'Maybe you should come with me to Beijing. I'll take care of you.'

'I'm not supposed to leave the village. I don't want you to be held responsible for breaking the rules. It would mean the end of your career.'

We walked in silence for several minutes trying to think of a solution to my problem. Finally he said, 'I have a friend who may be able to help us. I'll call him. Is there a telephone in the village?'

I laughed at his question. 'No,' I said. 'We'll have to go to the central post office in the city.'

We borrowed my brother's bicycle and rode it to Danyang. My husband called his friend at the National Defense University from a public phone in the post office. He had discussed my problems previously with his friend. The friend's father ran a business in the oil fields in western Henan province and might be able to arrange a job for me there – where no one could trace me. The condition was, however, that nobody – including my parents – know my whereabouts. He also did not want his father told of my political problems.

We returned to the village with a large package of firecrackers and fireworks. It was the eve of the Chinese New Year. 'We had bad luck this year,' my husband said. 'Maybe when these go off, they'll chase that bad luck away and we'll have lots of good luck in the New Year.' That night there were celebrations. Firecrackers exploded outside every home to drive away evil spirits, and rockets whooshed high into the air and exploded in bright colors. I saw some of the rockets disappear into the darkness and I thought how wonderful it might be if I could do that – suddenly fly off into the darkness and never be seen again.

At my family's New Year's Eve dinner my brother announced that he'd cancelled his wedding. His fiancée's family had learned of my situation and concluded it was not an opportune time to hold a wedding.

This news put everyone in a dark mood. As soon as dinner was over Lin Cheng and I excused ourselves and went to bed. I started to cry again. 'I'm still here for you,' my husband reminded me. 'Keep your head up. You can't give in. No matter what happens or what you do, I will always be here to help you,' he reassured me. 'I am your husband. I didn't marry you just for the good times.'

I started to talk about the plans we'd made when we married. We planned to live together in Beijing someday and to have a child. My continuing hope of that future was one of the things that kept me alive, I told him.

After a long pause he said, 'Meihong, I love you but we can never have children. You should let go of that dream as soon as possible. It can only bring you disappointment.'

His words sliced through one of the remaining cords that still joined us – a common dream of happiness with our own family. He loved me and he'd made enormous sacrifices for me. But the grim reality of what had happened to me, I now realized, had affected our marriage deeply.

'You have to understand our situation,' he said. 'Even if you come to Beijing someday and have a baby, the baby will be treated differently. He will be discriminated against and suffer because of his parents and their reputation. His life and career will be far less than either of us could want for him. That's not fair. And I won't do that to a child. If we stay married, we will live by ourselves without any children.'

If we stay married, I thought. If? I wondered if Lin Cheng realized he'd used that conditional word.

When Lin Cheng asked me what had happened to me at the Center I couldn't remember clearly nor could I explain it. I wasn't sure how I had transformed a simple assignment from the MSS and a request from the General into a personal catastrophe. What could I say had attracted me to Larry in the first place? Why did I feel the way I did when he held me and we danced? I was surprised at my own feelings. They were completely unexpected. I felt guilty for feeling good when he held me, when we danced, and when he touched my hand. Every time I made up my mind not to go for a walk with him again or to visit him again. But when he called I gave in. I wasn't sure why I couldn't resist. And if I didn't understand my own feelings, how could I hope to explain them to someone else? I was sure my affection and respect for Larry didn't diminish my love for Lin Cheng. I always assumed that someday Larry and I would part and we'd have fond memories of each other and we'd probably never forget our year in the Center. Larry would return to America and I'd return to my husband and my old life, I thought. I never intended to threaten my marriage or my future. But I had done just that.

That night I realized that despite his support for me upon

my release from custody, Lin Cheng's love was different from the love we'd shared in the past. On the surface, to those watching us, we still seemed, I was sure, the perfect couple, deeply in love. But that was an illusion. My initial romantic experience with him convinced me that love is always youthful, reckless, passionate, hopeful, respectful and forgiving. If it isn't these things, I believed, then it isn't really love. If it is these things, then it has the power to transform dreams into realities.

I listened to my husband say that his love for me was no longer hopeful. And he reminded me that our dreams – my dreams – would never become realities. When I heard him say this I realized that Lin Cheng's love for me was another casualty of my conduct at the Center.

For a long time I lay awake beside my husband that night and stared at the ceiling and repeated his last sentence silently to myself over and over again. Then I quietly cried myself to sleep.

iv

He was right. I had to accept the fact that I was no longer the person I had been only a few months earlier. Not only my career in the military had ended. Everything had changed. Everything in my life was going to be different from that day on.

The next morning I was visited by my best friend from high school, Zhong Yuhua. She had become a teacher at Qinghua University in Beijing and lived in a dormitory on campus. When we were alone she told me she'd heard what had happened to me. She asked what I was planning to do. I told her I wasn't sure. 'Come to Beijing,' she suggested, 'and live with me. Take a new name. Nobody will find you there. I'll help you.'

'Maybe someday,' I said, 'but not now,' I told her. 'I have other options at the moment.'

'You have my phone number in Beijing, don't you?' she asked before leaving.

'Yes,' I told her.

'Call me when you need me,' she said. 'You can start over in Beijing.'

'You'll hear from me,' I said.

'When?' she asked.

I remembered what the General advised and I said, 'Shortly after hell breaks loose in Beijing.'

'That soon?' she asked, and we both laughed. She held my hand as I walked her outside and said goodbye. 'Don't ever forget my offer,' she said, turning to me one last time before walking back to her parents' home.

'I won't,' I assured her. I watched her walk away and didn't think I'd see her again.

During the weeklong Chinese New Year's festival it is a custom to visit relatives and extend New Year's greetings. So my husband and I walked to the nearby villages to visit my aunts, uncles and cousins. I felt uneasy in their homes. No one asked about my arrest. But they all knew what had happened to me. I was now jobless, poor and without a future. Most of the visits were quiet encounters. My husband became increasingly uneasy as the hours passed. He stopped trying to participate in the forced and formal conversations. I only felt comfortable visiting Lingdi and her husband. They greeted me, embraced me and poured tea and served New Year's cakes. Lingdi held my hand while we talked. I felt as if I was the same person I'd always been while I sat in her house. Her affection for me hadn't changed. She knew what I was facing and what it was like to live as an outcast in the village. She tried to comfort me in the way my mother had comforted her after her return to Lishi from the labor camp.

After the celebration of New Year's Day we returned to the post office and called Lin Cheng's friend in Beijing. He said that I could go to rural Henan province and that someone there would take care of me. I'd be given a job. I wouldn't be reported. I wouldn't be watched.

We decided to go by ship up the Yangtze River. We could go as far as Wuhan and take a train the remaining distance to my haven. We had never taken a ship up the river before, so this was to be our first cruise together and it might well be our last, I realized.

I didn't tell my parents I was leaving. I wanted them to remain ignorant of my plans in order to protect them from inquiries by the PLA and the MSS. I'd find a way later to let them know I was safe.

Early the next morning Lin Cheng took the train to Nanjing to purchase tickets for us. I told him that I had to take care of something important before I joined him late that afternoon at the wharf in Nanjing. Since I knew I would not be back in Lishi in April for the Qing Ming festival, when the family tended the graves of our ancestors, I needed to bid farewell to my grandmother before departing.

V

I walked three miles to the village cemetery. It was the first time I'd been there alone.

The cemetery for Lishi and the nearby villages was thought to be haunted. In the 1960s someone in Beijing decided that burying the dead in caskets resulted in the loss of too much productive agricultural space. A law was passed requiring cremation of the deceased. During the Cultural Revolution, Red Guards came to our village, dug up the old graves, cremated what they found, compacted it and then covered the new remains on smaller plots of land. This angered and frightened the older villagers, who believed the Red Guards were disturbing the dead. The spirits of the dead were enraged by being dug up and burned, the villagers believed, and their ghosts roamed the cemetery after that, seeking revenge. Now no one dared go there unaccompanied. There were angry ghosts, it was said, waiting there to seize the living. But I was no longer afraid of ghosts. I was afraid of the living.

There are several hundred burial mounds in the cemetery. A small stone is placed at the head of each small mound, giving the name of the deceased and the dates of birth and death. All four of my grandparents are buried there.

Now, alone, I entered the cemetery and walked to my grandmother's grave. She was the woman who literally pulled me screaming and bloody into this world. Her grip on my head had been so tight, I was told, that she left her fingerprints on my forehead. I could see them clearly each time I looked in the mirror – small indentations in each side of my forehead. My grandmother also gave me my name, brought me up, followed my career and took enormous pride in my accomplishments. I loved her deeply and I missed her. She was the only one I could pour my heart out to now. I was happy she had been spared the shame of my expulsion from the PLA and my forced exile in the countryside. I suspect it would have broken her heart.

'I have to go away, Grandmother,' I said. Then I closed my eyes and tried to remember her face, her laugh, her scowl, her voice and the touch of her hand.

I was her pride and joy, she said so often. We also shared a tragic secret. Although I called her grandmother – and she was my grandmother in a legal sense – she was, in fact, not related by blood either to my father or to me.

vi

My grandmother's name was Zhu Xiaoying (Little Hero). She was born in 1905, when Tzu Hsi, the last Qing Dowager Empress, still ruled China. She was the third daughter of six children born to her parents, who were moderately well-to-do peasants. When Grandmother was very young, a distant relative with no children from another village came to her family and asked them to give her to them to raise. Her father agreed. Sons were a blessing to a family, but daughters were not. So she was given away.

One of the reasons her parents gave her away was that she resisted having her feet bound. Her mother and father attempted to force her to have bound feet, which was a common practice at the time, but every time they were bound she unwrapped them. When her parents discovered what she'd done, they beat her. Yet she persisted, no matter how many times she was beaten. She was strong-willed, unbending, and finally the family simply gave up. They concluded she would always be troublesome and would never amount to much or marry well. Distinguished men did not marry women with big feet.

Her adoptive parents, both educated people, were progressive and opposed foot binding. They were more concerned with her education. They treated her kindly, taught her how to read and write and provided her with books. She loved to read and adored her adoptive parents. But when Xiaoying was fourteen, her new mother died and her new father, fearing he could not raise her alone, returned her to her original family.

Upon her return, her father decided to marry her off as quickly as possible. In the countryside, at that time, fourteen was a marriageable age. She was a tall girl and beautiful in a rustic way. She was never delicate or fragile, in the way that women from the cities were. She never wore makeup. But she had large eyes and clear skin and long shining black hair. When men in the countryside saw her, they stared in openmouthed wonder.

Although she lived and worked in the village, people said she did not look like any other peasant woman. The way she dressed and carried herself when she walked, the way she looked people in the eye and the assertiveness of her voice set her apart.

One morning, when my grandmother was alone in her parents' house, the village head entered the house and tried to get into her bed. She fought him off. He vowed to return another day and have his way with her. But before that happened she struck back. She went to two of her older sisters that day and told them what had happened. They had married two brothers who were sons of a warlord and members of a secret society.

Two nights later, the village head was awakened from his sleep by two masked men who dragged him outside and beat him. Before leaving him cowering in front of his house, they warned him, 'Don't you ever touch Xiaoying again. Don't you ever speak to her again. If you do, there will be a bullet waiting for you.'

The village head was terrified. He never came near my grandmother again. In fact, when he saw her approaching on the road, he ran away and hid. When other men in the village heard what had happened, they too feared coming near her. She was safe in the village, but her father could find no prospective husband for her.

Finally, in frustration, her father hired matchmakers. After several days the matchmakers said they had located a good family – surnamed Xu – with a son of marrying age. The son resided in Shanghai, where he ran the family business – a shoe manufacturing company.

A fortune teller was employed to pick a propitious date for the wedding. On that day, the Xu family sent eight porters and a sedan chair to carry Xiaoying to their home. Her family followed behind in a solemn procession.

When my grandmother and her family arrived at the Xu home, they were told that the groom was not there yet. He was in Shanghai finishing important business. Nonetheless, the wedding ceremony should proceed without him because this was the lucky day for the wedding.

In the traditional wedding ceremony of that time the bride was obligated to kowtow to her new in-laws, to their ancestors and to her husband. During the ceremony her face was covered with a red silk cloth, so she could not see the pictures of the ancestors or the faces of the new in-laws. Suddenly she sensed someone standing next to her and she assumed it was her husband, who had arrived late. She became very anxious about pleasing him. So she kowtowed solemnly to the pictures of the ancestors and the family members and in the direction of her new husband.

But when she was finished they lifted the red cloth covering her face, and she found she had kowtowed not to her husband but to a large red rooster. This, according to local tradition, was the substitute for an absent groom. That night, her wedding night, she was locked in a wedding chamber with the rooster.

Despite the fact that the Xu family was only following an established tradition, she was deeply embarrassed by this. She was angry at her husband even before she met him, though he explained later that his absence was no fault of his own. For the rest of her life she blamed him for not being at their wedding.

Her husband arrived five days after the wedding ceremony. She took an instant dislike to him. For one thing, at just over five feet tall, he was much shorter than his wife.

When she returned to her father's house a week after her wedding, she refused to walk beside her new husband. She insisted he walk several feet behind her so people would not notice their difference in height. When her father greeted her, the first thing she said to him was 'Why did you marry me to this little man?'

'Because he had money and because he did not object to marrying a girl with big feet,' he shot back at her. 'You brought this on yourself, Xiaoying. Had you allowed us to bind your feet, today you would have a husband as tall as your sisters'. Don't blame me.'

He was a short man, but not bad-looking. He was stylish and dapper and quite out of place in the countryside. He was a successful Shanghai businessman and he considered himself cosmopolitan and dressed the part. He wore only well-tailored Western-style wool suits, a fedora tilted at a rakish angle and expensive custom-made shoes. He sported a gold key chain and he carried his money in a genuine leather wallet.

She spent one month with her husband in his village home. Then he returned to Shanghai and she remained in the village house.

As the wife of the heir to the Xu family land and interests, her primary duty became the care and comfort of her in-laws. In those times it was the custom for a young woman who married into another family to become a servant to that family. Her duties were to work for the family and produce sons. When her own sons married, their wives would become her servants. For a woman like my grandmother, who was independent, literate, intelligent and restless, this was a particularly difficult burden.

Since there was but one son in the family, Xiaoying was the only daughter-in-law in the household. She had no one with whom to share her labors. So she arose at four o'clock each morning to begin her day. She prepared and served breakfast for her in-laws. Then she fed the farm animals – pigs, sheep, chickens, water buffalo and rabbits. When she'd finished and cleaned the stalls, she walked to the fields to tend the crops.

She had to learn from others about tending the crops and the animals because, when she was young, she never imagined she would live the life of a peasant. Her talents were in other areas. The teachers who educated her had prepared her for the life of wife and companion of a scholar. But after her marriage, her husband and his family refused to allow her to read or write. Her husband was threatened by her intelligence and talent. Knowing she was more accomplished than anyone else in his family, he did not wish her to assume an arrogant attitude toward either his mother or his sisters, who were illiterate. He had only finished grammar school himself. By the time he had mastered the abacus his father believed he'd had enough formal education. He wanted his son to know enough to work with numbers so he would never be cheated in business. Anything else, he insisted, was a waste.

During the first ten years of her marriage, my grandmother did not become pregnant and her failure to give her husband a son became a major concern for the Xu family. Grandmother decided to move to Shanghai and live with her husband. She immediately noticed that many young women flirted openly with her husband and competed for his attention. According to a village tradition, if a woman did not bear her husband a son within a reasonable period of time, her husband could 'send her away' and take a new wife or another wife. She wondered how long before one of those women might replace her as his wife.

So she made a surprising proposal to her husband. She told him, 'I have a cousin in Shanghai. Her husband died recently. She has three children – all of them boys. She is only in her late twenties and she seems to have a talent for producing male children. She has little income since her husband died, and she needs money to feed her children. We can pay her to have a son for us.'

Grandfather was interested.

Grandmother promised she would not be jealous and the three of them could keep the arrangement a secret. She suggested that the woman be asked to move into their house with her sons and to work as the housekeeper until she had the child, then she would be rewarded with a generous lump sum.

The woman was invited to meet Grandfather and he found her to be very beautiful. My grandmother told her of the plan. After some discussion about compensation, she agreed.

So the woman lived with my grandparents and worked as a housekeeper in the family. After one month the woman became pregnant. Grandmother then told Grandfather to stop sleeping with her. The goal of the arrangement had been achieved.

But she discovered that Grandfather continued to sleep with the woman, that an emotional attachment had developed between the two and that the woman might be scheming to replace her in the household after she bore a son.

Then came a bigger surprise. One week later Grandmother discovered that she had morning sickness. She had become pregnant, in fact, during the same week as her cousin. When she was sure she was expecting a child, she told her cousin to leave. She demanded that Grandfather pay the woman immediately and send her back to the countryside.

Grandmother was sure she would have a son. But when she gave birth she was devastated to discover she had a daughter.

It was a difficult delivery, and my grandmother was anxious about it. She was so afraid, she told me years later, because so much was at stake. When the child was finally delivered, Grandmother was completely exhausted. After she found she had given birth to a girl she burst into tears. She was inconsolable. She cradled the newborn girl in her arms and talked to her and asked her over and over again why she could not have been a boy. What had gone wrong? The newborn child kept her eyes closed and slept in my grandmother's arms without making a sound. 'I've been waiting all these years for you,' Grandmother told her. 'Now I became pregnant and it is you. Why? Why do girls bring so much misery into the world?' she asked.

Grandfather waited outside the bedroom where his wife gave birth. He was concerned and anxious himself. He only wanted to hear one phrase that morning: 'You have a son.' When he was told that he had a daughter, he was crushed.

When he entered the room to see Grandmother, he could not even look at his new daughter. 'What shall we do now?' he asked.

She confessed to him weakly, 'I don't know what to do. I am so sorry.'

But Grandfather said he had secretly formulated a plan in case his wife gave birth to a girl. 'There is a worker in my factory,' he told her, 'and he has four sons. The worker's wife gave birth yesterday to a boy. They don't want any more sons and they are willing to give the new child away. I'll talk to him to see if we can make a trade – our daughter for their son. We can then tell people that you gave birth to a son. No one will suspect.'

Grandmother was in a vulnerable condition at that moment. If the decision was to be made, her husband said, it had to be made quickly, so no one would know the difference. Grandmother saw the disappointment in her husband's face, saw the way he refused even to look at his newborn daughter. She agreed to the trade.

'All right,' she said. 'I was given to another family when I was a child. My new parents were kinder to me than my real parents. Perhaps she can have a good life with them. Let me clean her up first.'

She asked Grandfather to leave the room. Then she took out a small cotton blanket she had purchased in a store in Shanghai. The blanket had delicate lace around the edges, and a hundred tiny figures of children at play embroidered into it. She planned to use it to wrap her new son and present him to his father. Now she used it, delicately and lovingly, to clean the body of her newborn girl. When she was washing the new child, she told me, the little girl opened her eyes for the first time and looked up at her and at that moment Grandmother began to have second thoughts about the trade.

When she had finished cleaning her daughter, Grandmother folded the wet blanket, soiled with her own blood, and flecked with tiny strands of the little girl's crown of raven hair, and placed it under the bed.

She wrapped the girl in a clean blanket, took one last look into her child's beautiful eyes and then folded the blanket over her face and handed the bundle to Grandfather, who was waiting outside the door. She then returned to her bed and fell into a fitful sleep.

An hour later Grandfather returned with a baby boy. He handed the child to Grandmother, who unwrapped him and immediately nursed him. She asked Grandfather about the other family. He assured her that they were delighted to have a new daughter. Now, he said, they could tell everyone that he had a son. He was very pleased with the trade.

But Grandmother was not happy. She could not forget the little girl and the look in her eyes, a look of silent wonder at the world into which she had been born and at the woman who had carried her. There had been an emotional bonding between mother and daughter in the few moments the two had spent together.

She thought about it for three days and started to ask herself over and over again, 'My God, what have I done? That was my daughter. I love my daughter. I want my daughter back.'

Then she told her husband she wanted him to retrieve the little girl. 'We can keep both of them,' she said. 'We can have a son and a daughter. We can tell everyone I had twins.'

This angered Grandfather. 'Damn you, forget her! She is gone,' he shouted. 'She is not your daughter anymore. She belongs to someone else. I paid them and the deal is completed now. You have a son. Take care of him.'

'I can't forget my girl,' Grandmother cried. 'I see her every time I close my eyes.'

'Then tell yourself she died,' he advised her.

Grandmother was haunted more each day by the memory of the little girl. She cried all the time. She lost her appetite. Her milk dried up. Grandfather hired a wet nurse to feed his son. During every conversation she had with her husband Grandmother begged him to return her daughter. And he, just as adamantly, refused.

At first Grandfather argued with her about bringing the girl back. Then he simply would not talk about it. When she started to question him, he left the room.

For two years, her requests for news about the girl were met with silence. Then, when the boy turned two, my grand-mother noticed some unusual features in him. They led her to a shocking conclusion.

One evening she asked her husband about their son, rather than about their daughter.

'What would you like to know?' he asked.

'He really is your son, isn't he?' she asked, startling him. 'He is your flesh and blood. Isn't that true?'

'Why would you say that?' he asked, visibly unsettled. 'He is the child of one of the factory workers.'

'But the older he gets, the more he looks like you,' she pointed out. 'Look at his ears. They are your ears.' My grandfather's ears stuck out a little bit and the boy had the same ears. 'Look at his cheeks and his eyes,' she said. 'They are like yours. And his hands are like yours and his walk is like yours. He is truly your son, isn't he? This is the son you produced with my cousin, isn't it?'

Feeling trapped, Grandfather finally confessed. 'Yes. You are right. He is the son your cousin bore for us. But that was your idea, don't you remember? It isn't my fault.'

Grandmother felt betrayed. 'Then where did you take my daughter?' she asked him. 'Did you give our daughter to that woman?'

'No, I didn't,' he said. 'She could not afford another child.'

Grandmother became angrier. 'Where is my baby girl? What did you do with her? Who has her?'

Grandfather left the apartment without answering. When he returned later that night, she continued asking him about the girl, and again received no response. Grandfather simply clammed up about it, hoping she would forget the girl. But after the passage of two years, she had become even more obsessed with finding her lost child. She stopped sleeping in the same bed with her husband. In fact, she never slept in the same bed with him again.

'Tell me where you took my daughter,' she demanded. 'If that woman did not take her, then who did? Where is she?'

One evening, in anger and resignation, he told my grandmother, 'I gave her to a very good family. She will have a good life. The father is a schoolteacher in Shanghai. He and his wife have no other children. That is the whole story. I am not going to say another word about it.'

But Grandmother was not satisfied. She demanded, 'Where do they live? In what district? On what street?'

Her husband responded, 'It's no use asking. I will never tell you. I promised them I would not tell anyone else about it.'

So Grandmother set out on her own to find her daughter. First she visited everyone she knew, all of my grandfather's friends and business associates. Then she visited the homes of the workers in the factory. She visited orphanages and spoke with the nurses about her missing child. She placed advertisements in the newspaper. She posted signs on walls offering monetary rewards for anyone who found the girl. But no one knew where the girl was.

Finally she bought a little gong and struck it to attract attention on the street in the business district of Shanghai. Each morning, no matter what the weather, she headed for the streets. She made loud proclamations on the street corners asking for information about a little lost girl.

People complained to my grandfather that she was crazy and a public nuisance as well as an embarrassment to the family. He asked her again and again to stop, but she refused to listen to him.

Finally, he struck a bargain with her. He said if she would promise not to go on the street anymore, he would tell her where the girl was.

Reluctantly, she agreed to his conditions. And so he told her, 'I threw her into the garbage outside the factory and left her there. She's dead. She's been dead from the morning I took her from this house.'

For a few moments my grandmother was completely

unhinged by this revelation. But then she said, 'That's not true! She isn't dead. I'm sure she cried after you left her and someone picked her out of the garbage. I'm sure she is still alive somewhere in Shanghai. I am going to find her.'

Grandfather insisted, 'No, she is dead. I know she is dead. I didn't throw her in the garbage. I threw her into the river. She drowned. I saw her sink in the water. She is dead. Forget her. Forget her, damn you!'

After China was taken over by the Communist Party in 1949, Grandfather's factory was confiscated. He was paid a small salary and drafted by the Party to manage the factory for the government. Unable to suffer his wife any longer, he sent her to his village home, where she raised the son who eventually became my father. Back in the village the lost girl was a well-kept secret and nobody knew that my father was not Grandmother's own child.

When my mother married into the Xu family, Grandmother made many demands on her and acted the part of the traditional mother-in-law toward the new daughter-in-law. But during the final months of my mother's first pregnancy, Grandmother changed. She cared for her, cooked for her and treated her like her own child.

After three days at labor, my mother gave birth to me on the morning of December 6, 1963. My father could not bear to listen to the crying and screaming, and took a chair outside the house and waited in the cold with friends to hear if he had a son or a daughter.

As I was about to be born, I became stuck. My mother was bleeding heavily, and my grandmother concluded that if she did not intervene, my mother would bleed to death and her baby would die. So she reached deep inside my mother with her fingertips and grasped each side of my head, and turned me and guided me into the world.

All of the sheets and towels in the house became soaked with blood. As soon as my mother completed the delivery, she lost consciousness. During the next day she lingered between life and death. Grandmother remained at her bedside constantly until she was sure my mother would recover.

My father, as the only son and heir in the Xu family, wanted a son to carry on the family name. When my grandmother went outside and made the announcement to my father that he had a new daughter, he showed little enthusiasm. But my grandmother was ecstatic. 'We should be celebrating,' she told them. 'Now we have a daughter in the family.'

Because of the profusion of blood from my delivery on the sheets and towels, Grandmother wanted to give me a name that would denote the difficulty and the triumph that my birth represented to her. So she named me Meihong, or Beautiful Red.

vii

At the age of eighty-two, Grandmother took the train to Nanjing to visit me at the military institute. I arranged for her to stay in a special guesthouse for four weeks. She cooked my meals and hand-washed my clothes. She even washed my bedding and hung it on a line to dry. When my friends watched her working and saw her energy, they could not believe she was eighty-two.

Her mind remained sharp and her body was healthy and strong. When we went for long walks in the evening, she was never tired. It was during her stay that she told me the story of her life and I promised to keep her secret.

At the end of her visit I accompanied her to the Nanjing train station. I embraced her and kissed her one last time before the train pulled away. I waved to her from the station platform and blew her kisses and cried as her train disappeared in the distance. I still vividly remember seeing her sitting there at the window, straight and tall and smiling, gazing back at me and slowly waving.

Three months later, on July 20, 1987, I received a telegram from home stating, 'Grandmother died. Please return home immediately.' I hurried home but by the time I arrived Grandmother had already been cremated and her ashes buried. That night my mother told me that Grandmother didn't die a natural death. She had hanged herself.

I asked my mother what they had done with my grandmother's personal belongings. They hadn't been disturbed, she said. I volunteered to go through them.

Grandmother kept all of her cherished memorabilia in a box next to her bed in her room. I wanted to go through it to see if I could find anything that might indicate why she killed herself.

So I went to her room, sat on her bed and opened the box. I noticed tiny black flakes on the floor around the box, like little paint chips.

Inside the box was a photograph of me in uniform. Beneath it were photographs of Grandmother with her sisters when they were all very young. There were none of her with her husband and, indeed, nothing that might suggest she had ever been married to him. The letters I'd sent her over the years were tied together neatly with a pink ribbon.

At the bottom of the box, neatly folded, was a very old delicately embroidered white cotton blanket that had been badly stained. I lifted it out of the box, placed it across my knees and carefully unfolded it. On the blanket were embroidered the fading images of a hundred children. My grandmother had never washed it after cleaning her daughter with it fifty-four years earlier. The sheet was encrusted with dried blood that had turned black and brittle over the years. When I opened the blanket the dried blood crumbled and came loose and fell to the floor like a million tiny slivers of stained glass.

I ran my fingers slowly around the children someone had stitched into the garment. I examined the tiny flakes of blood and the little filaments of black hair that still adhered to the blanket.

I refolded the blanket and returned it to the box. Then I put back the other items exactly the way she had arranged them. I closed the box and slid it to where she'd left it. I told my father to keep it in a safe place. It contained the story of his mother's life.

viii

I remained at my grandmother's grave most of the morning thinking of her, talking to her, explaining why I was leaving. I asked her to give me the courage to keep my head up and to fight for a new life.

Finally, I returned to Danyang and caught the train to Nanjing. I took a bus to the wharf, where I met Lin Cheng.

We boarded the ship and located the compartment that we shared with two other people. One of them, I noticed, was in uniform. Every time I looked at him, I became uneasy. What was he doing here? I asked my husband if anyone saw him when he bought the ticket. He said he didn't think so.

The soldier struck up a conversation with us. He said he worked in the Guangzhou Military District and he had just been to Nanjing to visit his parents. 'You look like you are from the PLA,' he said. 'Aren't you?' I assumed he'd noticed something distinct in my bearing – the way I kept my back straight and my shoulders pulled back – something all military cadets practiced until it became second nature.

I told him I was. He asked where I was assigned. I told him I was from the Institute in Nanjing. He said, 'I know this will sound like a coincidence, but last night I had dinner with your political commissar. He is a good friend of my father. What is your name?'

I made up a name. I could hardly believe my bad luck. If this soldier figured out who I was and told the political commissar in Nanjing, all of my effort to escape would come to nothing. They would easily trace me. I felt uneasy. The New Year's firecrackers hadn't worked.

I excused myself and told my husband I was hungry and wanted to go to the dining room.

The dining room was dirty and crowded. The food was expensive and bad.

I lost my appetite. I said I needed to get some air. We went up to the deck. It was raining but we didn't mind. We were alone. We stood at the ship's railing in the rain and talked about the past several days and watched the shoreline slip past.

EIGHT

Mao's Child

The floor before my bed is bright:
Moonlight – like hoarfrost – in my room.
I lift my head and watch the moon.
I drop my head and think of home.

— LI BAI

i

From the deck of the ship Wuhan appeared to be a large, crowded and dreary place. We were confronted at the foot of the runway by throngs of desperate men eager to be porters. They scurried anxiously around arriving passengers and begged to be allowed to carry their luggage. Each of the men told a story of personal misfortune – hungry children, sick wife, no job, no food, no home. A shockingly thin man about forty years old approached us and bowed slavishly several times and said he hadn't eaten for three days. He was barefoot and wet from the rain. Lin Cheng handed him our luggage, and just as he began leading us away from the wharf, one of my bags broke open. Everything inside, all of my clothing and toiletries, fell onto the muddy street. I wasn't sure if I should laugh or cry. 'Can anything else go wrong?' I asked myself, glaring up for a second at the slate sky. The porter apologized and seemed terrified – as if he expected me to strike him. But I assured him it wasn't his fault, and the three of us got down on our knees in the street and hurriedly stuffed my soiled belongings back into the bag and then tied it shut.

A short distance from the wharf we found a bus to take us to the train station. Lin Cheng paid the porter and gave him a generous tip. The porter was so pleased that he insisted on boarding the bus with us and helping us find a seat and a place for our bags. Then he waited just outside until we pulled away. He smiled and waved and shouted goodbye as though we were close relatives.

The huge, cavernous train station in Wuhan is one of the largest in China. We sat on our bags until the arrival of our train was announced. At that moment we became part of a tidal wave of anxious people suddenly rushing to the station platform. The cars were unheated and unventilated. People stood tightly packed together and it seemed every man in the car smoked furiously. The air was blue with smoke. The journey took nearly four hours. It was so crowded that once I put my hands in my coat pockets, I couldn't get them out. Men coughed up phlegm and spit it onto the floor and onto the shoes of immobilized fellow passengers. Some people succeeded, after a struggle, in unpacking their meals. They dropped the wrappings and scraps around them. The awful clatter and squeak of the wheels made conversation impossible. I thought that hell must be very much like this and I tried to remember what it was like to breathe fresh air. I closed my eyes and for the first time in my life I fell asleep standing up.

When the train squealed to a stop the doors were flung open by the attendants. Hundreds of people who had been waiting along the tracks rushed and blocked the open door and then bulldozed their way into the car. For a moment the inrushing mob prevented the exit of those already inside who were trying to get out. There was a tremendous crush. Women and children screamed and cried, and men swore and shouted threats. Those battering their way into the car seemed oblivious to the protests of those trying to get out. They were afraid of being left at the station and those inside the train were afraid of being unable to get off.

Lin Cheng and I locked arms and he pulled me to the aisle and then we pushed our way toward the exit, holding tightly to our bags, hoping the handles wouldn't break or the sides wouldn't split open. When we became entangled in the luggage of other passengers we lifted our bags over our heads and continued steadily inching our way toward the door. After several minutes we made it, wedged our way through and jumped to the platform. People spilled out one side of the door and frantic travelers madly pushed their way in the other. Through the windows we could see several dozen people caught in the crowd inside, unable to move toward the door. As we walked away from the train, a bell sounded and the attendants boarded the train and pulled the doors closed behind them. We heard people inside protesting and shouting at the top of their lungs, insisting that they had to get off. But the attendants paid no attention to them and stared blankly down at the platform.

The lights in the train station had been switched off and the platform was unlit. The only illumination came from nearby streetlights. We could barely distinguish the shadowy forms of the masses of people around us, some sitting on their luggage waiting for another train, some moving slowly away from the tracks toward the station and nearby streets.

We had to take a bus to a settlement several hours away where my life in exile was to begin. We started to walk with the crowd along the railroad siding. We had gone only a few steps when I slipped and nearly fell to the ground. A pungent fetid odor rose from the ground. I bent down to see what I'd slipped on. 'Oh, God, no,' I sighed when I recognized it. I was standing on a slick layer of human waste. Thousands of people had waited for their trains along the tracks. Refusing to surrender their strategic positions beside the tracks, adults and children had simply squatted a few feet away in the dark and relieved themselves.

When we got to the street several hawkers approached us soliciting business for hotels. One young man pointed to a hotel a few blocks down the street and said it was clean and inexpensive and had a vacancy. It was midnight. The bus terminal wouldn't open until the next morning. We decided to check in.

The hotel manager in the dimly lit lobby quoted a price that was twice what we'd expected to pay. But we were exhausted and in no mood to argue. We paid the manager and asked for the key. The manager said that none of the rooms in the hotel had locks. But the hotel was safe, he swore.

Our room was illuminated by a single unshaded overhead lightbulb that was controlled by a switch at the end of the hall. The manager said he didn't want people to waste electricity, so he'd allow us just ten minutes before he turned the light off.

The bedsheets had not been changed for weeks and so we

decided to sleep on the couch. We worried that someone might sneak into the room and steal our bags if we slept at the same time. Lin Cheng told me that I could sleep first and that he would stay awake and watch the door. He braced a chair against the doorknob. I finally managed to doze off. When I awoke hours later, Lin Cheng was sound asleep on the floor beside the couch. Our bags had not been touched and the chair was still in place. It was already early afternoon.

As we walked to the bus station, I complained about the hotel. Lin Cheng reminded me that life was difficult for most people in China. Those without connections or without a good work unit – and I was now one of those people – enjoyed no luxuries. Perhaps during my years in the PLA I'd forgotten how hard life was for the masses, he suggested. 'We stayed in an inexpensive hotel last night,' he said, 'but you should remember that most people in this country can't even afford that.'

I had to accept the fact that the life I'd led was gone for good, he said. I had to adjust and lower my expectations and my tastes and learn to live like the people I saw around me on the street.

I listened in silence. But I thought to myself, 'If this is really to be my new life, if I am expected to live without dignity or decency, then what is the use of living at all? How long can I stand it,' I wondered, 'before I go insane?'

The fifty-mile bus trip to the headquarters of the oil company where I'd be working took three hours. As we bounced and jerked along, people jostled one another and stared silently out the windows at the desolate frozen countryside. The fields were barren and the hard furrows of earth were covered with a dusting of snow. Peasants in drab clothes walked slowly along the side of the road carrying children and pulling wagons loaded with sacks of supplies and fodder for the farm animals. Each wagon carried several adults sitting atop the cargo, staring blankly ahead. Everyone seemed mute or stunned, our groaning bus invisible to them.

I saw a little girl standing outside a large barn a few meters off the road. She was holding a bundle of hay, feeding it little by little to an old brown horse. The animal lazily pulled the fodder from the girl's hand, and after it did, she reached up and petted its nose, tenderly. It looked like she was singing to the horse. The squeal of our brakes startled the horse and the girl turned and looked in our direction. Our eyes met. She flashed a broad smile and waved at me as if she recognized me.

I turned to Lin Cheng to tell him about the girl. 'I remember doing that,' I whispered to him before I noticed he was asleep. I didn't want to wake him.

'I remember,' I repeated to myself. 'That was me. I did that. I sang to the farm animals, too. It wasn't that long ago.'

I was now returning to everything I'd once dreamed of escaping. This bus and the ship and the train carried me through time as well as space, slowly pulling me to my past as well as to my future. Yesterday and tomorrow were gradually blending. My life had come full circle.

ii

When I was her age, during school vacations I had a job caring for the village's herd of water buffalo. For a ten-year-old child, tending the buffalo was exhausting work. Each day I carried a sickle to cut grass for them and walked them to the river to drink. I guided them on solid and safe paths along the dikes in order to make sure they did not get injured, lost or stolen. At night I herded them into a pen. When it rained and when there was thunder and lightning, the animals became restless and jittery and sometimes ran away. But I got along well with them.

They could recognize my scent and the sound of my voice and they came to trust me and were comfortable in my presence. In the morning, when I let them out of their pen, I climbed on the back of one of the animals and stayed there throughout the day. One of the old females was particularly fond of me. When she saw me approaching she'd lower her head for me. Then, barefoot, I'd place each of my feet on the smooth part of each of her horns, and she'd carefully raise her head and I'd slide down onto her back.

I daydreamed when I was on her back and then narrated my dreams to all the animals. They seemed to listen to my words, grazing slowly and looking up curiously when I stopped talking, as if they were impatient for me to continue. My most persistent daydream was of becoming an officer in the PLA. The PLA uniform was the most beautiful garment I'd ever seen. I wanted to be just like Comrade Lei Feng, the heroic PLA martyr whose selfless and courageous exploits became the centerpiece of my education. I read storybooks about Lei Feng to the buffalo and promised them that someday I'd come back to them in a PLA uniform and have my picture taken and share my accomplishments with them.

My father's friend, 'Uncle' Xinglong was in the PLA for many years. Whenever he returned to the village in uniform everyone wanted to be near him and share a meal with him. The children followed wherever he walked and held his hand. He owned a camera and he had pictures taken of himself with all of the villagers. The pictures were pasted like religious icons to the walls of all the village homes. They served as reminders of the dreams the villagers had for their children.

The Army meant escape from the drudgery and banality of farm life. In the PLA you may obtain opportunities for further education, a better career and more connections. You could sing in a chorus, be part of an Army drama or dance troupe, march in Tiananmen, help the people, fly an airplane, ride in a submarine, see the world, defend the country, and play with guns. Getting into the PLA for peasants in China at that time was something like getting into heaven for a Christian. It was a wonderful, colorful new world where everyone dressed in a beautiful uniform and did good things for the motherland. It was impossible for peasant children in those days to get into college, secure an occupation in the city or get a change-of-residence permit for a better place in which to live. The PLA offered us the only ticket to our dreams.

Uncle Xinglong sometimes let me wear his PLA jacket and cap when he visited. Dressed in his clothing, I paraded back and forth in front of our house, pretending I was a soldier. I ran to the old female water buffalo, who had wet saucerlike eyes. I used her eyes as mirrors and gazed at myself in the uniform. I was in paradise. At the same time she gazed back at me in what I took to be wonderment. She recognized my scent and my voice but was somewhat confused by the oversized outfit. From the moment Uncle first placed his PLA cap on my head, I knew what I wanted to be.

Uncle Xinglong was the model soldier. He was kind and deferential and never pretentious. Since I was his favorite, he told me, 'When you grow up, Meihong, I will recruit you into the PLA. I will make you a soldier.'

That was my dream. During my long hours in the fields with the water buffalo I shared it with them. I asked the old female how she liked me in my uncle's uniform. Then I translated what I believe were her thoughts into my words. 'Perfect!' she was thinking, I assumed. 'Absolutely perfect.' Then I told her that after I returned and had my picture taken in a uniform with her I'd have to go away and fight the enemies of the people. But I'd survive and I'd always come back and visit her. When I told my dream to my classmates or my parents they reminded me of the difficulties of joining the PLA. The buffalo just listened patiently and I imagined that they, unlike the villagers, believed in my dreams. They alone understood me and knew I'd really leave this place someday and that when I came back, I'd come back as a hero.

When the sky started to darken and I realized rain might soon start falling, I tried to calm the animals by singing to them. But the only songs I knew were revolutionary songs I'd learned in school. Those songs were meant to excite and to quicken the heartbeat of the listener. I didn't know what effect they might have on the buffalo. I sang 'The East Is Red' and 'The Internationale' to the buffalo to see if I could soothe them. It worked. From the moment they heard me begin with 'Red in the east rises the sun, A man called Mao Zedong was born in China,' they became calm and listened to my voice. So I repeated the same songs over and over again and they remained serene and walked slowly from field to field until the first raindrops fell or they heard the sound of thunder. From that point on, singing was useless.

One morning the old female buffalo had difficulty leaving the pen. She limped badly and she couldn't follow the other animals. She was old and worn out now. Father examined her and concluded she could work no more. The decision was made to butcher her and divide her meat among the farmers in the village.

I'll never forget the day when the butchers killed my buffalo. When she saw one of the men approaching with ropes and the huge knife he carried she seemed to sense what he intended to do. She tried to pull away and run, but she was too old and too sick and couldn't move easily anymore. She spotted me standing nearby, and I could see the tears coming from her eyes as she looked at me and she began to bellow very loud. I think she wanted me to help her. I think she wanted me to repay her for all the afternoons she carried me through the fields. I cried when she looked at me and made her frightened sounds. Then suddenly she became quiet. As one of the men placed his hand on her neck and felt for the place to cut her, I began to sing softly 'The East Is Red,' her favorite song. She relaxed and continued looking at me. She recognized my voice and my song. She gave a great shudder when the knife was plunged into her throat and the blood exploded from her. She fell to her knees, gasped several times, choked on her blood, rolled onto her side, kicked the air violently several times, shuddered and died.

I knew how hard she worked pulling a plow through the fields or towing huge wagonloads of rice and wheat. In the winter I'd watched her help the workers move stones from the fields and carry large baskets of dirt to repair a dike. I knew how strong she was and I'd seen how gentle and kind she was, too. I loved her.

That evening when my mother served meat from the buffalo, I burst into tears and refused to eat.

I never again watched them kill any of the animals on the farm. I couldn't stand it.

iii

Even though my life on the farm was difficult and I worked long hours when I wasn't in the classroom, I was often reminded how lucky I was. My mother's childhood had been far more difficult than my own. In 1941, when she was born, the Japanese ruled the province and made their regional headquarters in nearby Danyang. Mother's world was narrowly circumscribed and her choices were few. She was from a very poor family and had little schooling. Her main concern, as a child, was finding enough to eat.

My mother's family name was also Xu, a common surname in the village. Her family was poor, but the poverty of the Xus was a relatively new status for them. My mother's grandfather and his father had been among the largest landowners in the village. The family was also wealthy in sons who were blessed with health, strength and intelligence.

One evening in the late-1920s, a local warlord and some of his men came through the village. They chose my great-grandfather's place to stay for the night. That night, Great-grandfather and his family slept outside while the warlord and his men slept in their beds. The warlord also had several large trunks carried into the house for the night.

In the morning he departed. But some of Great-grandfather's neighbors believed the warlord had left one of his trunks behind. Word of this quickly reached a group of bandits who operated in the area. A day later the bandit chief and a dozen of his men broke into my great-grandfather's home and demanded the warlord's trunk. Great-grandfather told them that the warlord had left nothing behind. The bandit chief ordered his men to beat Great-grandfather to force the truth from him. But Great-grandfather remained adamant. There was no trunk.

So the bandits bound Great-grandfather and his sons and marched them to the village square. Then they assembled all of the villagers and demanded to know where the trunk was. No one knew. The bandits brought a huge cooking pot from one of the homes, filled it with cooking oil and built a fire under it. Once the oil was boiling, they hoisted Great-grandfather into the air over the pot and told him he had one last chance to reveal where he was hiding the trunk.

Great-grandfather cried and begged for the men to let him go. His sons and his wife fell to their knees and pleaded for his life. But the bandits were in no mood to give mercy to someone they were convinced was concealing a treasure from them. Again and again the bandit chief demanded that Great-grandfather turn over the trunk. Again and again Great-grandfather said there was no trunk. Finally, tiring of the interrogation, the bandit chief gave a signal to his men and they dropped Great-grandfather into the boiling oil. There was an abbreviated scream of terror, a loud crackling and bubbling, and Great-grandfather was gone.

Great-grandfather's three sons were then lifted into the air and held over the pot where their father was cooking. The brothers cried and tried to free themselves as each of them was lowered to within a few inches of the boiling oil and ordered to surrender the warlord's trunk. And each of them in turn denied that the warlord had left behind any trunk.

The bandits finally concluded that the story of the trunk wasn't true. They released the three boys. But before they left they ransacked Great-grandfather's house, taking everything of value – food, tools, clothing, blankets, money, pots and pans. Then they loaded up all of the family's grain and seed and killed their farm animals. Finally, before departing, they set fire to the house.

When the bandits came into the village that morning, Great-grandfather was one of the wealthiest peasants in Lishi. That afternoon when they left, Great-grandfather was dead and his widow and sons were homeless. Eventually they were forced to sell all of their land in order to rebuild a home and to get medical treatment for my great-grandmother, who fell ill after her husband was murdered.

My grandfather never forgot what happened. He harbored an unquenchable thirst for revenge. He'd enjoyed good fortune in the past. He believed if there was a just god he'd enjoy it once more in the future. So he bided his time.

Before my mother was born, his wife bore him two daughters. But the girls were born sickly and there was not enough food for them and no medical care. They died. Grandfather could not afford caskets to bury his daughters, so he wrapped them in cotton coverlets and buried them in shallow graves near the village. People said that even though the infants who died were merely girls, my grandfather's heart was broken.

My mother, Yingdi, their third child, was born in 1941. Two sons and another daughter followed and survived.

My grandfather worked hard to feed his family. During the Japanese occupation, the short devils took most of his crops. So he worked from dawn to dusk but had neither enough food nor medical treatment for his many ailments since doctors were not available to villagers in those days. What food remained for his family was given first to his children and then to his wife. Grandfather lived on scraps and leftovers. His health deteriorated. His heart grew weak. People said that he worried about his children too much and he remembered what had happened to his father and he feared what the Japanese might do to his family. All of this worry took a heavy toll on him. But he never complained. He waited for justice.

After the Japanese were defeated and the civil war broke out, a Communist force liberated our village. Grandfather found in the Communist Party the god of justice he had been waiting for. He had opened his home to Communist Party agents who needed a place to hide from the Nationalist forces. Before the Communists won the civil war, Grandfather had become the first member of the Communist Party in our village.

The Party named him head of land redistribution and reform in the village and the surrounding area. The time for justice had arrived and justice in Lishi was my grandfather.

From 1949 on, the Communist Party and the Xu family enjoyed a close relationship. Those who had taken Xu land now had that land taken from them by the Party. Those who owned the largest parcels of land were labeled 'landlords' by the Party and after their land was confiscated they were publicly executed. The local warlord and the bandit chief and his men were captured and executed. Grandfather and his brothers were invited to attend the executions and they stood as close as possible to the bandit chief to hear him beg for mercy before a firing squad silenced him. But my mother told me years later that they enjoyed little satisfaction in watching the bandit chief die.

'The Party was our salvation,' Mother was reminded again and again when she was growing up. 'They saved us from starvation and warlordism and they gave us justice and land.'

Grandfather was a true believer in those days and worked tirelessly for the Party. He also worked for justice. He was, in fact, so fair in redistributing land that the local people came to respect him and the Party decided to publicize him as the ideal peasant Communist.

They brought him to neighboring villages to give speeches on the glories of the Party and on what it had done for Lishi. He talked about the old order of warlords and bandits and what had happened to his family. He told of the grasping Nationalists and he described the horrors of the Japanese occupation. Then he pointed out how everything had changed and how history had turned a corner. Chairman Mao Zedong was right, he said, the Chinese people had stood up at last. The peasant assemblies loved Grandfather's speeches and applauded and cheered him enthusiastically, later waiting in long lines to shake his hand.

Before long, however, most of Grandfather's time was spent making speeches rather than working on his land. He traveled to Danyang, Zhenjiang, Nanjing and other large cities to speak and soon he was the centerpiece of a Party delegation traveling by train through Jiangsu province and neighboring provinces telling the story of his family and his village and how everything had been changed for the better by the Party.

But Grandfather never aspired to be a celebrity. He had received no formal education, and he could neither read nor write. He was only a peasant and he loved working on the land, planting, cultivating and harvesting his crops and raising and caring for his family.

Grandfather eventually became unhappy in his new role and started to suspect that the Party was taking unfair advantage of his political passion. People didn't need him to tell them what the Party had accomplished, he told a senior Party cadre. All they had to do was look around them and they could see it.

He was told that the People and the Party needed local heroes. Peasants in the countryside needed to see and hear from peasants just like themselves. They needed to hear what had happened in other villages, such as Lishi. Grandfather's words were inspiring, he was told. They were like a trumpet call.

Grandfather began to doubt that. He spoke Mandarin with a heavy country accent and he often mispronounced words. He started to notice people in the audience snickering and laughing at him. After this happened several times, the Party appointed a group of young writers to compose long speeches and stories for Grandfather and to go over pronunciation with him before each of his appearances. Grandfather couldn't read them and so they were read to him over and over again until he memorized them word for word.

The speechwriters used words and idioms that were incomprehensible to Grandfather and he found himself reciting speeches he couldn't understand. Again, he asked to be sent home but was refused. His unhappiness increased. When he was on the stage, applause punctuated his speeches, but it also interrupted his train of thought and he sometimes forgot where he was. He repeated long passages or skipped paragraphs and his narrative seemed disjointed and illogical. People shook their heads when they heard his fractured syntax and his persistent mispronunciations.

When he persisted in his appeals to be sent home, his credentials as a genuine Communist and his dedication to the Party were called into question. He worried more and more about his farm and family. He became self-conscious on the stage and made more and more mistakes. Some of the Party cadres accused him of consciously trying to ridicule the Party with his inept performances. Grandfather burst into tears and said he just wanted to work on his land. Why couldn't they understand that? He was not a hero. He was a Communist but he was also a man with responsibilities to his wife and children.

Grandfather was never a healthy man. After traveling for the Party for several more months he began to experience pain in his chest. He fainted on the stage in the middle of a long speech in Zhenjiang and was rushed to a hospital. The doctors said he was just tired.

He warned the Party cadre that the memorization and the speaking tours were killing him. They laughed and said it was nonsense, that he was strong as a water buffalo. A good night's sleep was all he needed.

Three days later while speaking at an outdoor rally in Nanjing, Grandfather hesitated in the middle of a sentence as though he was suffering another memory loss. Then he clutched at his chest, doubled over and collapsed on the stage. Thinking he had only fainted again, the Party cadre loosened his collar, fanned him to give him fresh air and then carried him into a nearby building to rest. By the time they found a table and laid him on it, he was dead.

The Party brought his body to his family in Lishi and held a ceremonial service in the village and praised Grandfather as a hero. He had been forced to work so hard under the old order, they said, that his heart literally wore out.

Grandfather's reputation grew to mythic proportions following his death. A short book was written about him and students in the local schools studied his life and work. In the schoolbooks Grandfather never lost his train of thought, never mispronounced a word, was never laughed at and never grew tired or disillusioned. Nothing at all was said about Grandfather's requests to return to his family and his desire to live a simple life far from the propaganda stage.

iv

My grandmother's health declined after her husband's death. She tired easily and did not have enough strength to go to work in the fields. Soon she became bedridden.

As a result of this double family misfortune, my mother, as

the eldest daughter in the family, became the head of her household. Illiterate like her mother and father, at the age of twelve she went to work full-time in the fields. She became responsible for providing food and shelter for her mother, her younger sister aged two, and two younger brothers, aged seven and five. Until this day, Mother believes she was deprived of her childhood.

She got up before dawn each day and worked until dark in the fields. The adults at first laughed at her because they didn't believe she would last long in the fields at her age. But she had no choice. If her family was to survive, she had to do whatever work was required. Eventually she won the praise of the other peasants who labored beside her.

By the time she was fifteen she'd saved enough money to send her brothers and sister to a village school. She insisted that they not work with her in the fields. She wanted something better for them. Eventually, her younger sister graduated from grammar school and both of her brothers graduated from high school. Both boys became Party members and the elder later became Party secretary for the brigade.

In 1960, when my mother was nineteen, China suffered a great calamity. The Communist Party's Great Leap Forward brought famine to the countryside. In five years nearly 30 million people starved to death. Peasants were ordered to produce steel in backyard furnaces and to work on public projects rather than cultivate their crops. An initial food shortage became much worse the next year. The only food available had to be purchased at expensive city markets. Those who couldn't afford it starved.

Mother and her cousin Lingdi learned that there were factory jobs available for young women in Shenyang in north-eastern China. So the girls said goodbye to their families and took the train to Shenyang. My mother placed her elder brother in charge of the family during her absence and promised to send money to him every month.

Mother returned home at the end of the spring of 1962, fearing her mother was near death. Her family had become emaciated and listless and were hungry all the time, but with the money she sent home, they had been able to buy enough food on the black market in Danyang to stay alive. There was no doubt that Mother had saved her family while many villagers died of starvation.

V

When Mother returned from Shenyang she had reached the marrying age. Grandmother encouraged matchmakers to find her daughter a good husband.

Mother had a reputation as a determined, strong-willed, hardworking and intelligent young woman as well as a good and faithful daughter. Everyone knew she kept her family from starving and she paid for the education of her brothers and sister. Local matchmakers approached her with several promising proposals. But for many months Mother was unmoved by their offers.

Then a neighbor told her about a young man in the village from another Xu family who had just graduated from a college near Zhenjiang and had become the farm's new veterinarian.

When a matchmaker introduced the young veterinarian to my mother in 1962, the two found they liked each other very much. After talking with him several times Mother found he embodied all the qualities she wanted in a husband. He was honest and self-effacing. He had a good sense of humor. He was one of the few educated people Mother ever met and he held an important position on the collective farm.

They were married on National Day, October 1, 1962. On their wedding day my mother packed her belongings in an old cardboard suitcase and walked to her new husband's home. The suitcase contained her entire dowry. She assured her mother and her brothers and sister that they had not lost her and that she would still provide for them as she had done in the past. She kept her promise.

vi

Fourteen months later, in December 1963, the Year of the Rabbit, I was born. At that time China was still suffering from a famine. As a consequence, throughout her pregnancy, Mother had nothing to eat except watery porridge. As a newborn, I weighed less than five pounds. My father's mother, who delivered me, told me years later that I had been only the size of a baby rabbit.

I did not have enough strength to suck and could not start Mother's milk flowing. For the first two days after my birth my mother was very weak. Since no milk or other baby food was available at that time, the only solution they could find was to have Mother nurse her younger sister (who was twelve at the time) until the milk started to flow and then to nurse me. It worked and I survived because of it. My auntie and I became very close as I was growing up and she loved to recall the story of how she had saved me from starvation when I was just a little rabbit.

The farm administrators granted Mother forty-five days of paid leave after I was born. After that she returned to work in the fields. Grandmother cared for me while Mother worked. Along with other elder women from the village, Grandmother carried me to the fields twice each day for feedings – at nine in the morning and three in the afternoon. At those times, the nursing mothers who were at work walked to the edge of the fields, found some shade or shelter and sat to nurse their babies. When Mother was finished feeding me she returned to work and Grandmother carried me home.

At that time everyone was instructed to study and memorize three critical articles (*Lao San Pian*) by Mao. I overheard my parents reciting Chairman Mao's words again and again. When I began to speak, among my first words were: 'WE ARE AFRAID OF NEITHER HARDSHIP NOR DEATH,' 'SERVE THE PEOPLE WHOLEHEARTEDLY,' and 'WE SHOULD

LEARN FROM THE OLD FOOLISH MAN WHO MOVED THE MOUNTAIN.'

When I was two years old Mother decided to put my talent on display. She carried me to Party meetings and during the recess stood me on a table in front of the room and had me recite sayings of Chairman Mao. I would push out my chest and turn my face to the heaven and shout out the familiar supernal aphorisms of the Great Helmsman.

The meetings customarily lasted three or four hours, and following a long day's work, many people found it impossible to stay awake during the proceedings. They dozed off while long monotonous speeches were delivered or lists of statistics and production figures were recited. When the Party secretary noticed a dozen or more people in his audience with their eyes closed and their heads slumped forward, he summoned me to the stage to shout out the words of Mao and awaken the sleeping cadres. Thus I became a living alarm clock for Chairman Mao and the Party.

Yet my mother noticed a disconcerting materialist conceit in my performances. I was not satisfied with applause alone. I wanted a reward for my recitations. After one of my early performances the Party secretary handed me a fistful of peanuts. From that point on, much to Mother's embarrassment, I refused to speak if I did not see the peanuts first. She stood me on a table and whispered for me to begin a recitation and I clamped my mouth shut. My uncle always carried peanuts in his pocket and when I refused to speak, he handed several of them to me. I instantly started shouting out patriotic slogans and awakened several slumbering Party members. It was amazing, my mother moaned at home later, because there I stood reciting the Communist Party line while behaving like a grasping little capitalist. She said I had unfortunately inherited traits from each of my grandfathers. I remember her repeating over and over as I ate my peanuts, 'Oh, Meihong, what will become of you?'

My brother was born in August 1965. Everyone was delighted that at last the Xu family had a son to carry on the family name. When my brother was two and a half, my grandmother took both of us to Shanghai to visit Grandfather.

Because of the way the Party treated him following liberation – at first they made him work as a janitor in his own company and later appointed him manager with a janitor's salary – Grandfather hated Chairman Mao and the Communists. And although he often complained openly, the Party tolerated his dissent because they needed him to manage his large factory for them. His words and his behavior, however, became dangerous for his family after the start of the Cultural Revolution in 1966. At that time if someone was overheard saying anything in the least critical about the Party or Mao or any government official they were sentenced to prison or were executed. But I remember Grandfather was unfazed by the warnings about outspoken criticism of the government and he still boldly expressed his feelings.

Once when he came to visit us in the village, my father and I went to meet him at the train station. Even as he stepped from the train Grandfather was complaining about Party policies, the Red Guard and Chairman Mao. He said the Party leadership was foolish and that they understood nothing about economics or production. They were schemers and hooligans, he insisted, and no better than warlords. They were incapable of comprehending the contributions of men like himself who provided jobs and entry-level careers for young men and women from the impoverished countryside. Capitalists were not the enemy of China, he said. They were its salvation. The Communists were the enemy.

Because I was an ardent little Communist at the time I didn't want him to talk like that – especially not in front of other people. My father worried also and tried to get Grandfather to shut up or to talk about the weather or the scenery. Father constantly responded to Grandfather by changing the subject, but Grandfather paid no attention to him and continued his ranting against the Party. He couldn't open his mouth, it seemed, without saying something hateful about Chairman Mao or Mao's wife, Jiang Qing. It was his obsession and his passion. The country was going to hell economically, he pointed out. The government was responsible for more starvation than either the Kuomintang or the Japanese. We were rushing backward under Chairman Mao. The Great Hall of the

People was the world's largest lunatic asylum.

Whenever Grandfather launched one of his tirades my father shut all the windows and doors, fearing he would be overheard and arrested. But Grandfather reacted by speaking even louder. Again and again my grandmother warned that he was 'tickling the tiger's ass' as if he did not watch his mouth we would all have to pay for his stupidity. Grandfather responded by saying the tiger was all ass. But while everyone else in the family waited for Grandfather to be struck down, he was never touched by the government and he never changed his ways.

I remained in Shanghai with my grandparents for six weeks. We returned to Lishi when my mother asked Grandmother to come home to aid with the delivery of her third child. I had been unaware that my mother was expecting.

We took the train to Danyang the next day. My sister was born three days later. On the day she was born Mother worked ten hours in the fields and returned home about 6 P.M. She prepared dinner for all of us and we sat down for the evening meal. Then Mother suddenly stood up, grimaced and swayed dizzily back and forth, finally steadied herself and announced that she was ready to deliver her child. Grandmother led her to a section of the house that was partitioned off with sheets draped over a cord. Father raced on his bicycle to a nearby village to fetch a doctor to assist in the delivery. The doctor arrived a short time later, dressed in white and carrying her little bag of instruments. She hurried into the house and pulled the partition closed behind her as she prepared to examine my mother.

Everything that was happening was a mystery to me. I had no idea at all where babies came from. The adults in the house, supervised by my grandmother, boiled water and carried towels and sheets back and forth. Eventually, unable to contain my curiosity, I quietly crept into the enclosure where Mother was lying on a bed crying and moaning. I felt sorry for her. I nearly burst into tears. The doctor was standing over her wearing a surgical mask and rubber gloves. I thought she was hurting Mother. I returned to my chair in the kitchen. I didn't know what to do.

The next morning my grandmother awakened me with the

news that I had a new baby sister.

My mother had difficulty with the delivery and was hospitalized for three weeks after the birth. She had to take medicine and couldn't nurse her new daughter. Grandmother therefore carried my baby sister to the homes of other women who were nursing and had them feed her.

Since I was the eldest child, it became my responsibility to care for the two younger children in the family. Grandmother fashioned a sling from cloth and wrapped it around me and under my arms and over my shoulders. Then she strapped my sister to my back so I could carry her with me. I was only six at the time, but Grandmother told me I now had adult responsibilities.

vii

I started grammar school when I was seven. The school was in the nearby village, a twenty-minute walk from our house. Constructed by the peasants from bricks they had made in their village, the school was crowded and several classes met simultaneously in one room. Teachers divided the students by grade level and while one group was given instruction the others did their homework. The school day lasted from 7 A.M. until 4 P.M. six days a week with three weeks of vacation in the winter and three months in the summer. Each fall we had a two-week break to help with the harvest.

Our curriculum stressed political education over conventional academic studies. On the first day in class we were each given our own copy of Chairman Mao's Little Red Book. A large picture of Chairman Mao stared down on us beatifically from the front of the classroom and at the back of the classroom hung a large-character dictum composed by Mao: 'STUDY HARD AND MAKE PROGRESS EVERY DAY.'

Each morning when the teacher entered the room we jumped to attention. She then recited a phrase from the Little Red Book and we repeated it, at the top of our lungs. Then everyone sang 'The East Is Red.' At the end of the school day we stood and recited another phrase from the Little Red Book and then sang 'The Internationale.'

In the lower grades we studied Chinese literature and history through simple stories and exercises and spent several hours each day practicing writing Chinese characters. We also studied math, science and politics. Every lesson was geared toward making us good Party followers rather than independent analytical thinkers. Obedience and conformity were the Confucian subtext of our education, even though Confucius himself was out of favor with the Party.

Part of each school day was devoted to physical education. Of course, our exercises also had a political component. We learned how to jog long distances in order to confront an enemy and we worked on strengthening our arms and shoulders so we could throw hand grenades.

We practiced sprinting, high jumping and distance jumping and played games like Ping-Pong and basketball – a sport that we never realized had originated in America. We also learned to march in close order while carrying toy guns. As we moved up through the class levels, physical education became increasingly martial and less and less playful.

During our first school year we were required to fill out applications for membership in the Little Red Guards or *Hong Xiao Bing*, a group organized among youth in 1966 to assist the older Red Guards in spearheading the Cultural Revolution.

The teacher wrote model letters of application on the blackboard and we copied them word for word and then signed our names. This was a solemn exercise. It was the first time any of us applied for membership in a political organization. Our future might well depend on our acceptance into the group, the teacher reminded us. Although all students applied, only 20 percent of the applicants were accepted for membership each year. Some of the students were never accepted into the Little Red Guards, and this became a source of consternation and even shame to the student as well as to his family. Not making it into the group branded an individual an outsider, and outsiders in China were objects of suspicion.

I was as solemn and serious about this application as I had

ever been about anything before in my life. After we had completed the applications and turned them in there was a week of anxious waiting. Then we were summoned to an assembly and the teachers announced which students in the school had been accepted into the Little Red Guards. Each of us sat on the edge of his seat knowing how proud our parents would be if we were accepted and were able to wear the red scarf – the badge of the Little Red Guards. If we were not accepted we realized we would have to explain to our parents what had gone wrong.

Out of thirty applicants at my school, six were accepted on this first round of applications. I was one of the lucky six.

I was ecstatic. I ran all the way home to tell my mother the good news. I also had to ask her for the fifteen fen I needed to buy my red scarf the following day. She was proud of me and gladly gave me the money.

The next afternoon, when classes ended, a gathering of the Little Red Guards from all classes took place. Every teacher in the school was in attendance along with the school marching band. The new recruits stood and swore an oath of loyalty to Mao and the revolution. The principal congratulated each of us by name and shook our hand. The band then played revolutionary songs and we all shouted out the words.

I could not contain my joy that afternoon. I had taken the first step toward fulfilling what I was certain was my heroic red destiny.

When we had finished shouting revolutionary songs and slogans, we were told what was expected of us. We were to be model students. We were never to talk out of turn. We were to sit straight, walk with good posture, and earn the top grades in class. We were to be leaders.

After each of the inductees promised to embrace the principles of the group, the older members of the Red Guards came to each of us and gave us a red scarf and showed us how to knot it properly. I can still tie that knot. We were directed to wear the scarf every day. It was a sign to everyone who saw us of our patriotism, dedication and fearless revolutionary resolve.

During my first year in school I was also selected to be a

247

member of the Little Red Flowers, a children's dancing, singing and performing troupe. In the afternoons the Little Flowers practiced their performances and several times a year visited a neighboring school or village and put on a show. We performed plays and dramatic scenes all pretty much the same: PLA soldiers saving peasants from wicked landlords. Sometimes I played a PLA soldier, sometimes a poor peasant and sometimes the daughter of a landlord. The difference between right and wrong was easy to see.

During the harvest, when the peasants on the farm worked long hours without breaks, the Little Red Flowers marched to the fields and stood on the dikes and danced and sang patriotic songs and chanted slogans in order to revive the spirit of the workers. We used loudspeakers to amplify our voices and project them as far as possible in order to stir the hearts of our neighbors, parents and relatives. Sometimes, I recall, peasants watched us and I saw tears in their eyes. In those days I thought they were tears of pride. Today, I am no longer sure why they cried.

viii

Many campaigns took place during my years in primary school. Each of them aroused enthusiasm for Party programs or eradications or rectifications. Looking back I sometimes wonder how we found time for serious academic instruction since we were so energetically consumed with improving China and keeping it safe from its enemies.

One of the first national campaigns I remember reinforced my childhood dream of someday becoming a soldier. In that campaign the people were instructed to 'Learn from the PLA.' As part of the campaign soldiers came into the countryside and worked in the villages among the people, helping them and instructing them.

They arrived without fanfare one afternoon in Lishi. I wasn't aware of their presence until I met a group of soldiers quite by accident one afternoon on the way home from school. At that time I was frustrated by my difficult experience writing complex Chinese characters. I practiced over and over, but kept making mistakes. I was so upset, in fact, that I burst into tears while walking home with friends. My vision was blurred by tears and I was keeping my gaze to the ground when suddenly the students in front of me came to an abrupt stop and I bumped into them. I looked up and saw four tall men blocking our path. They were in uniform and I thought they were the most handsome men I had ever seen in my life.

One of them bent down beside me and asked, 'Why are you crying, Little Red Guard?'

'I can't write my characters,' I confessed. 'I just can't do it and everyone laughs at my writing.'

'Let me see if I can help you,' he responded. 'What is your name?'

'Xu Meihong.'

'Well, Xu Meihong, show me your notebook,' he said. I held it up and showed him my tortured characters.

'That isn't so bad,' he assured me. He knelt down beside me and then very slowly in large clean strokes made the characters for me. After doing that he put the pencil in my hand and guided it over and over, drawing the characters. I felt I was touched by a god. The other children were envious and awestruck by this dreamy interlude.

I could hardly breathe.

I saw them often in the next days and the soldier who'd helped me remembered my name. 'How is your writing, Xu Meihong?' he asked.

'Very good, Uncle PLA,' I replied. 'Excellent. I am studying hard.'

He smiled, saluted me and continued on his way.

The soldiers remained in our village for two weeks. Of course all the students fell in love with them. We thought their uniforms were beautiful – a rich green with vermilion piping and epaulets and stars. Their bright uniforms contrasted starkly with the drab formless outfits worn by the peasants.

The soldiers labored with the men and women in the village, helping in the fields and with construction. They worked long hours and camped in their quarters outside the villages. They cooked their own food and turned down all invitations by villagers to stay in their homes or to eat with them. They would take nothing from us, they said. They had only come to help us. The adults adored these healthy, happy young men as much as the children did. Incredibly, even my grandfather had something good to say about them.

When they had completed their work in Lishi they moved on to another village. They departed quietly early in the morning, without making any noise, just as inconspicuously as they had arrived. They put everything in order and cleaned up their camp before departing, leaving behind only affection, goodwill and a platoon of little dreamers.

ix

When I was in the third grade, our teacher told us that we were going to learn special marching – just like the PLA. Naturally, we were excited by the prospect. She asked each of us to bring a toy gun to school.

The next day some of the children showed up with toy guns their parents had purchased for them. Those whose parents were woodworkers had beautiful homemade guns. But most of us were pathetically armed. My father had no tools for shaping a rifle stock or rounding a gun barrel. So my weapon was just a rough pointed stick. Most of the students had weapons like mine. Students with the good guns were little stars in our class and everyone wanted to hold their guns and march with them.

When she saw our homemade guns the teacher frowned for a moment and then changed her request. She said we could carry any homemade weapon, not just a gun. A sword or spear might suffice.

We used our ingenuity. We cut tall bamboo shoots and our fathers fashioned crude curved sword blades and spear points from wood and tied them to the end of the bamboo like a traditional Chinese pike (*hong ying qiang*).

At school the students were forever comparing the craft and imagination that went into the construction of their weapons. We tried to make the tips and blades as sharp as possible so we could skewer any enemies of the people we might find – landlords, rightists, Americans or Russians – on the way to school.

At the end of each day we marched in tight formation around the school brandishing our crude weapons and shouting out patriotic slogans. We must have appeared from a distance like an army of evil Lilliputians. But we saw ourselves as heroes and protectors of the people. Armed as we were, we feared no enemy force.

Our teachers had begun to tell us frightening stories about the enemies of China. My father listened to his battery-powered radio and heard similar tales. The landlords were singled out because they were the most insidious. They hid among the people and carefully concealed their true agenda. Before 1949, we were taught, the landowners were extremely wealthy and they dressed in silk and had many servants and concubines. They overworked and abused the peasants on their lands. It was hell to be a poor peasant before liberation. We were told that life was much better since liberation and we thought it must be true, because nobody ever voiced disagreement with that statement – except, naturally, my grandfather.

But the landlords still lay in wait for their return to power, backed by their allies abroad. They kept all of their wealth buried and all of their records of loss and confiscation. If the revolution was overthrown they would rise up to take back their land and their wealth. They would bring out their record books and make sure all accounts were balanced and everything that was theirs returned. They worked quietly to weaken the government. We had to defend the government and the revolution in order not to be exploited and enslaved by the landlords.

Our teachers and the leaders of the Little Red Guards organized hunting expeditions Saturdays and Sundays and we combed the fields around Lishi for places where the landlords might have buried their account books or their gold. We never found any.

We also tried to find spies. They were everywhere, we were warned. They were disguised and swam like fish in the ocean of people, trying to be inconspicuous and to win converts to the counterrevolutionary cause. Every stranger was a suspect. Whenever a relative or friend from outside our village came to visit, he was required to report to the head of the village and to tell who he was, where he was from, whom he was visiting, how long he would stay and what the nature of his business was. If he wanted to stay overnight he needed special permission. A permanent file was maintained on every outsider who visited.

We developed a siege mentality. Teachers and Party cadres repeatedly reminded us that there was danger at every turn. We were told that our only security was in finding the enemy before he could strike. So we watched for anyone who behaved suspiciously. We had an obligation to protect Mao, to protect the revolution and to protect our motherland.

In order to provide practical training for what we'd learned in school our teachers organized scores of field trips for us. On those trips we wore our ersatz PLA uniforms and brought our weapons. We were required also to carry our own bottle of water and a white cloth tied on our right arm to use as a bandage in case we were wounded during an enemy attack. Across our backs we each carried a rolled quilt and an extra pair of cloth shoes.

We assembled at school to begin our own little version of the Long March. For kids of eight or nine this was a big adventure. We marched down the road shouting patriotic slogans such as 'WE WILL DO OUR BEST FOR SOCIALISM,' 'WE WILL SACRIFICE OUR LIVES FOR THE COMMUNIST CAUSE,' 'DOWN WITH LANDLORDS,' 'DOWN WITH KUOMINTANG,' 'DOWN WITH THE AMERICAN IMPERIALISTS' and 'DOWN WITH THE U.S.S.R.'

As we marched along shouting slogans, the teacher would occasionally interrupt us by shouting, 'Hit the ground!' and we all dropped to the ground and lay completely still. Then she shouted, 'Bombs!' and some of the students immediately shielded their fellow students from bomb fragments by covering their classmates' bodies with their own.

After a few minutes she ordered us to resume our marching and shouting. We continued until she shouted, 'Enemy airplane,' and we fell to the ground again. Sometimes, when we came to a grove of trees with long branches, we broke off the lower branches and fastened them to our hats and uniforms to camouflage ourselves from enemy aircraft. It was an authentic military operation to us. I was training for real life. When we thought an airplane was overheard we would lie on the ground without moving a muscle. The teacher walked around and inspected us to make sure we were not moving. Then she ordered, 'All is clear. Get up and march on.'

We had a wonderful time playing at stealth and combat. Each of us imagined himself a little hero off to save the nation. There were never complaints. We were part of the continuing struggle for justice, part of the revolution, we were hunting down the enemy spies in the countryside and foiling enemy aircraft.

Sometimes, as with my aunt Lingdi, traitors were found within the village itself. Whenever I heard a commotion, I ran outside to watch the Red Guards denounce another class enemy. The Red Guards were ruthless and merciless, but they said they were trying to save the country from its enemies. So they dared not show mercy. They had hardened their hearts against the people who would enslave us again.

Determined to save ourselves by punishing the guilty, the rest of us joined in the chorus of denunciation. The children were given little red flags and we marched around behind the accused, berating them, throwing stones at them, demanding they confess, and shouting patriotic slogans. Entire families participated in the denunciation rituals. Each sought to outdo the others in their boisterous demonstrations of patriotism.

Those identified as enemies of the people were not punished only by public beatings, denunciations, humiliation and imprisonment. Some were wicked enough to merit execution. I witnessed several public executions when I was a child. It was considered important for children to see these in order to be shown real enemies of the state and to watch them suffer their richly deserved fate. Public executions became rallies and macabre patriotic spectacles for the whole village.

The condemned criminals might be from our village or from any other village or town in the county. The doomed men and women were marched onto the stage, usually with their hands and arms bound tightly behind them. They wore a sign around their necks listing their crimes and the name of each was written on the bottom of his or her sign and then x'd out. They were rebuked, punched, kicked, slapped, poked and denounced as hooligans or landlords or capitalist roaders or rightists or spies with relatives in Taiwan, Hong Kong or the United States. Then they were dragged from the stage and taken to a field at the edge of the village. Everyone followed along enthusiastically, shouting slogans and pausing now and then to listen for expressions of contrition or confessions or pleas for mercy from the accused.

When an execution took place the family of the criminal was required to pay thirty fen for each bullet used by the Public Security police. It was deemed unfair that the state should have to pay to dispose of the criminal. A common threat used by parents with disobedient children was 'I hope that on the day they execute you one bullet will be enough. You are not worth more than thirty fen. Don't ask your family to pay extra money to kill you, please!' It served as a stark reminder of where misbehavior or disobedience might lead a wayward child.

Often enough a criminal might move at the instant the bullet was fired or there would be a misfire or a bad bullet that simply stunned the condemned individual or knocked him to the ground. In those cases, the criminal often screamed or cried out for mercy and struggled to get to his feet and run away. If the bullet entered his head or neck but didn't kill him, he lay flopping around on the ground, his mouth moving without making a sound, his eyes wide open and bulging out, just like a fish thrown onto dry land. When that happened the crowd screamed condemnations and a Public Security officer placed his foot or knee on the condemned man's back and put his pistol against his head or in his ear and fired again.

I heard no dissent – with the exception of my grandfather – over public executions. They were carried out methodically and coldly. No one asked if the convicted criminal really deserved the fate he suffered, if his trial had been fair or even if he'd had a trial. Those who were executed deserved it, we believed, and everyone benefited by their disposal.

Of course, the relatives of the condemned were sad. But they dared not show their sadness in public or they would be accused of complicity or disloyalty. So they had to witness the execution and, in a sense, endorse it.

Although traitors and hooligans had corrupt souls, this did not necessarily mean that their internal organs could not serve the state. Sometimes doctors from various hospitals attended an execution. As soon as the bullet was fired into the head of the criminal, he was rushed to a nearby tent or room to have some of his organs removed for transplant. If a condemned man's heart was to be removed, he was shot in the back of the head or neck. But if his eyes were to be used, he was shot in the back of the heart.

Later, I learned that execution quotas were issued by the Party and the Public Security Bureau. Every province, county, district and village had to fulfill a quota. The quotas had nothing at all to do with the crime rate. Like everything else in China, they were politically determined. What the state needed to demonstrate overrode any other considerations. In one case, a young man from our village was arrested late one night for attempted rape. He had gotten drunk and sneaked into his girlfriend's house. But he went to the wrong room and tried to embrace her sister. The police were summoned and the young man was taken away. The next morning a sign was posted in the village saying he had been executed for 'hooliganism.' The quota was filled.

In retrospect, what disturbs me most about those episodes was that I was not bothered by them at the time. All of us – adults and children – had been so steeped in hysteria and group thinking for so long that what we witnessed seemed necessary and natural. We believed we could save ourselves only by sacrificing the lives of our alleged enemies. We never imagined for a moment that we were being manipulated by our own leaders. Indeed, such facts would have been frightening to us at the time, indicating that someone had planted seeds of doubt and disloyalty in our minds. Our response, naturally, would be to find that someone and to eradicate him.

X

Since enemies of the people might be anywhere, our teachers encouraged us to describe in detail our home life in order to uncover evidence of treachery and disloyalty. We were instructed to watch the activities of our parents or our brothers and sisters because they might be class enemies. Our primary loyalty, we were told, must be to the Party and the revolution.

Of course, this presented an opportunity for children whose parents strictly disciplined them or beat them when they misbehaved. It was not uncommon in the village for parents to strike their children for not doing their homework or for failing to do their chores. Such punishment of children was a traditional practice.

To avenge themselves, some children went into the street or came to school and suddenly blurted out an antirevolutionary slogan, such as 'Down with the Communist Party!' or 'Down with Chairman Mao!' If they were heard – and they usually were since that was their intent – they were detained by the authorities. The children were interrogated and asked where they had heard such words. That was the moment for sweet revenge. 'My father said that,' a child might say, or 'I heard my mother say those words.' One or both of the parents were immediately seized and questioned. If they confessed to their crimes, they got off with a lengthy self-criticism followed by reeducation by Party authorities in the village. If they were reluctant to confess they might be dragged before a general community meeting, forced to wear a huge dunce cap and be denounced by the entire village for refusing to own up to their counterrevolutionary statements and for corrupting their children.

Corporal punishment of children declined. Parents came up with a more patriotic method of punishing troublesome children. They insisted that when you misbehaved you were disobeying the instructions of Chairman Mao to be a good citizen. They demanded that you kneel – sometimes for hours – before the portrait of Mao and ask for his forgiveness by repeating, 'Chairman Mao, I am so sorry. I am wrong. I've decided to be your good child.'

The world had been turned upside down. Of course, my paternal grandfather hated these spectacles and said that the only people guilty of a crime and the only enemies of the people he could see were the Red Guards. We cringed when he said that and as always we hurried to shut the windows and doors. One time when Grandfather came for a visit he sat down to talk with me about my activities in the Little Red Guards. I told him about the enemies surrounding us and the slogans and songs we'd learned and the people who'd been caught and denounced.

Then he said, 'Meihong, I have a question for you. Your grandparents and your parents raised you. We gave you food to eat and clothes to wear. We have never mistreated you. Now, if your mother or father – if any of us in this family – asked you to do something and then if you were told that Chairman Mao had said that it was not good, what would you do? Would you do what we asked or would you follow Chairman Mao's wishes?'

I responded immediately, 'Of course, I wouldn't do anything Chairman Mao didn't want us to do. I would never disobey Chairman Mao.'

My grandfather became angry at this. 'What have they done to you?' he asked. 'You don't even know what kind of a man Mao is. You have never seen him. Why would you listen to him and not your parents or your grandparents?'

I responded to his questions by shouting a slogan: 'Without Chairman Mao, there would be no new China.' Then I repeated what I had been taught in school: 'Without Chairman Mao there would be no parents or grandparents and there would be no me. So we should all thank him because without him we would not exist. I love him for that. Of course I should listen to him, because my family could be wrong, but Chairman Mao could never be wrong. We have enemies all round us, everywhere. Even in our family.'

My grandfather turned bright red and his eyes narrowed and he hissed, 'We have wasted our time with you, haven't we? What a wasted little life.'

When my mother returned home that evening I told her about my exchange with Grandfather and she said she was proud of my response. Then she told me, 'You are right. You should listen first to Chairman Mao. Don't listen to your grandfather. He is too old. His mind is not clear any longer.' She also made me promise never to repeat Grandfather's words to anyone else. I knew I should report him. I thought about it often. But I just couldn't do it.

My father's radio-listening habits also bothered me. He loved to listen to his radio – a battery-operated *Hong Deng* or Red Lantern radio that was given to him by Grandfather. Each night at eight o'clock he listened to a national news broadcast. But late at night or early in the morning, when he thought everyone else was asleep, he'd listen to the BBC and the Voice of America (VOA) broadcasts in Chinese. I was disturbed by this. Our teachers told us to report anyone who listened to foreign radio broadcasts, but I had not turned my father in. I worried about him and became suspicious of Grandfather for giving us such a devilish machine. It was dangerous, I was sure, to allow the toxins from the capitalist and imperialist world to seep into our village through the radio. Why would my father do such a thing if he was not cooperating with our enemies? I suspected my father was a spy receiving secret coded information via radio from the Americans or the Taiwanese. I grew nervous when I heard the broadcasts and expected the Public Security people to come smashing through the door at any moment to arrest him and take him away and then to ask me why I hadn't reported him.

The VOA reports told how poor Chinese were and they said critical things about our government. I refused to believe a word of it. But at the same time I found the reports fascinating and could not stop listening. I could not understand how people in the United States and Britain who were exploited and kept in poverty by capitalists could be allowed to repeat such lies about China. I found solace in the belief that no Chinese citizen in his right mind could possibly believe the stories broadcast on the VOA and the BBC. Not a word of it was true, I was sure.

xi

When my father traveled from village to village to treat the animals, peasants whose pets had litters sometimes gave him a puppy or a kitten and he would bring one home for me. The pets provided genuine joy for us. But invariably the Red Guards or Party officials announced that owning a dog or cat was a violation of Party doctrine. Keeping a pet, they said, was a carryover from the old regime, a practice of the bourgeoisie. Besides, dogs wasted too much food and polluted our environment. They also told us that dogs carried germs and sometimes went mad and bit people, who then contracted rabies or other diseases. Consequently, we were ordered to kill our pets.

Whenever these orders were issued the children cried. They saw no reason to give up a pet. The policy of the Party was inconsistent and confusing. A year or more might pass when nobody cared if you had a pet. Then the Party would suddenly declare an anti-pet campaign.

They sent around a dog-killing team to search all the houses in the village. If you hadn't killed your dog by then, they killed it for you. Members of the team came through the village carrying ropes, clubs and knives and terrified the children. The police were authorized to walk through the village and to kill any dog they saw. They were also allowed to take the dead animal home to eat – an additional incentive for them.

Domesticated pets were not the only enemies of the Communist Party. There were national campaigns to kill rats and mice as well. We were told that they ate the crops and carried germs. So the Little Red Guards and the peasants were organized to go into the fields to hunt and kill rodents.

We carried spades, hoes, picks and pointed bamboo shoots as we went from dike to dike looking for the holes where the rats and mice lived. Whenever we found a suspicious hole we poured water in it and dug our way in to get the rodents. When they finally came scurrying out we beat or slashed them as they tried to run away. We were required to save the carcass and turn it over to a team leader, who kept a tally of how many kills we made. Those who killed the most were named model peasants or students.

It reached bizarre levels. I sat down under a tree one hot afternoon and rested for a time in the shade and watched scores of my classmates racing along a nearby dike swinging clubs, knives and cleavers screaming, 'Kill it! Kill it! Kill it!' at the top of their lungs as they pursued a rat.

Whenever a snake crawled out of one of the holes we killed it also. The snake was then divided up between the hunters, because snake meat was considered a delicacy.

While the rat-killing campaign was in full swing, the Party announced a fly-killing campaign. So the students were sent out to kill as many flies as possible. Of course, we weren't merely required to kill the little pests. We had to recover their tiny smashed carcasses, place them in a box, and take them to school to be counted. We were each given a quota of a hundred dead flies a day. Each student carried several empty matchboxes to keep dead flies in. This was taken to school and emptied and the teacher carefully counted and recorded the numbers for us. Eventually, the village named the most successful fly killer and posted his name.

No sooner had the rat and fly campaign ended than local Party cadres announced a campaign to raise food production in the village. But there was a peculiar problem. They discovered that there was not enough fertilizer for the fields that year. Party officials said that we could not ask county or province officials to provide fertilizer for us, since that would constitute a loss of face. We had to find fertilizer for ourselves. So students were sent out every afternoon, led by the Little Red

Guards, with large baskets to gather fertilizer for the fields.

What we collected was weighed and those most successful in gathering up a heavy basket of fertilizer received little badges and medals and their names were posted on the school wall. The fertilizer we collected, of course, was simply the waste from humans and animals. So the enthusiastic and patriotic students learned the art and science of gathering the most waste in the shortest amount of time. Of course, the first thing each of us did was to defecate in our own basket. Then we ran out and followed the water buffalo around the fields, because their droppings were the biggest and wettest and heaviest of all. After students selected a buffalo they followed it, sometimes jerking on its tail to encourage it. Others, less fortunate, followed dogs – if any survived the latest anti-pet campaign – around the village and picked up their droppings with a little shovel. The slowest students had to pick up droppings from the pigs, rabbits, chickens and birds. That was the most tedious and fruitless task of all. The campaign to gather fertilizer lasted about three months each year for several years. Everyone wanted to be recognized as the champion fertilizer gatherer. Intense competition led to cheating. When we picked up droppings of the water buffalo, we mixed in a little straw to add weight. If it was picked up from the ground, then a little dirt was always scooped up with it. Some of the students mixed in rocks with the droppings to add weight and win plaudits.

After filling our baskets we went to the head of the village and the baskets were weighed. He wrote down the weight of our basket and praised us for our work for the revolution.

xii

When I was six years old the Chinese government put up its first Earth satellite. Dongfanghong-1, or The East Is Red-1, was put into orbit in late April 1970. An announcement came to us on the radio of the success of our space program. We were told to watch for it at night – and to listen for it. It was said that it was broadcasting music – 'The East Is Red' of course – and that if we listened carefully we could hear it in the night. So at night everyone in the village gathered outside and watched the sky for The East Is Red-1. I don't remember ever seeing it. But many people insisted they saw it and pointed and shouted and then other people also agreed that they saw it and everyone stared at the sky and pointed and we listened quietly. And then someone would say, 'Do you hear it?' and someone else would answer, 'Yes, I hear the music,' and others, afraid of being accused of having rightist eyes and ears, also said they could see it and hear it. I don't recall ever hearing it, but I listened hard. It was as though God were crossing the sky. And after enough people agreed that they saw it and heard it, they would break into song, singing 'The East Is Red,' in celebration of the greatness of Chairman Mao. And pretty soon everyone joined in and sang with gusto and pride. Then, after an hour or so, someone suggested it was gone now, and others agreed and we all returned to our homes, filled with awe at what our country had accomplished.

When I remember those times now, it seems to me that everyone was reduced to the mental status of children, and children were raised to the status of adults. The world truly did turn upside down in that sense. The local Party cadre listened to the radio or received directives from Beijing and relayed instructions from Chairman Mao for this or for that campaign – catch flies or kill pests or pick up animal droppings. Then there would be a rally and everyone would bring his little red flag and the Little Red Guards wore their scarves and uniforms. And then we shouted and sang and learned new slogans or songs. When our enthusiasm flagged, a new campaign began or a new enemy was uncovered. A group of journalists might come to the village, as they did regularly, and write articles about our enthusiasm or our demonstrations. When we learned they were on the way or were already present, we dropped whatever we were doing to join in a rally and, in a sense, to perform for them. Everyone performed exactly as expected.

xiii

My last semester of grammar school began in January 1976. On the morning of January 8, 1976, I was preparing for school while listening to my father's radio. The national news was being broadcast when suddenly there was a long silence. This was followed by slow sad music that played for several minutes. I stopped dressing and stood still next to my bed waiting to hear the resumption of the news. Music like that indicated that someone important had died.

The announcer came on the radio again and said that Premier Zhou Enlai had died. My heart sank. I felt sick. Chairman Mao was the greatest man in the country, without question. But Zhou Enlai was the most loved. He was like a member of every Chinese family. When my mother heard the news she burst into tears. I began crying and could not stop.

At school we were given little white paper flowers to wear. The eyes of all of the teachers were swollen and red from crying. I felt it was the beginning of a terrible time.

People told stories about Zhou Enlai and his long service to China. Then on Qing Ming Day, April 5, 1976, when we celebrate our ancestors and clean their grave sites, a large crowd gathered in Tiananmen Square to put flowers at the Monument to the People in memory of Zhou. But on the radio it was reported that counterrevolutionaries and hooligans had gathered and were chased away by the police and armed workers. The situation, which might have become much more serious, was resolved quickly.

When we heard this story we were stunned and confused. How could so many hooligans and counterrevolutionaries in Beijing take to the streets to openly defy the government? Who were they? Why did the hooligans love our late premier? This was the first indication we had that enemies of Chairman Mao and the Cultural Revolution were numerous, organized and bold enough to express their dissent openly. And since these dissenters praised the policies of Zhou Enlai, some of us wondered to ourselves about unity within the Communist Party. How could the followers of China's most beloved leader (Zhou) and China's greatest leader (Mao) be opposed to each other? At the time, there was no official explanation. Still, we couldn't help but wonder what was going on in Beijing.

During that spring of 1976, a debate began in China between the advocates of traditional higher education and its opponents. Deng Xiaoping, who had championed the reopening of the universities and the restoration of academic testing to place talented students in the schools, was teetering on the brink of power again. He fell from power before summer. Hard-liners who opposed Deng thought that an education in the conventional sense was useless. They said that many of those who'd gathered in Tiananmen Square and threatened the government were students and intellectuals whose education spoiled them and turned them into counterrevolutionaries. Labor and hard work were the best teachers and were the best way to serve the people, they alleged. Traditional education in a university or a high school easily ruined a young person, it was said, and alienated him from the people and the Party.

The debate was carried on in my village and in my own home. Since I was finishing grammar school that spring, my personal future was at stake. My parents disagreed over whether I should continue on to middle school or go to work in the fields as a laborer.

My uncle was Party secretary of the brigade. He believed reading more books would only encourage me to feel superior to the workers around me. 'The most important thing in life,' he insisted, 'is for a young person to have a red heart. If she goes to school and studies poetry and history, the more she learns, the worse she will turn out. She will turn against the revolution and the Party. A good heart is more important to the country than being a bookworm.'

At a local farm meeting that spring, a Party official asked, 'Why in the world should our children study math or literature? The most important thing is to know about Marxism and Leninism and the thoughts of Chairman Mao. That is all we need to know.'

My parents disagreed about my education. My mother's reasons were economic more than ideological. She pointed out that we were poor and that if I went to work in the fields I could add to our income and make life a little better for everyone in the family. The family resources could then be conserved for the education of my brother. She was not against education for me in principle, but she wanted me to understand that we would be better off if I went to work. Besides, an education doesn't make any difference in a girl's life in the village.

My father, on the other hand, favored a further education for me. He had attended a good high school in Danyang and had studied in college to become a veterinarian. He had not been spoiled or alienated by his education, he said. He was a Party member and his experience indicated, he insisted, that a higher education might enhance my ability to earn an income. He was therefore willing to invest the modest tuition required, he said.

Father prevailed. But there was a compromise. Mother told me they had decided that I could attend a middle school for two years. But to continue after that and attend high school would be useless. When I was fourteen, she said, I would become a full-time worker on the farm.

I was happy, of course, with her decision to let me continue my education, but heartbroken that it would be for only two years. I loved school. I was first in my class in every subject we studied. Again and again I was named a model student. If I could attend high school, I thought, I could go on to a military academy and become a PLA officer. I could fulfill my dreams. I didn't know how I could change my mother's mind. I could only keep working hard and hope.

xiv

In the summer of 1976, a few weeks after school ended, the Tangshan earthquake devastated China. The earthquake struck on July 29 in Tangshan, one hundred miles southeast of

Beijing in Hebei province. It was especially terrifying to me since I had never before experienced anything like it.

The night of July 28 had been unusually hot in the village and I was unable to sleep. I awakened early – before anyone else was up – and poured water into a large wooden container to bathe in. I climbed in, certain that no one else was awake and my privacy would not be interrupted.

I was relaxing in the tub in the gray of the morning, when I felt something like an explosion. This was followed by a severe shaking of the entire house. The water sloshed from side to side in the tub and splashed out onto the floor. I tried to stand, but the shaking of the floor made it impossible. When it stopped, I jumped from the tub and ran outside screaming. I hadn't even stopped to wrap a towel around myself. I stood outside, petrified, shaking and totally naked.

Up and down the village paths people were running around outside screaming and crying, terrified by the quake. Some of them were proclaiming it was the end of the world. I didn't realize I was naked until I noticed several of the neighbors staring at me. I felt more fear than shame and didn't go back into the house, but instead covered myself with my hands. My parents and brother and sister came outside, also crying and hysterical.

My father turned on his radio, but the government news services refused to say anything about the quake – perhaps for fear that it made us vulnerable to an attack by our enemies. The only guidance we received from the government was to sleep outside. (Later we heard that initial estimates were that 655,000 people had been killed in the quake and 779,000 injured in Hebei province alone.)

Of course, the villagers of Lishi obeyed. In the next days and months it was as though we were one big clan or tribe again. In the central square of the village the people put up a huge plastic tent. The problem with the structure was that although it sheltered us from the rain and from the bright sunlight, it did not protect us from the heat. There were no airholes cut in the top of the tent and no windows. There was only a large opening to go in or out, and that was closed at night to keep out mosquitoes.

Inside the tent the temperature rose to well over 100 degrees day and night. The flies and mosquitoes were only slightly deterred by the tent and feasted on the exhausted villagers. People fainted before going to sleep and some had to go outside again and again during the night to fan themselves. But the Party cadre would not cut windows or airholes for fear of letting in even more flies and mosquitoes. As a result, we cooked night after night in our communal tents. It was hell.

When classes resumed in September we were instructed to stay outside the school building and even beyond the shade of its walls, which might collapse in another earthquake. There were no trees nearby, so we studied under the sun. September was particularly hot that year. Our skin burned and we perspired and soaked our clothing.

I wondered if things could possibly get any worse. Then they did.

At 4 P.M. on September 9, 1976, we heard the news that truly shook our world. When we first switched on the radio, we heard only solemn music playing for an hour.

My father became tense as he listened. He had no idea what to expect. All we knew for sure was that something bad had happened again. Listening to it this time, and remembering the deaths of Zhou Enlai in January and then Zhu De, a close associate of Mao and an early revolutionary leader, in July, I felt heartsick. Who might it be this time?

Then a newsman's voice came on the radio. He spoke slowly. It seemed that he waited several seconds between each of his words. He said, 'Our great beloved Chairman Mao Zedong has passed away.'

I couldn't move. To me, this was an official announcement that God had died.

My mother, who had been lying in bed listening to the music and the news, immediately burst into tears. I heard shouts outside as people rushed from their houses moaning and crying.

With the death of Mao an old world died for all of us and a new age began. At the time we believed that the sun had died and that the new age would be one of darkness for China. But we were wrong, we found. We soon discovered we had been living in darkness without knowing it and the new age – which we initially feared – quickly brought us change and light.

XV

I thought about my childhood years in the village for a long time after seeing the little girl feeding the horse and looking up to smile at me. She seemed as full of happiness as I had been when I was her age.

It was early evening and was growing dark outside when we finally arrived at our destination. The bus stopped and we gathered our luggage and got off. 'Where are we?' I asked.

'Near your new home,' Lin Cheng replied. 'We have to walk a short distance. It's about half a mile away.' We stood and picked up our bags and pushed our way through the crowd to the rear exit of the bus. As soon as we had stepped to the ground, the driver closed the door and the bus pulled away, leaving us alone next to a small unoccupied bus station. I saw a cluster of houses and smokestacks in the distance.

'That's it,' Lin Cheng said, pointing to the buildings. We began walking down the road toward the settlement. We walked slowly, side by side, like two lost and tired souls looking for shelter. The wind picked up as we walked and I stopped for a moment to pull my scarf over my nose and mouth.

I looked up for an instant and through a break in the clouds saw a shooting star streak across the evening sky. Didn't a shooting star mean good luck? I couldn't remember. I asked Lin Cheng, but he said he couldn't remember either.

NINE

Twelve Pandas

Early rays of sun illumine the parade grounds
and these handsome girls heroic in the wind
with rifles five feet long.
Daughters of China with a marvelous will, you
prefer hardy uniforms to colorful silk.

— MAO ZEDONG, 'Militia Women' (February
1961)

i

W e were greeted by a guard inside the headquarters of the
Nanyang Oil Company. Lin Cheng gave our names and
said we had an appointment with the supervisor of the facility.
The guard made a phone call, and the supervisor appeared
several minutes later. He was friendly and said his son in Beijing
had told him about us and he'd been expecting us. We chatted
for a few moments. He seemed convinced he was helping a
friend of his son escape from family difficulties for a time.

We stayed in his home that night. He told me I could live in
his house with his family, earning my keep by helping with
cooking and chores. He found me a job selling instant noodles
on the street.

My husband remained with me for two nights and then
returned to Beijing. On the morning of his departure I accompanied him as far as the bus stop outside the facility. Before we
parted I gave him a letter I'd written to my parents and asked him
to mail it as soon as he arrived in Beijing. In the letter, I told my
parents I was doing well and was busy with my new job and
would not be able to write to them often. I gave no indication that
I was not in Beijing.

From the bus station I walked directly to work on the street
to sell instant noodles. I felt completely out of place. None of
the people I worked with had even a basic education. They
didn't speak Mandarin and their greatest passion was making a
one-fen profit from each bag of noodles. They gawked at me as
if I was from another planet.

Each day I got up at 5.30 A.M. to clean the rooms in the
house where I lived. Then I prepared breakfast. I was also
supposed to go to the company dining room to fetch six

271

thermos bottles of hot water for the supervisor and his wife to use when they got up. As soon as they were up I served them tea and made the bed for them.

I had a ninety-minute break at lunchtime. During that period I'd hurry home to make lunch for the family. When everyone had finished, I cleaned up after them and washed the dishes.

After work I cooked and served dinner and washed the dishes and the clothing for the family. No television, radio or newspaper was available to me. I was no more than a servant in the household. The only bright moment of my day was when I received a letter from Lin Cheng. He provided my only hope and connection to the outside world.

Lin Cheng's words were always cordial, concerned and sympathetic. I wrote back to him every day and asked the supervisor's wife to address the envelopes for me and had them sent to Lin Cheng's friend, who then hand-delivered them to him. I took this precaution so my whereabouts could not be detected by anyone who intercepted my letters. His letters were addressed to the supervisor's wife. My new co-workers laughed at me because I wrote so many letters and didn't understand why I budgeted so much of my salary for the post office.

One month after I began my new job I received a letter from Lin Cheng with news I dreaded. 'I have thought it over,' he began, 'and I feel I must tell you now that I no longer love you. I want to get a divorce as soon as possible. I know you are facing the most difficult time in your life. But pretending that I still love you would be to mislead you, and I won't do that. We each have our own lives to live now. Please don't be angry with me. In time I think you will understand why this is necessary.'

I went to my room, locked the door behind me and cried for the rest of the evening. The next morning I started to cry again. I didn't leave the room. When the supervisor's wife came to my door and asked what was wrong, I told her I was sick. That evening I finally came out of my room and prepared dinner for the supervisor and his wife. I cried as I cooked and my tears fell into the food. They watched me but said nothing.

I sat in a chair next to the window that night thinking about my life. I saw no reason to continue it. I thought about stepping into the path of one of the oil trucks that passed me on the road each evening when I returned home from work. I could snuff out my life in a second, I thought. Painlessly. It would just take one step. I thought about composing a suicide note and sending it to Lin Cheng. Then I decided against it because I really wasn't sure how to explain what had happened to me. I was still confused and I just couldn't find the right words. All I knew for sure was that I was tired of living. I decided I'd let Lin Cheng tell my family and friends in his own words what he thought had happened. Perhaps he'd tell them I'd been the victim of an accident while visiting a friend in Nanyang. Perhaps they'd believe him and forgive me for the shame I brought them.

I sat in the dark, crying softly, feeling unloved, unwanted, unneeded and doomed. I crossed my arms on the windowsill and rested my head against them. As I did, I felt something cold against my face. I sat up and noticed the small silver bracelet still locked snugly around my wrist. I had never removed it. And I'd completely forgotten it.

I recalled the afternoon Larry gave it to me and promised it would bring me luck. If it weren't for the bracelet, I could almost believe he'd never existed.

I sat at the window staring at the night sky and slipped the tiny silver links through my fingers. About midnight I was distracted for a moment by a flash of light in the distance. Another shooting star? I watched the sky and minutes later saw the flash again. It wasn't a shooting star after all. It was just a searchlight, somewhere far away, slicing silently through the darkness.

ii

My life was over, I kept telling myself. I'd never felt such deep darkness and sadness before. The last time I'd cried with such hopelessness was after I'd heard of the death of Chairman Mao. At that time I was sure I'd never smile again.

Then I remembered that I'd been wrong. Mao's death, in fact, opened a door for me to a new life.

The death of Mao and the arrest of his wife and her associates marked the start of a period of dramatic change for everyone in China. The Great Proletarian Cultural Revolution was abandoned. Victims of the hysteria of the past decade were gradually released from prisons and work camps and returned home to start their lives over again. Those who had been expelled from the Communist Party were restored to membership and many victims of the purges of the period were posthumously exonerated.

Deng Xiaoping eased control of the government from Hua Guofeng. Maoists were removed from positions of power in the Party and replaced by Deng's friends. Deng announced his intentions to modernize China, to deemphasize class struggle and politics. He instituted dozens of basic reforms and stressed the importance of pragmatism rather than pure ideology in government policies. Among the reforms he introduced were fundamental changes in the educational system. Universities and colleges that had stopped functioning during the Cultural Revolution and were taken over by political factions were returned to the academic administrators and teachers. Examinations rather than class origins were reinstituted to determine qualifications for admission. Political education was deemphasized in school and genuine academic achievement became the primary goal of education.

A wide variety of new books and new editions of old books suddenly became available. A large bookstore opened in Danyang and did a brisk business. The Danyang library also became a crowded and busy place as students hungry for education tirelessly studied and prepared for entrance examinations to good high schools and to colleges and universities.

There were no more political crusades for the students, no hunting for fertilizer or landlords on the weekends. Teachers were restored to the pedestals they traditionally occupied in China. They convinced us that the only way to escape a life of labor in the fields was to labor hard in the classroom and to prepare to achieve a high score in the high school and college entrance exams. Not a minute was to be wasted. And so we read our books and recited our lessons with the same energy and enthusiasm we'd demonstrated in our earlier political campaigns. Under this situation, Mother changed her mind and let me continue with my education rather than relegating me to working on the farm.

I completed middle school in the spring of 1978 and earned a high enough score on the high school examination to qualify to study in Danyang High School, one of the most prestigious high schools in Jiangsu province. While nationwide only 4 percent of China's high school graduates qualified for admission to a university, 50 percent of the graduates of Danyang High School gained admission to universities.

I continued to study tirelessly day and night and was rewarded for my efforts by being one of only two students in my class inducted into the Communist Youth League during my first semester in high school. The induction ceremony was even more moving to me than my earlier induction into the Little Red Guards. My parents were extremely proud of my accomplishments. At a school assembly I was called to the front of the room. I stood in the midst of other members of the League and swore a solemn oath pledging always to stand by the Communist Party. Then everyone stood and sang the national anthem of China and 'The Internationale.' I was given a red pin to wear every day on my blouse over my heart. On the pin were engraved the words 'Member of the Communist Youth League.'

Following the completion of my third year in Danyang High School I took the college entrance examination. The examination was rigorous – eighteen hours of tests in six subjects spread over three days. On the third day, after returning home from a six-hour exam, I shut myself in the bedroom and composed a letter to the president of the PLA Institute for International Relations. The Institute was my dream school since its mission was to educate and train the future leaders of the PLA as well as of the country. For the first time since 1965 the Institute had announced it would recruit female cadets for admission in the fall of 1981. Admission, it was announced, was to be based on academic accomplishment and test scores rather than on family background and personal connections.

Only twelve females would be selected from the applicants throughout the country. Although my high school academic advisor cautioned me that my chances for admission to the school were slim due to the limited number of recuits taken on and, despite the PLA's announcement, many top military officers would try to use their influence to have their own daughters admitted to the Institute, I nevertheless put the Institute at the top of my list of choices.

I'm not sure how I came up with the idea of writing a letter to support my application. Perhaps it was a combination of my faith in the desire of the PLA to recruit the very best candidates – and I needed to point out in my own words why I believed I was among the very best – and my reading of stories about people in power always on the lookout for talented youngsters. I had everything to gain, I felt, and nothing to lose by writing. I worked on my five-page letter until midnight. I introduced myself to the school's president and told him of my background, my education, my aspirations and my determination. I told him I'd always dreamed of being a member of the PLA and that now I was ready to fulfill that dream if he would only give me the opportunity. I promised that if I gained admission to the school I would be the best and most enthusiastic student he'd ever seen.

Three weeks later I received my scores, which were among the highest in my county. Then I was directed to three different hospitals, where I was given special physical examinations for admission to the Army. In late July officers from the PLA Institute for International Relations visited my high school on three occasions to interview me in both English and Chinese.

On August 18, 1981, I was informed that I had been selected as one of the twelve girls admitted to the PLA Institute. As soon as I received the official admission letter, I ran to the field to share the news with my mother. When she heard of my good fortune, she turned to those working around her and shouted. 'My daughter has been accepted at the PLA Institute!' 'Congratulations,' the villagers shouted back. 'You are lucky to have a good daughter like her.' Later Mother told me that was the happiest day in her life. I was the first individual in her family ever to attend a university. She told me she felt even her ancestors were proud of my accomplishment on that day.

We walked home together that afternoon. She cooked a big meal for me and then we rode my father's bicycle to the homes of our relatives in nearby villages to share the news. Late that night Father set off firecrackers he'd saved from the Spring Festival for the special occasion. He confided in me that he would not have saved them if he hadn't had faith that I'd succeed.

My parents accompanied me on the train to Nanjing one week later. Despite the fact that we were only two hours away from this large city, neither my mother nor my father had ever been there. Before we left our village, people told us that Nanjing was the most beautiful city in China and that I would love it there. I reminded them that not only would I be living in the most beautiful city in China but I'd also be wearing a PLA uniform. I was seventeen years old and all of my dreams were coming true.

Officials from the PLA Institute were waiting at the train station to greet arriving cadets and transport them by bus to the school. When we climbed aboard the bus, three young uniformed men helped us with our bags and found seats for us. The ride to the Institute took more than an hour.

I was anxious to see the place I'd dreamed of since my childhood. As we approached the school, I saw armed sentries guarding the gate. The high wall around the compound was topped with barbed wire, giving the place a mysterious touch but also the appearance of a prison rather than a school. Everyone on the bus became silent as the sentries pushed the gate open and we drove inside. My heart was racing and tears welled up in my eyes. I was holding my mother's hand and quivering with anticipation.

iii

W e were driven to a large central parade ground, where the bus stopped and everyone got out. The senior cadets raced to their quarters, leaving my parents and me behind.

Two orderlies came for us. One escorted my parents to a guesthouse and the other directed me to follow him.

He led me to an office building, where a PLA officer greeted me. He was a pleasant and personable man, smiled broadly, shook my hand and introduced himself as Officer Ying. He was one of the three officers to supervise all new cadets of English major. Ying examined my papers and extended an official welcome to me from the Institute. 'Ha! You are the one who wrote to the president,' he said. 'That was a wonderful letter. The president sends his greetings to you.'

Ying led me to the second floor of the building which served as quarters for the twelve female cadets. There were six rooms. Three of them were bedrooms, two smaller ones were storage rooms, and one was a washroom with cold-water faucets and a partitioned bathroom with five toilets. There was no shower and no tub.

Twelve bed frames were the only furnishings on the second floor. Two young women who arrived earlier sat forlornly on one of the bed frames, waiting quietly for other female cadets to arrive. They were happy to see me.

Ying led us to a supply building to pick up the things we'd need to live in the barracks. We were issued mattresses, coverlets and mosquito netting. Each of us was also provided with three small bowls, a spoon, a pair of chopsticks, a thermos, a washbasin and a short wooden stool to sit on at meetings and assemblies.

That evening I had dinner with my parents and new class-mates in the campus dining room. The place was large enough to accommodate more than 1,500 cadets. After dinner we walked through the campus and I said goodbye to my parents. I was required to attend an exercise session early in the morning and wouldn't be able to see them off at the train station.

At six o'clock the next morning I was awakened by a shrill bugle call followed by loud martial music played over the Institute's public-address system. An orderly shouted outside the door that we had five minutes to get to the parade ground. Once there, we were directed to stand in a straight line and to sound off when an officer called our names. Only about thirty cadets were present. We were all early arrivers. The officer led us in morning exercises for one hour. Then we returned to our rooms to make our beds and wash up. Then we went to breakfast. That was the routine during the first three days at the Institute – we exercised in the morning, cleaned our room, ate in the dining room and walked around the campus and talked.

Four days after my arrival all new and returning cadets were on campus and settled in their quarters. The fall semester commenced officially on 1 September. All the new cadets of English major (120 of us) gathered in a big meeting room. Ying called our names one by one, then was quiet for a moment before telling us, solemnly, why we had been selected from among thousands of applicants from throughout China, and what we might expect in the future.

'This school,' he began, 'is unique to China. No other school like it exists. No other school trains its students for the work you will be asked to do. We are part of the PLA's Second Bureau – Erbu – Military Intelligence. We deal both with the collection of information abroad and with counterintelligence within China. Those will become your primary tasks after you graduate.

'You will find that many people in China and abroad are curious about this place and interested in finding out what they can about us. In order to protect our security, you are never to talk about this school, about what goes on here, with anyone. Not with your parents, not with your friends. You will never describe your classes and activities in a private or public place with your friends or your fellow cadets. You will never take your notes or textbooks out of the campus. You will never tell anyone what books you are assigned to read and what books are available in the library. You will never tell anyone how many cadets are here or who the faculty members and commanding officers are. You will never tell anyone how many buildings are here or how they are situated. You will never tell anyone how you are trained or with what weapons.

'You will never tell anyone the location of this school. There is not a map in China with this institute's location on it. Our own buses will pick you up at the train station or downtown Nanjing and bring you here. Your address at the institute will be a post office box number only. You will tell no one your telephone number. You may call individuals but they may not call you here.

'Some of this may not seem important to you now. But in time you will learn the reasons for this secrecy. The makeup of our corps of cadets is a national secret. You must remember that absolutely everything that happens to you here, everything that you do here, everything that you hear here, is never to be discussed outside these walls. The penalty for breaching these rules will be most serious.'

We were excited and drawn closer together by the revelations, the secrets and responsibilities we shared. We were made to feel that we were part of an elite, blessed and important band of young people.

The meeting lasted about one hour. Then the twelve of us female cadets returned to our barracks. Ying joined us shortly. We were asked to introduce ourselves and to say a few words about our background and our expectations. Ying assured us that we were like no other girls in China. We were the first female cadets recruited by the institute since 1965. The important role we would play in maintaining the security of our country was emphasized. The sacrifices we could expect to make were listed. One by one, he called our names again and asked us if we were willing to make the required sacrifices for our motherland:

Xu Meihong (Beautiful Red)
Tao Xiaoying (Little Hero)
Chen Taohui (Waves of Wisdom)
Xia Haiou (Seagull)
Zhu Hong (Red)
Qu Yuanyuan (Beauty)
He Lianzhen (Precious Lotus)
Chen Nishang (Neon-Lighted Dress)
Gao Ming (Nimble)
Zhang Hong (Deep Water)
Sun Yanrong (Honored Swallow)
Meng Qiuqing (Pretty and Delicate)

Each of us in turn answered, firmly, 'yes.'

He announced that we were designated a special squad in the school's Company 13. I had been selected along with He Lianzhen as the leaders of our group. Then he said, 'You're special. You are not just part of Company 13. You are the "Twelve Pandas" – twelve national treasures. Live up to it. Work hard.'

Before leaving, he said something that we would hear repeated by our officers nearly every week for the next four years. At the time none of us appreciated the full truth of it. 'We will train you, feed you, clothe you and care for you for a thousand days,' he said. 'But we will only need you for one moment. Be ready!'

Our spirits and expectations were high. Military life would be tough but we welcomed the hardship. We were prepared for the discipline. When our day came, we wanted to be ready.

iv

For the next few weeks we studied the regulations and rituals of military life, memorized the names of our commanding officers, did vigorous daily exercises and learned to march in formation and scrubbed and cleaned our quarters and the classrooms. Finally, we were given our uniforms. When we put them on the first time and buttoned the tunics and adjusted the caps we could hardly conceal our pride.

To celebrate the National Day (1 October) we had a huge ceremony. It was mandatory that everybody in the Institute attend the event. The Institute's cadets were divided into thirteen companies. Companies 1 through 3 were trained specifically to work with our military attachés. Companies 4 through 6 were trained to work in Japan, Germany, France, Vietnam, and other Asian, European, and Middle Eastern countries and in Taiwan and Hong Kong. Companies 7 through 9 were trained to work in Russia. Companies 10 through 13 were trained to work in English-speaking countries. We assembled by company on the parade ground and then marched into the auditorium. On the way we sang – rather we shouted as loud as we could – our marching songs. We proceeded quickly to our assigned seats and then stood at attention until the hall was filled. An officer appeared on the stage and shouted in a shrill voice, 'Sit!' Instantly, with a great rustling and clatter, all 1,500 cadets and 500 officers and teachers in the auditorium sat.

For a moment there was complete silence. Then, from a far corner of the room a company of seniors broke into a rousing martial song. Everyone joined in. No sooner was the song finished than another company began another song. This was followed by yet another. It soon became clear to the new cadets that each of the companies competed to see who could sing the loudest. Before long we were growing hoarse from shouting the songs. There was no concern with singing in tune or in key. It was volume alone that counted. The point was to drown out the singing of nearby companies with as much gusto as possible, demonstrating the spirit, energy and lung power of your own company.

The most popular song that day was 'Three Disciplines and Eight Things to Remember,' which was merely the words of Mao set to music. The second most popular song was the National Anthem. A close third was 'The Red Flower' – the Red Flower indicating a model soldier. The words and melodies were simple, even childish, yet we roared them out as though each word was a promise and a challenge. After fifteen minutes of singing, an officer stood and signaled us to stop. Then someone ordered the female cadets of Company 13 to stand and sing. They wanted a better look at us. We stood, self-consciously, and sang 'The Red Flower.' When we finished, the boys hooted, stomped their feet and applauded for several minutes. We were embarrassed by this attention but at the same time very proud to be part of this crowd of enthusiastic and patriotic soldiers at last. Since our early youth we'd heard the singing PLA soldiers and dreamed of joining their ranks and now our dreams had come true.

Since we were the first girls at the Institute, we created some unusual problems. All three of our immediate superiors were in their early thirties, and all were clearly shy around us.

When they came to our quarters to speak with us and some of the girls were not completely dressed or if bras and underwear were drying in the washroom, they noticed them and blushed deeply and experienced difficulty speaking straight.

During the first week of orientation, the male students were given lectures on how to behave with females on the campus. 'We must warn you,' they were told, 'that it is strictly forbidden that there be any contact between you except in the most formal of circumstances. You are not to eat at the same table, you are not to make trouble, you are not to flirt. There is to be no courtship. There is to be no romance. You are to study and train here. That is all. If secret contacts are discovered you will be disciplined along with the woman. You could be expelled from the PLA and there will forever be a black mark on your record.'

The women were called together in our own meeting and also warned. We were reminded that our quarters were above the offices of the English Department, which would give us additional security on campus. Anyone coming to our rooms during the day would have to pass through the offices, which were staffed by officers and secretaries. They would be our daytime sentries. The boys were housed in three barracks further away. They could see our quarters, but were too far away to see in through the windows. Ying even put up a chalkboard and wrote two words in red chalk: 'BI XIAN' – *bi* meaning to escape and *xian* meaning suspicion. At the time, none of us could imagine allowing a romantic attachment to endanger our military career. We had come to the Institute only to study and train and serve and we intended to preserve our passion for soldiering alone.

V

We went through three months of intense military training before regular classes began. The training lasted from sunrise to sunset every day, six days a week. Until we completed basic training we were officially referred to as civilians in uniform.

We marched and maneuvered around the parade ground and then practiced the proper way to salute, talk, stand, run, jog, and sit. I thought I already knew how to do these things. But I was wrong. I learned that there is a proper PLA way to walk, and to sit, and to stand with good posture, the chin always up and the back straight. There was also a proper and improper way to hold and use chopsticks and we were shown that. We had to learn how to make a bed, how to hang our clothes, how to place our shoes under the bed, where to put our stool, how to arrange our pillow, how to lace and tie our shoes and so on. Nearly everything we did had to be learned anew. At night canteens were hung on hooks on the wall so that every girl's canteen was at exactly the same height.

The initial days of training were exhausting. Each morning at five-thirty reveille and martial music awakened us. We then drilled, had a brief break for breakfast, drilled again until lunch and then drilled after lunch until dinner. We practiced individually at first and then in larger and larger groups. There was a special squad for the student leaders with twelve boys and two girls. I was one of the two. We were trained to shout slogans in unison and to issue marching and running orders to the other cadets. At first it was an interesting and novel exercise. Then it became amusing and finally it was boring and exhausting. We stumbled to our beds at night and collapsed on them without even washing. We didn't move until the bugle call the next morning.

After we mastered the proper way to march and move about, we were given training in self-defense and weapons utilization. We learned kung fu and wrestling for hand-to-hand combat. This training continued throughout our years at the Institute. Mastery of martial arts, we were told, could be critical in escaping from difficult situations and saving our lives someday.

Each of us was issued a pistol – a 9 mm '54' model, which was copied from a Czechoslovakian weapon, and then the automatic and semi-automatic versions of the AK-47. We practiced with them on the firing range, and then learned to assemble, load, maintain and disassemble the weapons blind-folded, and to name each of the weapons' parts by touch. The reason for this training, we were told, was that the enemies of China might attack in the middle of the night and we had to be prepared to meet and defeat them.

Later we practiced hand-to-hand combat with bayonets and learned the best techniques for disarming and stabbing enemy soldiers (usually our assault on the enemy followed the familiar cry 'American soldiers, surrender! You are sur-rounded and all resistance is futile!'). From there we worked our way up the weapons chain, practicing with hand gre-nades, small artillery pieces, mortars and finally fieldpieces. This was not our main training, we were reminded later. We were training primarily for intelligence gathering and analy-sis, but combat training was an important skill that might be required in an emergency.

Our training was accompanied by intense political indoctri-nation. We were told repeatedly of the PLA's tradition of courage in combat against the Japanese, the Nationalists, the Americans, the Indians, the Russians and the Vietnamese. We were told of fierce struggles – the fight against the Americans at Pork Chop Hill in Korea and the bloody struggle in the mountains along the border with Vietnam that resulted in our forces breaking through to destroy a major Vietnamese city and to teach the Vietnamese a lesson. Along the border with India the PLA overwhelmed the enemy armies that outnumbered them. The Americans were kept in the lower half of the Korean peninsula. The Nationalists were expelled to Taiwan, and soon we would defeat them there. No one could stand up to the PLA, we learned. We were in training to carry on the glorious tradition and to be the best soldiers in the world.

Near the end of the training we had several emergency drills. These were supposed to serve as a practical test for all we'd learned as well as a rehearsal for a real international crisis. When the bugle sounded the alarm in the middle of the night we were supposed to be out of our beds and into our uniforms in twenty seconds. Then we had to prepare our packs and assemble at the parade ground. Because we were going into combat we had been instructed to tie a cloth around our left arm to be used as a tourniquet or bandage in case we were wounded. All preparations had to be made in complete darkness because of the danger of enemy aircraft spotting our post if even a single light came on. We were instructed to familiarize ourselves with the layout of our room and to be sure we could find everything we needed in the dark.

One morning in the last week of basic training we were awakened at three o'clock by a series of bugle blasts. We knew what this meant. We sprang from our beds. Some of the women, still half asleep, became entangled in their mosquito netting, tearing it down or stumbling and falling on it or tipping over their beds. We struggled into our uniforms, grabbed our packs, rolled up our coverlets, tied extra shoes to our packs, pulled a towel from our clothesline and tied it around our left arms, then raced down the stairs and out to the parade ground.

An officer was waiting for us and addressed us in an unusually serious tone. 'Comrades,' he announced, 'we have received word that China has been attacked by the United States.' We glanced back and forth at each other – this did not sound at all like a dress rehearsal. It seemed like the real thing.

'The Americans have crossed our borders and invaded our country,' he continued. 'As you know, this means all-out war. American marines have come up the Yangtze River and are at this moment ten miles from here. Our orders are to advance rapidly to the Yangtze and to meet and destroy them.

'We are to engage the Americans within the hour. We will gladly sacrifice ourselves this morning, if necessary, for the security and the survival of our country. And we are prepared for that task. We are eager for that. We welcome the challenge. Turn right! March!'

We turned and marched out through the gate into the darkness. Quickly our pace became a jog as we hurried off to fight the Americans.

Although we carried full packs, some of the women began to whisper that something important was missing from our supplies. We had not been issued our weapons or ammunition! As we proceeded toward the enemy we became increasingly concerned. How in the world were we supposed to fight the American marines? With kung fu?

We jogged on and on through the hot, humid morning. We were soon drenched with sweat and short of breath and one by one the women slowed and dropped behind. Only two of the twelve women made it as far as the river where the Americans were said to have landed. I was one of the hardy two.

As we neared the river we saw a ship anchored in midstream. The first ranks of men slowed and began to form a skirmish line – still without weapons. Was that the American ship anchored on the river? Someone whispered that it was.

Then as we advanced slowly to the riverbank we could make out the Chinese markings on the ship. Our commanders walked behind us with stopwatches. They announced that this was a drill. There were no marines. There would be no fight. We dropped to the ground, exhausted.

As the stragglers arrived at the river's edge, we were told to form a line to march back to the Institute immediately.

As we returned, we came upon some of the other men and women sitting beside the road, looking completely bedraggled. Those who had dropped out now weakly stepped back into line as we passed. Similar drills followed in the next days until there were no dropouts on the way to battle and our time getting into battle was reduced to that required by our commanders.

At the completion of our three months of basic training the Institute held a dress parade followed by a formal ceremony. Each of the twelve women was given a red ribbon for the collar of her uniform and a red star for her cap. There were no official ranks in the PLA at that time, but we were informed that we were all designated officers. We traded in our training uniforms for officer's uniforms. We, as officers, had four pockets in our tunics and the enlisted men had two. That was how rank was distinguished in an army without official rank.

vi

Physical conditioning, marching, and weapons-utilization training continued during the next four years, but the principal focus of our education shifted to language skills and intelligence gathering and analysis. Our most intensive courses concentrated on developing fluency in English. Without English communication skills, we were told, we could never fulfill our assigned tasks.

Part of each day, consequently, was spent listening to colloquial English and another part of the day to reading and translating written English. We needed equal facility in colloquial and technical English because PLA officers stationed in listening posts throughout China monitored American military and diplomatic communications and private telephone conversations originating in Southeast Asia and the western Pacific region. America's Sixth and Seventh fleets were a critical target of our monitors. Telephone and radio communications from the fleets were recorded for analysis. We listened to taped intercepts of American naval personnel calling their families from various ports in Asia or from aboard their ships. We were shocked, sometimes, to hear an American naval officer call his wife in the United States and then moments later call his mistress in the Philippines or Hong Kong and use exactly the same romantic idioms.

The conversations we heard not only helped us learn English expressions but also aroused in us a contempt for American moral standards. Our officers, of course, encouraged the development of such negative feelings. We were hearing firsthand, they said, the duplicity, decadence and tawdriness of America. We were shocked and amazed at what we heard. Romance and love, to us, were still largely textbook concepts. None of the twelve women had even held hands with a man. We expected romance to be fully as noble and pure as it was in the novels and stories we read. We read Jane Austen, Charlotte Brontë,

Margaret Mitchell and Ernest Hemingway and we were daz-
zled by films like *The Sound of Music*, but we'd never imagined
language like that overheard in monitoring American service-
men. Truly, they were nothing at all like the high-minded
officers who commanded the PLA, we believed. The world
would be a better place, we knew, when America's power and
reach abated and her influence retreated to her own shores.

Our classroom reading is best described as eclectic. We read
classic English and American novels along with modern fiction
and nonfiction in order to acquaint ourselves with evolving
idiomatic expressions. For development of our technical
vocabulary we studied military manuals, newspapers, maga-
zines, journals and reports provided to headquarters in Beijing
and then duplicated for our use.

We also studied American politics and international relations, film and popular culture, so that we could better understand Americans and carry on a fairly sophisticated
conversation with them. We learned the proper way to eat
with Western utensils and before we graduated became adept
at Western ballroom dancing. These, too, were skills that could
someday open doors to new friendships and information
sources, we were told.

Years later, however, when I met Americans and lived with
them at the Center for Chinese and American Studies in
Nanjing, I discovered how outdated our training had been. I
had difficulty understanding the latest American idioms. I also
learned that Americans our age didn't do ballroom dancing
anymore, nor did they listen to the kind of music or watch
the kind of movies we enjoyed. We had been practicing to
interact with an America that no longer existed. While we
thought we were preparing to fit into American society
someday, our lessons made us seem quaint to the Americans.
I recall taking to the dance floor at a party with Americans
and dancing with another Chinese student. The Americans
stood aside and watched us, amused by the formal steps we
had mastered. When the music changed to loud rock, the
Americans danced and the Chinese stood and gaped at them,
either unable to follow their steps or too restrained and shy
to try.

As the weeks passed, our studies in pronunciation, transcription of rapid dictation, note taking, speed reading and analysis and vocabulary building intensified. There were regular exams on the materials covered and critiques of our work and progress. I recall in the early classes going over and over the same technical manuals and writing and rewriting again and again translations of those documents in order to get them down precisely. We were required to dispense with dictionaries and we were told to construct an English dictionary in our mind.

New classes were regularly added to our curriculum. During the second semester we added a class on military geography. This involved fieldwork in determining direction and finding our way over the landscape with a compass or with natural indicators – the sun, shadows, moss on trees and so on. We learned basic survival techniques and how to read military maps and to make maps freehand. We practiced the estimation of distances and altitudes of hills and mountains.

Often in the evening we watched training films from air forces in the West and of naval maneuvers of the American fleet. We learned to identify different classes of naval vessels and weapons and missiles. We visited a Chinese naval base and went aboard submarines and frigates and asked the officers and enlisted men about their experiences and their expertise.

A Thursday afternoon class concentrated on Party policy. We read the directives of the Party, analyses of the current world situation and China's international stance. Sometimes the materials we read were described to us as 'sensitive materials with limited circulation' and so we were led to believe that we had been drawn into a trusted inner circle of the Party – even though we were not yet Party members – that we were special and that extraordinary things were expected of us in return.

About 90 percent of the new cadets were in the Communist Youth League – the organization from which Party members were drawn. League members met in small study groups on a weekly basis. We expected, through our study and hard work, to earn membership in the Communist Party. Our sessions were held for one or two hours in the afternoon. Following each session a squad leader wrote a report on everything that transpired at the meeting, who said what and so on. Sometimes in the meetings we were required to write an essay about our thoughts on a selected subject or on ourselves. We were reminded and warned again and again in the sessions that keeping personal secrets, in a sense of personal life, was forbidden. Nothing was to be concealed from the League and, above them, from Party officials. The League and Party line was: 'There is nothing – absolutely nothing – that you cannot share with the Party.' So, in accordance with that principle, each of us wrote our private thoughts, and then if they were not revealing enough, were required to write them again. They were collected and read aloud to the group and then criticized for selfish attitudes or for intimations of bourgeois values or political ignorance. We were also required to keep a diary in our rooms and these also were collected from time to time and read, or we were directed to exchange diaries and read them aloud to each other and to the group.

The intent of these sessions was to raise and sharpen our political consciousness. The result, however, was not what the League and the Party expected. We learned to dissimulate and act. Whenever you are absolutely certain that what you write will be read aloud in front of a group and added to your permanent personnel file, you naturally become cautious and self-censoring in putting words on paper. We filled our diaries with folksy politically correct fabrications. We learned early what Party and League leaders wanted to hear and that is what we wrote. They loved to listen to prevarications. In fact, they preferred them. They seemed to believe if we wrote these fables again and again that eventually we'd believe them. So gradually we learned not only to lie on a regular basis but to tell big, colorful, incredible lies about our love and respect for all of our senior officers and for all of our fellow cadets even if we found them brutish or ignorant. If any of us betrayed our misgivings about commanders or classmates, the result would be long reeducation sessions and black marks on our records.

Well-crafted lies could lift us into the ranks of the officially blessed of the League, the Army and the Party. And, ironically, even though we learned these powerful organizations easily mistook lies and exaggerations for truth – and we supplied many of those lies – still, we worked hard to become accepted members.

We developed a public and a private persona. The public persona never challenged or questioned the established order of things or officially sanctioned wisdom. The private persona felt doubts and fears and had questions and misgivings. In the dark, at night, the twelve of us whispered our thoughts to each other, laughed at some of our commanding officers and questioned what we'd been told to believe. We came to trust only each other and to share our real feelings only when we were in our quarters.

We were drawn closely to each other by the secrets we shared. We were protective of the group and became as close as sisters. We felt little sense of competition with each other but instead saw ourselves as a group apart from the rest of the Institute and the rest of the world. We listened sympathetically to each other's concerns, cared for each other when one of us became sick, covered for each other, lied for each other when necessary and respected and loved each other. During the next four years, despite external pressures that tested our loyalties, our affection and respect endured.

All of us experienced misgivings and disappointments from time to time. By the end of our first year some of the women wondered if they'd made an unwise choice in coming to a PLA school. Our friends in civilian universities enjoyed a far less disciplined life. Already, some of our patriotic ardor was starting to dissipate. But we could never indicate that to our commanders and instructors. We could never openly question or challenge them but we could, in the privacy of our barracks, ask and say anything we wished. In the face of doubt, we hoped for the best and trusted that the larger part of our childhood dreams might in the end be redeemed. And we continued to cultivate our two faces. While the PLA counted twelve girls in our company, we knew there were twenty-four.

vii

O ur most enjoyable and inspiring classes in our first year were those on the history of the PLA and the study of its great battles and leaders. The wars in Korea and in Vietnam were examined in detail and veterans gave us dramatic eyewitness accounts of what they had done and seen in those conflicts.

One afternoon we were summoned to a general assembly to listen to the personal account of a hero from the war against Vietnam – the so-called Pedagogical War of 1979. His national reputation was already well established when he addressed us.

The official story alleged that during a Vietnamese assault on his position, the soldier stood his ground against overwhelming odds, and when a grenade landed near his position, he threw himself on it in order to save the lives of his fellow soldiers. As a result of his selfless and heroic act, he'd lost a leg.

When he told us of the fierce fighting at the front and of the sacrifice he willingly made, we were deeply moved. Many cadets were in tears when he finished speaking. He was the first great military hero we'd heard at the Institute and the younger cadets were inspired by his words and wondered if the time came for us to make a sacrifice whether we could be as selfless and patriotic as he had been.

Moments after we left the auditorium where he spoke, however, we overheard senior cadets complaining about him. They suggested that everything the veteran said was a lie. They'd heard him and read about him in the past. Some of them had fathers and brothers who'd fought in the war against Vietnam. They said they knew the real story and were resentful of the show that he had just put on for us. 'Don't believe a word of what they tell you about Vietnam,' one cadet said. 'It's all just bullshit.'

The hero, they said, was in fact a coward who'd planned to desert his unit. He had been stationed with a unit on the

Vietnam border and he was petrified by the prospect of actual combat. He devised a scheme that might allow him to be sent home. He planned to throw one of his own grenades over a bunker and then to pretend he had suffered a severe concussion from the blast of an enemy grenade. But he didn't toss the grenade far enough and it bounced back down the bunker towards him, exploded and blew off his leg.

His commanding officer, after discovering what happened, was reluctant to report the incident since he believed it would result in criticism of his command. How could he allow his troops to become so demoralized? So he reported that the soldier had been injured by an enemy grenade. In fact, he even embellished the story by saying that the injured soldier had thrown himself on the grenade to save his comrades. He thought that would be the end of it. He was wrong.

The account impressed the PLA headquarters staff in Beijing. When higher-ups in the PLA read the report, they sent a propaganda team to the front to interview the soldier and his commanding officer. Both of them lied to the team, sticking to their original story. The account was forwarded to Beijing and the wounded soldier was rewarded by immediate induction into the Communist Party and honored as a national hero.

The soldier knew of no way to stop the spread of the story without getting into deeper trouble. So he went along with the fabrication. When he was released from a PLA hospital he was sent on a national speaking tour to drum up continued support for the fight with Vietnam.

In our quarters we discussed the alleged hero. All of us knew men and women who'd fought in Vietnam in 1979. Some of the young men from my village, including one who worked for my father, had gone to fight in Vietnam. These men returned home 'changed,' people said. Some were melancholy much of the time and others seemed detached from the world around them. Still others were belligerent and outspoken and drank too much after coming home. I'd never before heard a single heroic eyewitness account of the struggle. When the veterans did speak about their experiences it was generally with bitterness and anger. But the hero who spoke at the Institute was different. Who was telling the truth? Or could all of the veterans be telling the truth? We wondered if our own government and officers might lie to us. And if so, why?

We read official PLA accounts of the Vietnam war and studied the tactics of the fight against the Vietnamese in the mountains near the border between the two countries. Every PLA soldier was courageous and did his duty, the official account said.

One day a 'war hero' who'd graduated from the Institute came through Nanjing and was invited to speak to the cadets. Prior to his speech he was given a special award. Nobody, however, had asked him what he had to say about Vietnam. The commanding officers assumed he'd adhere to the Party line and talk about the glories of defending the motherland.

His speech was unforgettable. 'We were sent to the front to fight the Vietnamese,' he began. 'And we had nothing against the Vietnamese and we didn't want to fight them. All we fought for was life. We wanted to live. It was a filthy business.' He went on for more than an hour telling us the horrors of the conflict in Vietnam, of the killing of prisoners by both sides, of the destruction of villages for no reason other than uncontrollable rage.

'At the front you could not lie,' he said. 'At the front you learn the truth quickly. And we learned to see through all the lies and the propaganda. We learned to see that we were simply used by the Party and that our life meant nothing to them. Several times we were shelled by our own artillery batteries,' he said. 'Some of my comrades went mad at the front. It's true. I saw it happen. Some went crazy and attacked our own officers.'

We were spellbound by his passionate recollection. His words were like drops of acid falling on our illusions. The officers on the stage with him were so shocked by his account that they apparently were unable to interrupt him or to order that his microphone be turned off. One senior officer finally stood and approached him, but the veteran turned and gave the officer a withering glare and the officer retreated to his chair.

'Yes,' he continued. 'It is true. Some of our soldiers attacked our own officers. One enraged soldier walked into a conference in the headquarters of his division and killed every officer there with an automatic weapon. When he was finished with the officers, he killed himself.

'And why did this common soldier commit such a crime? Because he was refused leave to go home and see his dying mother. When he received news that his mother was ill and he asked for leave, his commanding officer told him, 'China is your mother. You must be concerned with her now.'

When the soldier finished speaking the room was silent. After a moment one of our commanders took the microphone and apologized to the cadets and said the man was obviously not well. They would make sure, he said, that he would never again address PLA cadets. The damage he had done with his lies would take weeks to repair, the commander said. He turned to the soldier and said, 'Something happened to you. You are not the same soldier who attended this school. You are not welcome to come back here again, ever.'

We could not help but notice that his account was consistent with the accounts of the conflict given by the senior cadets and by the veterans we saw and heard in Nanjing. And these accounts were nothing at all like the official PLA version of the war. Our skepticism was growing.

viii

We experienced yet another troubling revelation in the spring of our first year. March is officially designated 'Civilization Month' by the PLA. We dreaded it. During the month the military launches a nationwide campaign to set an example for civilians. Classes were of secondary importance during the month and cleaning and performing good deeds were of primary importance.

We cleaned everything – every window, floor, toilet, shower and tile. We climbed trees and cut old branches and removed dead leaves. We used stiff brushes and cleaning powder to scrub the surface of every concrete floor. Our rooms were cleaned over and over again. Then we cleaned the dining room and the kitchen. We even cleaned the outside of every building and the roofs. Someone was stationed outside our quarters to pick up any leaves that fell from the trees before final inspection. The campus was spotless.

When we had finished cleaning our campus and passed inspection we were sent into the countryside to clean the homes of the peasants and to 'make them love the PLA.' We hated this task, but had to put on a friendly face. The twelve women went as a group to a nearby village one morning to clean the homes of the peasants. As we marched into the village singing a revolutionary song, I saw the children staring at us and I was reminded of the soldiers who'd visited my village when I was young and how they had impressed all of us and their help had been genuinely appreciated.

But things were different now. An elderly man in his seventies came to us while we were cleaning his house and said, 'I really don't know why you come here and do this. I enjoy being dirty. I don't like my house being clean. Please, after today, don't come back.'

We had thought he was going to thank us and praise the spirit of the PLA and we tried to conceal our disappointment and embarrassment that quite the opposite was true. While we continued working, photographers from the PLA took pictures of us. PLA journalists wrote long glowing accounts of our efforts and of the appreciation and love the peasants showed us for our labors. But we could tell that the peasants didn't want us there and they realized we were working for the sake of ourselves and not for them. This was just an act. I saw disgust in their faces when we gathered their children around us and posed for a photographer. Something fundamental had changed in the relationship between the peasants and the PLA since I was a child. I wasn't sure why the changes had taken place but suspected it might have something to do with the persistence of poverty in the countryside that contrasted so sharply with the prosperity of the nearby cities and of the PLA facilities.

When we finished our work in the village we were required to write a report on our activities. Without comparing notes, none of us told of the old man's request or of the cool reception we'd received from the peasants. Our reports sounded like official PLA dispatches, praising friendly peasants and describing our own joy at being able to help them. I realized then that we had absorbed the very values we questioned.

When we'd finished them our reports were broadcast over the loudspeakers on campus during our meals and in the evening. I was embarrassed to hear the exaggeratedly positive report I'd written and the ones the other women had turned in. Later we learned that many male cadets went into Nanjing 'to help the sick and the elderly cross the streets and get on and off buses.' I heard that many of them also made up those tales. Nobody checked to see if they were true. When we heard our own reports we could not help but give a guilty smile to each other. We'd learned that as long as we wrote glowing reports about our good deeds we made our superiors happy. We posed as heroes without doing anything other than writing heroic self-serving reports about our selflessness. As long as good deeds were on paper that was real enough. I began to see how optimistic PLA reports from the front in the Vietnam war had been composed. The writers had probably been soldiers exactly like us.

ix

A final eye-opening revelation came during graduation ceremonies for the senior cadets in July 1982, which were held shortly before we were dismissed for our summer vacation.

Prior to the official graduation ceremony, senior cadets were given their future assignments. All of us had come to the Institute and studied hard in the full expectation that someday we would, as commissioned PLA officers, be given important assignments. Now we learned this might not happen. A few minutes before the final graduation ceremony we heard that fifteen graduating cadets had been assigned to Tibet. We had talked about Tibet often. We were told by cadets whose friends had been sent there that life was dangerous and difficult in Tibet. Despite government reports to the contrary, soldiers wrote back that the Tibetans did not want us there. The people were unfriendly or openly hostile. No Chinese soldier felt safe when he was alone, particularly at night. There were constant acts of terrorism against the soldiers – bombs thrown into a movie theater or shots fired at them in the countryside and vandalism of PLA equipment. Our soldiers hated all Tibetans and dismissed them as animals and barbarians. The feeling was apparently mutual. Assignment to Tibet was considered tantamount to being sent to hell. It meant not merely isolation in a remote and unfriendly place but also a dead end to a military career. No soldier stationed in Tibet had the chance to make the connections or the reputation necessary to rise in the ranks of the PLA. Each year spent in Tibet meant another year out of the mainstream of military affairs. To languish in such a place was something like a slow death of one's career. And literally to die in such a place, most soldiers believed, was a complete and meaningless waste.

Moreover, even in the temporary absence of hostility and terrorism, soldiers reported that life in Tibet was a constant misery. They suffered from dizziness, headaches and nose-bleeds. They could not play sports for more than a few minutes without becoming completely exhausted. They couldn't grow their own vegetables and they had to eat canned food. Newspapers arrived fifteen days late and they were unable to receive television broadcasts from China. The assignments in Tibet were long and soldiers were allowed to return home only once every three years. It was impossible to start a family of one's own there, they said, since there were few Chinese women in Tibet. Marrying a Tibetan was, of course, utterly unthinkable.

In 1981, when assignments were made for Tibet, the commanders of the Institute made a fundamental error. They relied heavily on the sense of self-sacrifice and patriotism of the cadets. They convinced themselves that because of the education and indoctrination we'd received during our stay at the Institute any recruit would accept any assignment without protest. And although that was what everyone said, very few cadets actually believed that. After all, cadets with parents who were officers in the PLA or high-ranking cadre in the Party had them pull strings to get them into the Institute. The expectation was that education at the Institute was merely a stepping-stone to something glorious in China or abroad. Those from the most influential families, after graduation, expected to serve either in a metropolitan area of China or in some prestigious post abroad. Although hardship assignments had to be given out, the unspoken assumption was that they would go to cadets who came to the Institute from the countryside and had no connections. The same system of favoritism, in other words, that operated in the PLA and in the Party outside the Institute, it was assumed by many cadets, should operate inside the Institute. Unfortunately, in 1981 the Institute's commanders overlooked this important principle and their oversight led to an embarrassing and explosive episode following our graduation banquet.

At the official graduation ceremony the name of each senior was called and his assignment was announced. The soldier was then supposed to come forward and say how pleased he was to make a sacrifice for his country and to serve in his assigned post. Those sent to the best posts in Beijing or Shanghai or Nanjing were pleased and said so. But those assigned to Tibet were sullen and silent when their names were called.

When the ceremony was over we marched to the dining room for a lavish banquet. Many pictures were taken. All of the officers were present, sitting at a head table. The young men assigned to Tibet sat together commiserating. Fellow cadets who had been given the best assignments came to their table, shook hands, embraced and took pictures. But the more fortunate cadets dared not express their happiness because it would only remind those bound for Tibet of their misfortune.

Beer and wine were served. The graduating seniors consumed large amounts of both in drinking dozens of toasts to each other. The tables were soon cluttered with empty beer and wine bottles and the seniors shouted for more.

As the evening passed, the senior cadets became more intoxicated, outspoken and rowdy. They unbuttoned their tunics and their faces reddened. I could sense something ominous happening as their toasts became louder. Then one of the cadets assigned to Tibet stood on his chair to give a speech. Several others at his table tapped on beer bottles to get everyone's attention.

We were stunned by his slurred and drunken words. 'During our first year here,' he began, pointing to the table of the officers, 'you told us we were being trained for important assignments and that what we did was critical for our country. Well,' he shouted, 'now we know that you were just full of shit. And you know it, too. Everyone in this room knows it.'

His words were answered by cheers from the other cadets at his table. He paused for a moment and then waved for the cheering to stop. The officers glared in disbelief at the young man. He glared right back. 'Every one of you, every single one of you, is full of bullshit. You lied to us every day. And when we're gone to Tibet, you'll still be here to lie to the new cadets,' he said, sweeping his hand in a wide arc over the audience of cadets. 'But they can't say they weren't warned. Not after tonight.'

One by one the senior officers stood and walked from the room. As they left, he denounced them by name, referring to each as a 'bullshitter.'

'God damn you,' he said, as they made their exit. 'You bullshitters will pay for what you have done. Mark my words. You will pay.

'We came here and we gave you our youth. And what did you do with it? You turned it into bullshit. You took our lives and our dreams and you gave us these goddamned uniforms. And they're bullshit too.'

Every time he finished a sentence, more seniors pounded on the tables and shouted their approval. One after another, those being sent to Tibet stood on their chairs and denounced the commanding officers and the Institute and proclaimed that everything that happened there was a deception.

They continued their denunciation until the beer and wine were gone. Then, like an angry mob, the seniors stormed out of the hall. They went to the kitchen and seized the remaining cases of beer and wine and carried the booty to their barracks. Within minutes we could hear them tearing up their quarters, smashing the windows, breaking the lightbulbs, throwing furniture into the courtyard. Several young officers returned to the dining room to escort the women back to our quarters. They advised us to lock the door, turn off the lights and stay away from the windows. The seniors were 'totally out of control.' We could hardly believe what was happening.

The sound of breaking glass continued for nearly an hour. The seniors stripped to their underwear and sat outside drinking, singing, chanting and throwing empty bottles through windows. We huddled around our window and watched them. Several times they stood and raised their bottles to us and drank a toast before collapsing on the lawn.

The commander of the Institute issued an order that night saying that as long as the seniors remained on campus, they were not to be approached. They were just letting off steam, he said. But no one would be allowed outside the gate and extra sentries were posted.

In the middle of the night it rained. There was thunder and lightning but above the clatter of nature we could still hear the young men outside cursing and complaining and railing against their commanding officers. Eventually, the seniors stumbled to their quarters and went to sleep.

Early the next morning we were awakened by the roar of the engines of several trucks. One of the girls ran to the window to see what was happening and shouted, 'They are coming to take them away!' We dressed and ran outside to the parade ground. All of the senior cadets were gathered outside their barracks. Some of them were embracing, others were shaking hands. One by one they threw their packs into the trucks and climbed up after them.

When they saw us approaching they became quiet. We had never spoken personally to each other. But we had listened to them talk in classrooms and in assemblies. This was an awkward moment. We watched them and they watched us for several seconds, no one saying a word. Then the engine of one of the trucks roared and the vehicle started to pull away. The noise seemed to shatter the barrier that had separated the male and female cadets for the entire year. One of the women suddenly shouted, 'Goodbye. Take care of yourself. We will never forget you.'

The departing cadets waved to us from the trucks and shouted back, 'We will never forget you either! Long live Company 13!'

We were overwhelmed with sadness. Soon all of us were shouting goodbye and many of us were crying. We felt so sorry for them. 'We will remember you,' we told them. 'You will always be in our hearts.'

Someone started to sing 'The Internationale' and we all joined in and shouted it out at the top of our lungs. The trucks rolled slowly toward the gate and the men still waved goodbye and we cried and sang at the same time.

Then they were gone and it was quiet again. The little dust devils kicked up by the trucks whirled around us on the parade ground as we stood together, overcome with emotion. We comforted each other, embraced and returned to our quarters.

We all felt sad and helpless and a bit afraid at that moment. We imagined our classmates and ourselves, three years in the future, leaving the Institute like that, bound for Tibet. It was a horrible and a frightening thought. We gathered in a circle in our quarters and whispered about the events of the past night and the morning. All of us had worked hard and faced intense competition in order to come here, we agreed. The officers told us that we were the elite, the best students in the country and that we were being trained for sensitive assignments. But Tibet? Would we spend our lives there? After all our work and sacrifice and after all our big dreams, would they do that to us?

Some of the girls started to cry. One girl asked if we weren't sacrificing too much by coming to the Institute. 'No fun, no romance, no dating,' she said. 'Study, run, exercise, self-criticism, martial arts. What for? Tibet? Three more years of work and sacrifice for that?'

But we were trapped and we knew it. We had no choice. We had agreed that in exchange for our education we would go wherever the PLA sent us. We just never imagined it would be to Tibet. And if not Tibet, what if we were sent off to other remote posts in western China or sent to teach or serve at a military post in some other out-of-the-way place? We believed we were making sacrifices in order to serve someday in important positions – not to be exiled to a dead-end post.

Someone remembered one of the seniors saying, 'You will have to pay!' He stood and pointed at the table of the twelve women and said, 'You will have to pay for everything they give you. You get a uniform and free room and board and tuition. All you have to give back is the rest of your life. Remember my words.'

His words haunted us now. Was the Institute really preparing us for important assignments or was it the graveyard of our dreams?

'Bullshit,' one of the women whispered during a pause in our conversation. We all looked up at her in disbelief. 'Bullshit,' she said, a little louder this time, imitating the tone of the seniors who had denounced the commanders. We giggled at her casual profanity. We held hands and repeated her word, 'Bullshit!' and then we couldn't stop laughing.

On the train home that summer, two of the senior men from the Institute sat in the same compartment with me. They were on their way to their homes to visit their parents before proceeding to their new posts in Beijing. Both of them cautioned me about the coming years. 'Be careful, don't be too aggressive or too active,' they said, 'because they will select you as someone eager to make a sacrifice for them. If you are too good and work too hard for them they will take advantage of you. Other students will envy you and the officers will exploit your eagerness. They'll say, "Oh, Xu Meihong is patriotic, she will do whatever we ask of her." And then they will give you an assignment in Tibet or some other godforsaken place. So stay in the middle, always. In your grades, on the shooting range, in the exercises, in everything. Stay in the middle and you will go far.'

X

I returned to the Institute in August to start my second year. One of the first things we learned from the other cadets upon our return was that half a dozen of the seniors sent to Tibet had deserted before arriving in Lhasa. The PLA had tried to hunt them down and to force them to serve in that distant post, but they resisted and refused. Their punishment was expulsion from the PLA and a black mark on their record. The Army wanted to keep their protests out of the news and prevent it from demoralizing other cadets and hoped that leniency might perhaps quiet the turncoats. Also, the men were well connected and supported by their parents. The commanders at the Institute did not wish to arouse the anger of influential critics. Each of the deserters, we were told, because of the language skills they'd acquired at the Institute, had immediately taken good-paying jobs with joint ventures in the same cities where they'd expected to be assigned by the PLA. We were shocked at how easily they'd slipped from the military harness and found new freedom. There was a kind of heroism in their defiance of PLA authority, we felt, and although we knew they'd done wrong we couldn't help but feel a bit of admiration for them.

The Institute's commanders learned from their mistake in the spring of 1982. After that the cadets selected for service in Tibet were young men of peasant background without any influential connections. These men prized Party membership – which was given along with their assignment to Tibet – and certificates attesting to their heroic status. They saw the sacrifice of service in the Himalayas as an honor. Thus, they became grateful and convenient victims for the PLA and there were no more insurrections following graduation ceremonies at the Institute.

By our senior year all twelve girls at the Institute were both bolder and more melancholy than we'd been in the past. We found boyfriends, defied our commanding officers in small acts of rebellion and were increasingly aware that we would soon be going our separate ways after being together for four years. We also faced the fact that each of us owed the PLA fifteen years of service as repayment for our education and training. I looked at that service obligation and reflected on the dreams I'd had on entering the Institute and I couldn't help but conclude that I should have followed the advice of some of my high school teachers who recommended that I attend a civilian university. My years in the Institute in Nanjing, I felt, except for meeting Lin Cheng, had been largely a waste.

On the day our final banquet was held and we were handed our degrees, we twelve women had our picture taken as a group for the last time. We smiled and laughed and joked with each other, but there was a deep sadness at our parting. We had depended on each other for support and strength for four years. We trusted and protected each other. We remembered our first days at the Institute when we received our uniforms and went through the exercise sessions and then the emergency drills. Now we were so different, wiser and more mature and skeptical than we had been four years earlier. We'd received the education and training we had been promised by the PLA. But we had also learned much outside the classroom from each other. And along the way we'd lost most of our optimism and our youthful dreams.

There remains a sacred chamber in my memory for the women of my company. We breathed the same air day and night for four years, practiced on the same parade grounds, studied in the same classrooms, slept in the same rooms, laughed and cried together. We loved each other and showed it daily in our acts. We shared everything and kept no secrets from each other. We dreamed and then lost the same dreams, enjoyed the same successes and suffered the same disappointments.

When we first came to Nanjing we were young and innocent and red and they told us we were national treasures. And we were.

xi

Night after night in Nanyang, alone in my room, I remembered my days at the Institute and the eleven women I'd shared those years with. It was so strange to look around me now and see where the road from the Institute had taken me. Everything I'd ever dreamed was ashes now – my idealism, my faith, my hope, my career, my husband and soon my life. I wondered if the other women from the group could understand or sympathize with my plight or if they'd ever know how much I missed them now.

TEN

Remember

The horses will keep on running, and the
dancers – they will keep on dancing.

— DENG XIAOPING

i

At the end of each day I returned from work on the street of the Nanyang Oil Company to my room. I walked along the side of the road used by the big oil trucks heading for the city of Nanyang. One after another they rumbled past, each pushing out a wake of fumes and dust that ascended and stained the evening sky a dismal sepia.

As I walked, I saw how simple it might be to step in front of a truck and end my life in the blink of an eye. Many times I stood unmoving at the roadside for several minutes and tried to summon the courage to take that step. I'm still not sure why I could not do it. I wonder, though, if my hesitation wasn't the result of a fragment of hope still hooked on a shard of memory. I'd seen the whimsy of fate and sudden reversals of fortune in the past. Though I found little to live for I held on to life.

I became quiet and uncommunicative and increasingly detached from the world around me. I passed through life like a sleepwalker. One evening while cutting vegetables for dinner I accidentally sliced through the skin on one of my fingers. I was aware only of a slight sting and paid no attention to it. Several minutes later I noticed the water in the bowl I was using was scarlet and only then did I discover what I'd done.

After turning off the lamp at night I lay in bed staring out the window at the stars and listening to the nocturnal whisper of the wind pushing through a grove of nearby trees. I closed my eyes and lured back visions of life before I arrived in Nanjing. I fixed on a happy day – a felicitous moment, even – and tasted its sweetness until sleep mercifully swallowed me.

When the waxy light of a new day woke me I realized I was still tethered to life. I rose dutifully and began again my daily routine. I dressed, started a fire and prepared breakfast, rinsed my face without looking into the mirror, pulled on my sweater, jacket and scarf and walked to work. Three days after I received Lin Cheng's letter asking for a divorce a telegram from him arrived. He said he'd had time to reconsider his request for a divorce and concluded he'd been wrong. He apologized and asked me to forgive him. 'I love you,' he said, 'and will never leave you. I'll do my utmost to help you and to help us get out of this terrible situation.' I realized that, like me, he was still struggling to untangle romantic recollections and hopes from the implacable imperatives we faced. His initial resolute pronouncement, I sensed, was tempered now by both memory and guilt. He was unsure as to what to do or what could be done.

I understood his vacillation. I felt it, too. I regretted all the heartbreak and trouble I'd caused. I often wondered if Lin Cheng was sorry he'd met me or what he thought now when he remembered our happy times together. But I didn't ask him those questions. Our first furtive meetings at the Institute and our innocent conspiracy to become lovers, the plans we'd made and the loyalty and affection we'd shown each other seemed to me now like something that happened to other people in another world I'd only imagined. Had it ever really happened to me or was it simply a passage in a novel I'd read?

We'd been so in love when we were young and innocent. But we became entangled in dark realities we never imagined existed. The world intruded and pulled us apart. Since autumn we had been moving in opposite directions. I understood Lin Cheng and his frustrations, weaknesses and elusive dreams. He stood beside me during difficult times. I was grateful for that. If our roles had been reversed, I wondered, could I have been stronger or more loyal than he? Because I respected and understood him I could not ask him to sacrifice any more of his life for me.

I took a bus to Nanyang to have my fortune told. Several workers spoke glowingly of a woman in the city who was a gifted seer. They said she'd inherited her supernatural powers from her mother and grandmother. I found the old woman telling fortunes on the street, charging five yuan for a session. I handed her the money and she folded it and put it in her shoe. Then she asked me to remove my gloves and she studied my palms carefully and looked into my eyes for a long time. 'Your marriage is in grave danger,' she told me in a low, concerned voice. 'Your husband is very troubled about the relationship.' I was startled by her prescience.

'Go on,' I said excitedly. 'What else do you see? What will happen?'

She studied my palms again and traced the lines in them with her finger. Then she concluded, 'You will leave this place soon. You will travel far. Very far. You will have many adventures. You will have a child – one child – no more. You will live a long life. You will live to see your great-grandchildren.'

Then she released my hands and said she could see no more. I handed her another five yuan and her powers miraculously returned. She studied my palms some more.

'If you wish to save your marriage,' she said, 'you must remain here. You must visit a temple tomorrow. Light one hundred joss sticks. Then face the east and pray while they burn. The gods will hear your prayer and they will save your marriage.'

That night I didn't sleep. I read through Lin Cheng's letters again and again and thought about our happiest moments together – our wedding, our promises to each other and our dreams. My problem was not mine alone. My problem was already affecting his career in the military. He had not been promoted as expected following the Spring Festival. He had been scheduled to escort General Zhang Zhen, the president of the NDU, on a visit to the United States and Southeast Asia. But at the last minute he'd been removed from that duty and replaced by a junior officer. People looked at him differently since his wife was accused of involvement with an American agent. What's more, the conservative old guard in the PLA still suspected that Lin Cheng was part of an underground clique of officers. They were simply waiting for

313

an opportune moment to detain him and his co-conspirators.

If I left Lin Cheng, I reasoned, I might save him from suspicion and even arrest. In doing that, I felt, I might repay him for the embarrassment and suffering I'd caused him. He could start a new life and in time fulfill most of his dreams. And by accepting the consequences of my actions and letting go of what was surely already lost, I too might find, in time, peace in my decision. If I was beyond redemption, as I suspected I was, then there was no valid reason to accept Lin Cheng's offer of further sacrifice. I was very deeply touched by his declaration of love. And I would always cherish it. But I knew that whatever happiness and security life might still hold for me could never be secured in China. The General had advised me to wait for an opportune moment, a moment, perhaps, of national chaos, and then take advantage of it and leave China. Saving my husband required only that I accept reality. Saving myself meant waiting for a miracle to happen. I decided to try my best to do both.

I didn't go to the temple the next day. I didn't want to save my marriage anymore. He deserved a better life.

In early May I received a thick letter from Lin Cheng. He'd enclosed correspondence from my parents and my sister along with a short letter from my childhood friend Zhong Yuhua, who was teaching at Qinghua University in Beijing. Her message was brief. 'Dear Meihong,' she wrote. 'Do you remember our talk in Lishi? I must tell you now that hell has broken loose. Come to Beijing.'

I felt my heart start pounding. What was she talking about? I hadn't heard a radio or read a newspaper since leaving Nanjing three months ago. I hurried back to the mailroom and asked the clerk if she had any newspapers. She rummaged through the papers on her desk and found a week-old copy of *The People's Daily* and handed it to me.

There it was on the first page. Students and workers were in the streets in Beijing following a memorial service for the late Hu Yaobang. They were calling for an end to corruption and for democracy. Thousands of people were descending on Beijing to join the demonstrations and similar disruptions were beginning in other cities.

'Oh, God,' I said to myself. I was shaking so much I could hardly hold the paper. 'Thank you, God, thank you, thank you,' I whispered. The girl stared at me as though I was crazed.

I walked out of the mailroom, looked around me, thought of going back for dinner and decided against it. I stood in the same place for a long time contemplating my next move. I reached in my pocket to see if I had my wallet. I did. But I had no money with me. It made no difference, I thought. I didn't want to waste time going home. I'd get by. I knew what I had to do and I had to do it immediately.

I walked from the mailroom to the road and again stood there watching the trucks roll by. After several passed I spotted a driver I knew. I waved for him to stop. 'I need to get to Nanyang,' I told him. 'Can you give me a lift?'

'Sure,' he said, and smiled broadly. 'I can always use company. Especially that of a pretty girl.'

I climbed in beside him. 'You old hooligan!' I said, and pushed his shoulder. He laughed out loud and I laughed with him. I was suddenly happy and felt the irrational desire to embrace him. 'Can you take me to the Nanyang train station?' I asked.

'Sure,' he said. 'Are you leaving us?'

'Just for a few days,' I lied. 'I need to visit a sick friend.'

'Without any luggage?' he asked, giving me a skeptical look.

I didn't know what to say. But I didn't have to say anything, because he smiled broadly and said, 'I knew you'd leave here someday, Xu Meihong. You weren't made for this place. You don't fit in. Everybody here sees that. Just be careful.'

I almost burst into tears when he spoke. 'Thank you,' I said. 'I won't forget you. I won't forget this ride.' He smiled and nodded.

I watched out the window as we rolled down the long bumpy road. The oil derricks in the nearby fields rushed by and the people trudging along beside the road became a blur and I smiled and felt tears well up in my eyes.

I was anxious and excited at the same time. For a while I watched in the rearview mirror as the sun settled below the horizon, its light flickering through the haze of the afternoon sky like a forest fire far away. Then I turned my gaze to the lengthening shadow of our truck on the dark ribbon of road ahead. We were heading east into the night. The driver was humming an old love song and I was listening to him and smiling. Ahead of me was a starless darkness but beyond that darkness was a new day and, I prayed, a new world.

ii

The driver dropped me off at the train station and wished me luck. I asked him to tell the supervisor and his wife that I had to leave for Beijing and he promised he would.

Thousands of people crowded the station trying to buy tickets. I had no money, so I didn't have to worry about standing in a long line. I merely looked at the schedule and saw when the next train departed for Beijing. Then I plunged headlong into the sea of people rushing toward an exit and let myself be pushed along with them onto the long platform outside. Within minutes I was on the Beijing-bound train.

All I had to do after that, I knew, was elude the conductor for the next sixteen hours. Initially, I stood in an aisle with dozens of other passengers. I was wearing work clothes, so I blended in perfectly with the mass of those who could afford only standing-room tickets. Whenever I saw a conductor approaching to check tickets I made my way to the bathroom and locked the door.

The lights in the aisles were dimmed around midnight. Most seated passengers fell asleep. Others stood talking in hushed tones, smoking or staring out the window at the blackness surrounding us. I decided to take a calculated risk. I walked through several cars until I found an unoccupied compartment. I stepped inside and closed the door behind me. I was exhausted. I lay down on one of the bottom bunks in the compartment and fell asleep almost immediately.

I was awakened later by a man shaking me by the shoulder and asking gruffly, 'Hey, who do you think you are, anyway?

And what the hell are you doing in my bed?'

I sat up and rubbed my eyes and responded, 'This is my seat, sir.'

'The hell it is,' he said. 'It's mine. I am the senior engineer on this train and that's my bed.' I realized, with the lights now on, that this compartment was reserved for the train's engineers when they finished their shifts.

'But I work on the train, too,' I said. It was absurd, but I didn't know what else to say.

'What do you do?' he demanded.

'I'm . . . an assistant engineer.'

He exploded in laughter. 'That's good,' he said. 'Very good. I've never in my life seen an assistant engineer like you.'

The door opened and two more engineers stepped inside. 'Look what we have here,' the senior engineer said, pointing to me. 'We have another engineer on board.' They all laughed as they sat down across from me on the other bunk.

'What the hell?' the senior engineer roared. 'So you're stealing a ride to Beijing. Good for you. What's it to me anyway? You can stay. Just get into the top bunk. We're going to play cards down here. And we're going to smoke and we're going to swear and if you don't like it you can leave,' he said, smiling broadly and winking at me. He knew I wouldn't leave.

The gods must be watching over me, I thought. My luck seemed to have changed. I thanked the senior engineer over and over again and climbed up into the top bunk, which he pulled out for me. The four men sat on the bottom bunks facing each other with a small table between them. They smoked cigarettes one after another, opened and consumed several bottles of liquor and played cards.

I slept soundly while engineers entered and left the compartment during the night. The next morning I remained in the top bunk and the engineers brought me food. We sat and talked about things that were happening in Beijing. I had hundreds of questions for them, and although they had little firsthand information, they said they supported the calls for an end to corruption and more democracy. They had children, they said, and they wanted to see their children

317

grow up in a better China and not experience the same struggles and injustices they'd experienced. When we arrived in Beijing the senior engineer said he was sorry to see me go, because he'd enjoyed our talks. He asked if I needed anything, since he saw I carried no luggage. I asked him if he could 'loan' me bus fare to get to a friend's place. He reached into his pocket and pulled out two ten-yuan notes and handed them to me. 'Take this,' he said. I tried to give one of the bills back to him, but he pushed it away. 'Just stay out of trouble, assistant engineer,' he said.

'Thank you, senior engineer,' I responded. 'You are a kind man.'

He winked and waved. I hopped down off the train and walked with the crowd through the station and then up into the street. Thousands of students were arriving on trains, milling around outside the station, finding friends and hurrying off in all directions. I walked among them and listened to their excited chatter. Some were going to university campuses and some were heading for Tiananmen Square. I asked for directions and was shown where to catch the bus to Qinghua University. I watched out the window as I rode through Beijing. As I watched the commotion in the streets, I felt I was in the midst of a wonderful dream and I was right where I wanted to be – in the middle of it. I thought of the kindness and the generosity of the truck driver and the senior engineer, and I couldn't stop smiling. I glanced down at the tiny silver chain on my wrist and wondered if at last it was working its fabled magic.

iii

Zhong Yuhua was very happy to see me standing outside her door in my dusty work clothes. She pulled me into her room and then held my hands. 'Everything is going to be all right again,' she assured me. 'There's going to be a new future for us.'

The words spilled from her in a torrent as she tried to tell me everything that had happened in Beijing since the death of Hu Yaobang in mid-April. It was nearly unbelievable. The universities – including her own – had become centers of protest and insurrection. The indignation and anger after years of corruption and mismanagement erupted in public demonstrations and open defiance of the Party. Huge banners covered the walls of the universities calling for an end to the corruption and demanding democratic reforms. Li Peng and Deng Xiaoping were denounced and the numbers of those demanding change multiplied daily.

I'd never heard Yuhua speak with such optimism before. We were village girls and our expectations of change in China had been bracketed by official propaganda. Dramatic change, we'd been taught, would bring erosion and the destruction of socialism and eventually a return to anarchism, warlordism and the rule of landlords. Suddenly, those assumptions seemed absurd. Change could make things better, millions of students and workers concluded. The old order was crumbling by the hour.

We both believed that a new world was at hand and that the stains of the past would be washed away. There was a universal feeling that China had arrived at a turning point and that this was a good time to be alive. The people were going to stand up and make history again. Students who made plans to study abroad and in the fall of 1989 changed their plans and decided to stay in China and help bring a new world into existence.

Yuhua loaned me clean clothing and then we walked around the campus and listened to student speeches and read the posters displayed on nearly every wall. That evening I called Lin Cheng at the NDU and told him I was in Beijing. He immediately came to meet me.

That night Lin Cheng and I had dinner with a friend and his girlfriend, a college student. I said little during the evening but listened to the girl tell stories about the demonstrations and the excitement at her school. Later that night Lin Cheng told me how lucky he thought his friend was to have a girlfriend like that. At another time I might have let the

319

remark pass. But now, each word stung me. How very unlucky he was, I thought, to have a wife like me.

After dinner we were left alone and I told him that I wanted to apply for the divorce as quickly as possible. 'I am a burden to you,' I reminded him. 'We both know that, Lin Cheng. I will be a burden to you until I go away. I understand why you're uncertain about the divorce. But for your sake, as well as mine, it's necessary. I have to divorce you because I love you and want you to be happy.' When I stopped speaking it was quiet for a moment. Then each of us started to cry and we embraced for a long time and tasted each other's tears. We agreed we had to be strong and help each other. The past and all that had happened to us would always be ours. We had to settle for that alone now. And we had to accept the fact that the future was not ours. This was not all our fault, I felt. But it was our fate. And I believed in fate.

He agreed. Then he said he would do everything within his power to help me.

As soon as we'd decided to file for divorce, I experienced a peacefulness in my heart. We became best friends, loyal to each other on a different level now. He was still so kind and deferential. We held hands when we went for walks. We would kiss goodbye when we parted. I'd watch him arrive and leave. We had our meals together, cooked for each other and visited friends who thought we were the perfect couple again. People sometimes said, when they saw us holding hands or walking, that we were like newlyweds. But our days together were numbered. The moments were precious now.

iv

M y first concern after arranging to start divorce proceedings was finding a job so I could earn some money and not burden my husband or Yuhua any more.

After searching for a week I finally found employment

through an old military friend. He had been an officer at the NDU, had gone abroad and studied at Stanford University for a year and then returned to China and became a high ranking officer in Beijing. His wife managed a large air cargo business in China. The company had branch offices throughout the world. In the spring of 1989 they were planning to host a big international conference in Beijing. I was hired to manage the conference on a temporary basis.

The work was hard and the workdays were long but I didn't mind. I lost myself in my duties. Sometimes, during my lunch break, I walked to Tiananmen Square and mixed with the students and workers who were gathered there. I noticed hundreds of foreigners at the square – many of them Americans. I began to wonder if I'd been told the truth about Larry during my interrogation. Had he really left China or was that merely another lie the Colonel fed me? I even imagined that he might be in Beijing. I called the Jianguo Hotel several times to see if he'd checked in or made reservations. He hadn't. My curiosity increased. I decided finally to call Nanjing.

'But what if the Center operator recognizes my voice and traces my call?' I asked myself. 'Will she report me to the MSS or to the Institute?' I decided to take that risk. I had to find out what had happened to Larry.

I remembered Larry's room number at the Center. I asked the operator at the Center for room 506. The phone rang once and a woman answered. I asked to speak to Professor Engelmann.

'Who?' she said. 'I'm sorry. I don't know who that is.'

'You must know him,' I said. 'He's lived there and taught there since September. Can you tell me where he is?' I asked.

'I have no idea,' she said. 'I don't know him. I arrived here a few months ago, but I've never heard of him.' I described him, and she said again, 'I'm very sorry, I can't help you,' and hung up.

I thought about him during the next day and decided to make another call. I went back to the post office and phoned the Center again. I asked for Tao Xiaoying, my classmate and friend from the Institute who was studying at the Center at that time.

She immediately recognized my voice. 'Where are you?' she whispered.

'Beijing,' I replied. 'What happened to him?'

She responded, 'I can't tell you anything, because I don't know anything about him.' It was a tense conversation and I suspected her phone was tapped.

'Where is he?' I asked.

'I don't know.' Another long pause. Then she said, tersely, 'I have work to do. I can't talk anymore. Goodbye.' Then she hung up.

'Where is he?' I wondered. I suspected something terrible had happened to him. I called the Center a third time and asked for Carol Chu. I thought she had to know where he was. I was told she was in Shanghai and would not be back until the following day.

The next evening I called the Center again and asked for her. When she answered the phone I said, 'It's me.' She recognized my voice. I told her I was in Beijing. She was cautious and gave only brief answers to my questions. Neither of us used specific names.

'Are you OK?' she asked.

'Yes, I am,' I assured her. 'Where is our friend? Is he OK?'

'He's in Hong Kong or Thailand,' she said. 'I'm not sure. He's finishing his book. He's OK, too.'

'I'm coming to see you,' I said. 'I want to talk to you.'

'Why?' she asked.

'I need to talk with you.'

'When?'

'At the end of the month,' I told her.

'Call me when you arrive,' she said. Then we hung up.

I was sure I sensed fear in her voice.

When my employer's convention concluded at the end of May my boss thanked me for the work I'd done and asked if I'd stay on. I agreed but told her I'd like a brief break.

I used the money I'd earned to buy a train ticket to Nanjing.

V

My train was scheduled to leave for Nanjing at 10.30 P.M. Early in the day of my departure I received a phone call from the General. He'd gotten my number from Lin Cheng, he told me. He was now in Beijing attending a meeting at the PLA headquarters. He had been summoned there from Nanjing for the national emergency. He said he would send a driver for me and meet me at Kunming Lake that afternoon.

The first thing he asked me was why I'd returned so suddenly. I confided that I thought China might be undergoing a dramatic change.

'There will be no change,' he said. 'The Army is going to wipe out the students. If you wish to remain alive, please do not go near the square again.'

I did not want to believe this. At first I objected. 'This can't be true. Look at all the American correspondents there and the students from other countries. People are watching on television all over the world. This cannot happen. They won't do it.'

He smiled and shook his head and said, 'Where did you ever get such a silly idea? They *will* most certainly do it. Believe me, the Army is the Army. Power is what is most important to the rulers of this country. Don't you know that by now? How short is your memory? They don't care what foreigners think. They don't care what the students want. The demonstrators are threatening their power. That is what they are thinking about. So the students will die. You were in the Army. Don't be so naive.

'Listen, Meihong,' he concluded. 'You have caused them trouble once. If they catch you again, here, you are dead. You know that, don't you? Must I remind you of that?'

'Then what shall I do?'

'The student movement is not an important consideration

323

for you. It will be crushed. The most important thing for you to do is to get out of China.'

'I want to leave, but I don't know how.'

'You are smart. I think you can find a way.'

'I was thinking about ways,' I told him. 'I know someone who can help me find Larry. She's in Nanjing. I called the Center. I'm going there tonight.'

'Be very careful,' he said. 'This may be the best time to go but you have to be cautious. Keep your trip secret from everyone. Take advantage of the chaos here.'

As we parted, he told me again I should try to get to America. But he also warned me to prepare for disappointment. 'Americans are not like Chinese,' he said. 'The Chinese are loyal to personal friends. So this Larry Engelmann may not be willing to help you – you should be prepared to be rejected by him. Try to think of someone else who can help you. Don't count on any one person and don't expect any American to feel an obligation to you. Most of the past, you will find, is meaningless to the Americans.'

But I did have faith in Larry. I don't know why I was so certain of it. But I was. If there was one person in the whole world who would help me, no matter how difficult my situation, it was he. But how could I find him?

That night I took the train to Nanjing – a twenty-hour ride – standing all the way. After I arrived I checked into a small rooming house near Gulou. I remembered the young girl fixing shoes on the nearby street and Larry's conversation with her. She was gone now. I recalled sitting in the little park across the street from Gulou talking and laughing with Larry.

I called Carol from the post office. She answered after one ring and I told her I was in the city, not far away. She asked to meet me in front of Zhou's restaurant in one hour, exactly.

I waited anxiously for the minutes to pass. I was suddenly extremely nervous. I took a walk through the Nanjing University campus to calm myself and I saw the wall where I'd stood beside Larry the last night we'd walked together. The world around the Center was redolent with memories of good times for me.

I passed Zhou's and then stood in a storefront a few

buildings away. The time for our meeting passed. I looked at my watch every few seconds and wondered if something had gone wrong, if this might have been a plot and Carol had been detained by the police. I decided to wait for ten more minutes and if she didn't show up I'd return to my rooming house, check out and catch a train to Beijing. Five minutes later, I saw Carol approaching.

I pretended to be shopping. I looked at merchandise stacked on tables in front of the store. She didn't see me at first. She hesitated outside Zhou's, peered inside the restaurant and looked up and down the street. I stepped into the street and she saw me. But the moment our eyes met, I knew something was terribly wrong.

She looked frightened. She walked towards me and I stared past her up the street so she would continue walking by me. Then I waited for a minute and watched the street behind her, trying to see if she'd been followed. When I was sure she was alone I walked up beside her.

We turned down a small alley and then came out onto a main street and continued walking quickly. Each of us was nervous, looking behind us several times. Half a year earlier, when I was still a student in the Center, Carol had nothing good to say about China and the Chinese government. She'd told me many times how the best thing that ever happened to her family was leaving China and settling in America. But now she talked positively about China and the Party. 'I wrote a letter to my brother inviting him to visit China,' she said. 'I think China is going to be wonderful this summer.' She seemed to be saying lines she'd rehearsed. She measured her words carefully, as if we were being recorded. I asked what had happened to Larry. 'Oh, he is doing just fine,' she said. 'He's in Hong Kong finishing his book.' I asked if she was in touch with him and she said occasionally she wrote or heard from him.

'He asks about you every time he writes,' she said. 'I didn't know what happened, so I had nothing to tell him.'

I told her I needed to get in touch with Larry right away. 'I need your help,' I said. 'Can you give me his address and telephone number in Hong Kong?' I asked.

She didn't respond for several seconds and then she said,

'Have you any idea what you did to him?'

'What do you mean?' I asked.

'You signed a statement – the State Security Police showed it to the Chinese co-director and he told the American administrators about it.'

'What statement, Carol? I never did anything to hurt Larry. Truly.'

'Xu Meihong, tell the truth. You signed a statement saying Larry assaulted you at the Center. You . . .'

'I never signed or said anything like that, Carol. Never. You've got to believe me.'

'They showed it to the Chinese co-director. He described it to the Chinese students at one of their meetings to discredit Larry. The American authorities demanded he resign and leave China.'

'Carol, I never signed anything like that.'

'The American faculty tried to protect him. But he had to leave China. And he loved it here. People in the Center say you hurt him deliberately. Why? He did nothing to hurt you.'

'Carol, I played no part in that. I want to get in touch with him. I'll explain it all. Just tell me where he is.'

'No!' she said with blunt finality. 'Absolutely not.' Each of her words was like a stab at my heart. Neither of us spoke for a time and then she continued: 'I am not going to serve as your go-between. I am not going to help you. You can find somebody else to assist you in doing what you think you have to do.'

'If you feel that way, why did you agree to meet me?'

'I wanted to see you one more time, to tell you what had happened.' Carol sounded like a complete stranger talking to me.

'Carol, who told you these things about me?'

She ignored my questions and continued, 'You know, Meihong, Larry never believed you signed that statement. Till the day he left he thought you were forced to write it. I am sure Larry will be delighted to see you in California someday, if you ever make it there. But I don't want you to contact him while he's still in Asia because that would be a disaster. We both know if you ask him to help you he is just irrational enough to do it. I'll have no part of it.

'He's crazy, you know,' she continued. 'He keeps writing letters trying to find you or trying to find someone to find you. He sent everyone at the Center his business card and asked them to give it to you if they ever saw you. I threw mine away. I think others did, too. And I don't even read his letters anymore. He's obsessed with you. You have already hurt him. Are you planning to hurt him again? It will only be worse this time.'

We made a circle of the campus of Nanjing University. Finally as I saw we were nearing the Center again I realized that my one contact with Larry was beyond reach.

'Will you see him this summer?' I asked.

'Perhaps,' she said.

'I want you to give him something for me. Would you do that?'

'Not a letter,' she replied. 'I won't carry anything with your name or address on it.'

I was still wearing the bracelet Larry had given me. But I didn't want to part with that – not yet. It had gotten me through many difficult times and I thought now I'd probably need its good luck in the future. I was also wearing the watch that Carol and Larry had bought for me in Beijing to thank me for being their tour guide. I quickly unfastened the watch and handed it to her. 'I am very poor right now,' I said. 'This is the most valuable thing I own. I want you to give this to Larry when you see him. I think he will remember me when he sees it and will be reminded of our happy days in Beijing. I don't want to make trouble for him. And I don't want to bother him and I don't want to bother you. I've caused enough trouble.'

'All right,' she said. She took the watch and said goodbye. Then she turned and was gone. I watched her for several seconds and then turned and hurried back to my rooming house. Later, I learned that as soon as I was out of sight, she crossed the street, found an open sewer and dropped the watch into it. She told Larry later that she feared I might report the watch missing and file a complaint against her. Or perhaps there was even a recording device or an explosive in it, she feared. She was scared to death of me. But I appreciated the fact that she took her time to meet me that day and I'd always respect her courage. Others might not even have dared to answer my phone call.

That night in Nanjing I believed that Larry would soon have the watch and he would remember me and know I was still alive and missed him. It might take a long time, I thought, but if he really wants to find me, he will find me.

I left Nanjing the next evening, June 2, and arrived in Beijing on the afternoon of June 3.

vi

B eijing was hot and humid. I found a bus to take me to the NDU, which is outside Beijing. I planned to stay in Lin Cheng's quarters until I began my new job. Then I'd move into the company's dormitory.

On the way out of Beijing, I saw troops in trucks along the side of the street heading into the city. The trucks sat bumper to bumper and the officers were in cars racing up and down the line supervising the caravan. The soldiers were helmeted and in uniform and all had weapons at the ready as they rode. It reminded me of photographs I'd seen of the PLA going into battle. People walking along the street or on bicycles and in buses watched the soldiers and demanded they turn around and leave the city. Some people shook their fists and denounced them. The people in my bus erupted in shouting and yelling. They leaned far out the windows and yelled, 'Go back! Go back! Why are you coming to Beijing? Go home!' Others were swearing at them. But the soldiers stared straight ahead and refused to make eye contact. The trucks, without flags or any military insignia, continued slowly on their way into the city.

The soldiers were young – seventeen or eighteen years old – about the age I had been when I came into the Army. They looked like provincial forces, thoroughly awed and intimidated by the crowds.

That night Lin Cheng had invited a half dozen fellow officers to watch television with him in his apartment. While they watched the news they discussed what they'd heard about troop movements. Some had heard rumors that the soldiers carried tear gas and rubber bullets to clear Tiananmen Square. The consensus was that nobody would be hurt. There might be bruises and some demonstrators would be disabled by tear gas – but that was as serious as it would get.

We watched the evening news on TV. The news consisted of directives from the Party. The same words were repeated again and again: 'We recommend that all of the people on the streets go home, and people in Tiananmen Square please return to your campuses or your homes. Please do not remain outside.'

None of us could fall asleep that night. Everyone was talking, wondering what might happen. About midnight we heard the sound of distant gunfire. We were too far from Tiananmen to be hearing it from there. It was closer. Clearly, it was automatic weapons fire. The television stations were not broadcasting at that time, so we turned on the radio to listen to the Voice of America and the BBC. We heard that the troops had arrived at Tiananmen Square and were clearing it. We could not tell, beyond that, what was happening. So we simply sat around and talked and waited for the morning when local television broadcasts might fill us in on what happened.

About 6 A.M. a friend came to the door and told us, 'They killed the students. They killed them all.'

We turned on VOA again. They were saying that hundreds of students had been killed. They played recordings of the gunfire and the screaming and fighting. Then there were rumors on the campus and on the radio that fighting had broken out between different units of the Army.

We found a minivan later that morning to take us into the city. We wanted to see for ourselves what had happened. What we saw was unbelievable. Cars and military trucks were lined up along the streets where I'd seen them the previous afternoon. Now they were empty and burned. Some were still on fire, with thick smoke drifting off into the air in long threads. It was like a war movie. The closer we came to the center of the city, the more devastation we saw. The metal dividers placed in the middle of the road had been knocked down and crushed. Carcasses of cars and trucks lined the street all the way into the city. People were standing around watching them burn. I saw no soldiers in the street until we neared the center of the city, where we saw tanks rumbling up and down the boulevards.

Later that day we turned on the TV and heard newsmen announce that the PLA had achieved 'another victory' and that Beijing was under their control.

On my way out of the city I saw enraged crowds of people everywhere denouncing the brutality of the PLA. The soldiers had killed everyone – students, women, children, they said, 'from babies to ninety-year-olds' – and had randomly fired into the windows of apartments where they saw lights or movement.

There were also reports that enraged citizens had stopped trucks filled with soldiers and mobbed them. Officers lost control. Soldiers were killed. Someone said that an entire company had disappeared in Beijing. An entire company! 'They can't find them,' others said. 'They just disappeared,' and they laughed when they said it. Others said that the soldiers had been killed and cremated in the same way the soldiers had killed and burned the students.

People threw food and rocks and almost anything else they could pick up at the soldiers. Women and children on the balconies of buildings overlooking the street threw down potted plants, small appliances and books and bricks. Some of the troops tried to disguise themselves and hide. They threw away their tunics. But they were still recognized by their white Army shirts and military trousers. They were beaten senseless or killed by mobs.

It seemed China was no longer my country. What had been done secretly to individuals in the past now had been done publicly to masses of people before the eyes of the entire world. The Party and the PLA feared no one and did what they needed to do to stay in power.

I began my new job two weeks after the Tiananmen massacre. I'd worked only for four weeks before agents from the

Second Bureau of the PLA found me. They told my manager that I had serious political problems and that I was forbidden to be in contact with foreigners. They warned her that she was responsible if I violated that restriction. She told me the next day she could not keep me much longer and that I'd better make other plans.

Agents from the Second Bureau also went to my husband and warned him that his wife did not belong in Beijing. Non-Beijing residents were not allowed to remain in Beijing after the Tiananmen massacre. But he told them I needed to remain in Beijing while our divorce was pending. They cautioned him that he was responsible for reporting any wrongdoing he might suspect me of.

That night he called me and told me it would be best if I left the country as soon as possible. They would follow me all my life, he feared. 'There will never be a normal life for you in China again,' he said. 'You have to leave.'

'But how?' I asked. I was told that after June 4 the government traced international phone calls and censored all international correspondence. I couldn't afford getting caught contacting Larry. I sought the help of Yuhua. She introduced me to a friend from her university who was going to the University of Kansas in August. He agreed to mail a letter to Larry for me once he arrived in the United States. I composed a short formal letter. 'Dear Professor Engelmann,' I wrote. 'Do you remember a girl you met in China named Xu Meihong? She remembers you. She thinks of you often. She needs your help. If you remember her and you would like to help her, please contact me.' Then I wrote my phone number at work and the address of Yuhua at the Qinghua University faculty dormitory and requested that my real name not be used on the envelope. I signed my letter 'Yours always, Rose.'

I also provided the friend with Larry's office phone number and asked him to call before mailing the letter to make sure Larry was still at San Jose State University.

I thought it would take at least until the end of August for the letter to get to Larry. If there was no response in that time, then I'd conclude he didn't want to get in touch with me.

My time was running out. I expected to lose my job at any moment and to be forced out of Beijing and move to some remote place where it's impossible to contact the outside world. I had to get in touch with Larry as soon as possible. I decided to take another gamble and to call him from my office. I arrived at work early in the morning two days after the PLA officers spoke with my boss about me. I still had a piece of paper I'd folded carefully inside a book with his home and office phone numbers on it. I assumed the numbers had not been changed and that he might still be reached at them. I called at 7 A.M., when only one other worker was in the office with me. I knew it was late afternoon in California. A man answered. When I asked for Larry he said I had the wrong number and hung up before I could ask him another question. I thought I must have dialed incorrectly, so I dialed again, very slowly this time. The same man answered and I asked for Larry again, and again he said I had the wrong number. He was angrier this time and he told me to stop calling him. I didn't know what mistake I might be making. I'd never before dialed a foreign long-distance call, so I was sure I'd misdialed. I asked the other girl in the office, a good friend, to dial for me. The same man answered a third time.

The next day I called Larry's office. As I listened to the ringing, I felt a wave of panic. What if the line was tapped? I didn't want to take a chance, so I decided not to mention my name. Rather I prayed that he'd recognize my voice. A recorded voice came on – I recognized it as his – and he said he wasn't in the office and that the caller should leave a message. I said softly, as if I was afraid someone might overhear me, 'Professor Engelmann, I need your help. Please call . . .' but I was speaking so softly, the machine apparently concluded no one was on the line and cut me off.

I dialed again, and again the message played and this time I spoke louder: 'Professor Engelmann, I need your help. Please call me.' Then I hung up. I hadn't left any number, because I feared someone might intercept the call and find out what I was doing. I prayed he might recognize my voice, and perhaps trace caller ID to get my number. I wasn't sure.

Several days passed and I was no longer sure what I could do. I was running out of ideas on how to tell Larry where I was. Yet I clung desperately to my faith that one of us would figure out a way to find the other.

On a Friday morning – August 25 – I went to work early. I had been unable to sleep and was trying to think of another way to get in touch with Larry. I arrived at work at 7 A.M. I heard the phone ringing and another girl answered it. It was for me. She said it sounded like an international phone call. I tried to remain calm. I picked the phone up and said in English, 'Hello.'

The reply was 'Is this Xu Meihong?' the caller asked. I recognized the voice. I started to cry. Then he said, 'Don't cry. I have your letter. I remember you. And I love you.'

'Me, too,' I said.

'We have a lot to talk about,' he said.

'Yes,' I replied. 'I want to explain everything to you.'

He seemed to understand. Neither of us spoke for several seconds and then he asked, 'You need my help, don't you?"

'I need help. You're my last chance, Larry. I need to get out of China. I'm in trouble. Can you help me?'

'I can help you, Xu Meihong,' he said confidently. They were the sweetest and most assuring words I'd heard in months. 'I'll do anything for you,' he said. 'Anything at all. Just calm down, and think about what you want and we'll get it together.'

'You're not angry with me?'

'No. I never doubted you for a moment, Meihong. Not for a moment.'

'OK,' I said, taking a deep breath and trying to compose myself.

'Do you want to come to America?' he asked.

'Yes.'

'Then let's make it happen. Do you have a plan?'

'Not yet.'

'Then let's make one. Or two or three.'

'All right.'

'By the way,' he said, 'do you still have the bracelet I gave you?'

'Yes, of course I do.'

'Good, because I want it back when you get here,' he said, and then laughed.

I knew when I heard his voice that I'd been right about him all along. He promised to call again on Monday morning at the same hour. In fact, he called every day during the following week and wrote two long letters during the weekend – without putting a return address on them or signing them and mailing them to Yuhua's dorm on the campus of Qinghua University. Together we began to make our plans for me to leave China.

In truth I had no idea how he could help me get out. He asked about academic sponsorship but I said I was certain they would never let me have a passport to come to America as a student. That would amount to rewarding someone who was branded a criminal.

'I have one other idea,' he said. 'But it is fairly dramatic. What if you were the wife of an American citizen?' he asked. 'Would that make it easier?'

'It could. But would you do that for me?' I asked, surprised.

'Would I do that? I love you. Of course I'd do that.'

'That might be my best chance.'

'We could get divorced after you were settled here and you could live your own life then.'

I waited for a moment to see if he was joking. 'Why would I do that?' I asked. 'I love you.'

'I love you, too,' he assured me. 'I've thought of you every day since I left China in January, Meihong. I've thought about bringing you here. I've thought about dancing with you. I've thought about our walks. I've thought about every word we exchanged. Every word!'

'Me, too, Larry,' I confessed.

'And . . .' He paused for a moment before continuing. 'You've been with me – in my heart and in my thoughts for a year. You've been in my dreams. Every night. We're taking a chance. But I don't think we have much choice. If you'll have me, I'd be happy to marry you and be your husband as long as you need me and want me and love me. How does that sound?'

'Larry,' I told him, 'I'll always love you. You've been in my dreams, too. I'll never stop loving you and I'll never let anyone separate us again. Never.'

Our exchange was spontaneous and heartfelt. I think each of us was surprised by the firmness of our determination. Again there was a long pause. Then he laughed and I smiled as I recognized his optimistic confident laugh – a laugh that seemed to come from deep inside and dispelled my doubts about our ability to accomplish whatever we set out to do.

'How much trouble will this cause?' he asked. 'Do you think the government will give us much flak?'

'Larry, you can't imagine.'

'Do you believe in happy endings?' he asked. 'Like in the movies?'

'I don't know,' I said.

'Believe,' he said, 'because we are going to make this happen, no matter what they throw at us this time. They've had their turn. Now it's our turn. So let's give them a happy ending.'

vii

We set a time line. He would fly to China during the first week in January. That would give me time to make all other arrangements. He'd come in through Hong Kong on a non-American airline, Cathay Pacific. Perhaps in that way he'd be a less conspicuous target.

I had to complete the required paperwork and get all the necessary signatures for marrying a foreigner – not an easy task even for someone who had never been in trouble with the government. I had doubts I could do it at all. But whenever I despaired, Larry encouraged me and told me that most things were possible if I tried hard enough. We needed to continue trying, to be flexible and creative. He never seemed to despair.

The very first thing I had to do was to speed through my divorce from Lin Cheng. During the turmoil of the spring, our application for divorce had not been acted on. I asked Lin

Cheng to use his connections to get the divorce within days, if that was possible.

While I was making plans for a speedy divorce, my boss told me I'd have to leave the company immediately. She said that she'd tried to keep me but someone in the office had been watching me and making reports to the authorities. They knew I was receiving long-distance calls from the United States, she revealed. She'd taken enough risk for me but she couldn't do it any longer.

While I was removing my things from my desk, several of the people I worked with came to help me and to say goodbye. Some gave me notes with their phone numbers and addresses on them and said if I needed their help just to call them. In those post-Tiananmen days anyone who was in trouble with the government suddenly had numerous friends who wanted to do whatever they could to undermine or frustrate the government.

Lin Cheng pulled strings to get our divorce finalized in early December. We were required at that time to hand in our marriage certificates and pay fifty yuan to get the final decree. Lin Cheng wanted to keep our marriage certificate as a souvenir and to tell the authorities he'd lost it. But in the end he decided against that and instead took a picture of it.

We rode on his bicycle to the government bureau, where we signed the necessary documents and were given our divorce certificate. That evening he arranged for a military car to take me to the train station. He held my hand all the way. When I got out he said, 'Don't worry, Meihong. I believe in you. You've come a long way from your village. You are capable and deserving.'

I kissed him goodbye and turned to get on the train, but he pulled me around again and held me and said, 'I am sorry that I didn't make life better for us. I let you go because you deserve a better life in a better place. I don't even have anything valuable to give you when you leave.' He handed me the camera he'd purchased on his trip to America and insisted that I bring it with me.

Then he carried my bags onto the train and put them on the overhead rack for me. He hugged me again. 'Goodbye,' he said.

'Take care of yourself. Have a good life.'

He stood on the platform and watched the train leave. I thought it might be the last time I'd ever see him. I watched him through my tears until he was out of sight.

viii

I returned to my village and began a frantic paper chase the morning after my arrival. Larry notified me that he'd be arriving in Shanghai the evening of January 7. He'd arranged to remain in China for one week – which, I assumed, would give us enough time to get married. Then he planned to fly back to Hong Kong with our marriage certificate and begin work on his side on getting me into the United States.

But I had no idea how to get married to a foreigner. I sent a childhood friend to Nanjing to meet with the General to get the information. She returned that afternoon with a contact name and phone number. She also handed me a wedding gift from the General – an envelope containing 5,000 yuan. 'He said you will need this money to buy your way out,' my friend said.

I took the train to Nanjing and visited the General's friend. I was shown a list of the documents I'd need. They had no xerox machine to copy the forms of required documents, so I copied word for word an entire pamphlet on the processes of marrying a foreigner, step by step.

According to the processes detailed in the pamphlet, I had to get married in my home town, and the only office there that was designated to issue marriage certificates to Chinese citizens marrying foreigners was in Zhenjing, the country capital. This process made it easier for the authorities to check the applicant's background. I realized this was another way for the government to tighten its control over people with foreign connections. I feared that my name might be on their blacklist. If anything went wrong, and if the PLA was notified of my intent to marry Larry, I would end up in jail. But what choice did I have left? I decided to take all risks and go all out to fight for my love, life and freedom.

The first step was to obtain a certificate of singleness and permission to marry from the neighborhood committee. The committee customarily consists of old women in the neighborhood. They are usually adept at collecting rumors about all residents. After hearing my initial request, the two women of my neighborhood committee said they were busy and asked me to return the following afternoon. I knew this did not mean they were really too busy. It meant I had come asking a favor and had not brought gifts.

I took the train to Zhenjiang, and through a friend I was able to buy a carton of Marlboro cigarettes and a carton of Zhonghua cigarettes, a brand smoked only by high officials in China. The next day I visited the two women and gave them the cigarettes. They pushed back my gifts twice – this was the standard ritual – before reluctantly accepting them. Then they asked what they could do for me. I said I needed permission to marry but did not say 'a foreigner' since I knew that would create a big problem with these women. They gave me a standard application form to fill out. Under the name of the groom I wrote Larry's Chinese name and wrote it small – I'd planned this – so I could write it in English beside it later. For the work unit I wrote San Jose State University in Chinese. Then all that was required was for them to do the official chop (stamp). They asked me where this 'San Jose State University' was in China since they'd not heard of it. I told them it was a new university. 'No wonder,' they said. 'We've heard of Beijing University and Qinghua University but never San Jose State University. We are too old to keep up with these things anymore.' All I could do was thank God at that moment for their ignorance. They stamped the document and handed it to me.

The following day I went to the marriage registration bureau in Zhenjiang, and met the two officers who would actually issue the marriage certificate. I was interviewed for a half hour and they told me there would be no problem. What was required to be married, they said, was a certificate of singleness from my future husband, a document I belatedly discovered did not seem to exist in America.

He was also required to provide a letter of support and sponsorship, a bank statement telling what his accounts were, a statement from his employer confirming that he was employed, and a copy of his tax return.

Finally, they said I'd need a medical certificate for each of us, including an AIDS test, before we could be married.

I decided to get the medical exams right away – before Larry arrived in China – in order to save time. More importantly, if Larry went to any hospital in China, he'd immediately attract attention and it would be very difficult to escape the notice of the local MSS.

I had a close friend who was a head nurse at the Danyang People's Hospital. I visited her at the hospital and told her what I needed. She was nervous but willing to help. The next morning we picked up the application forms at the hospital and went to the head physician, a sixty-year-old man who had very poor eyesight. I told him I was transferring to Zhenjiang from Danyang with my husband and we needed the physical exam reports immediately. The physician said he would see us right away as a favor to my girlfriend. Then I had to tell him the husband wasn't there. I said he was on a business trip and would not return for ten days. But Zhenjiang needed the papers right away, so I needed his signature and official stamp. My girlfriend suggested that we could get the document signed first and then do the exam later. The doctor thought for a moment and then took the form and started to ask questions about me and Larry regarding our height and weight. 'Your husband is 1.84 meters?' he asked. 'That's very tall.'

'Yes,' I said. 'He's a basketball player.'

'Why do you need an AIDS test?' he asked. 'This seems very unusual.'

'My husband is in the PLA,' I said. 'The military has special requirements for their examination.'

The doctor looked puzzled. 'Oh, so he's a soldier,' he said, and seemed for a moment to be convinced of the legitimacy of what I was asking him to do. He checked several of the boxes on the form. Then he noticed the form was already dated 'January 10, 1990.' He asked about it and I said, 'I'm sorry, that was a mistake. Can we just leave it like that instead of starting over with a new form?'

The final thing I needed him to do was to stamp the pictures attached to the form. 'Something is wrong with this photo,' he said. 'This man is not Chinese.'

I had to take a chance and I blurted out, 'You're right, Doctor. He's not Han like us. He's from a minority group in Xinjiang.'

'Oh, I see,' the doctor said. 'He looks like a . . . like a Uighur. Is he?'

'Yes, he is,' I said. 'His ancestors were even part Russian.'

'Now I understand,' the doctor said.

I could hardly believe the string of lies I'd gotten away with. My future husband – a Uighur PLA officer basketball player! What a combination.

In Zhenjiang I arranged for us to stay at the Jinshan Hotel. I told the front desk that I was from the Foreign Affairs Office and I wanted to put up an American there. They were very nice and reserved two rooms for me immediately. I felt sad and ironic that I was trained to use these skills in lying to escape and survive in an enemy country and now I had to apply them in my own country.

The day Larry arrived, I went to Shanghai and checked into a hotel. His flight was scheduled to arrive at 6 P.M. At 4 P.M. someone knocked on my hotel-room door. I opened it and saw a soldier standing there in uniform. I nearly fainted. He didn't look like an enlisted man – he looked like an officer. For a moment I thought he'd come to arrest me. But instead he said, 'I've been sent by a friend to take you to the airport to pick up your friend.' I felt relieved. I knew who the friend was.

He parked the car in the airport lot and walked with me to the terminal so he could carry Larry's luggage. All along, in the back of my mind, I had a suspicion that someone high up in the MSS might be orchestrating everything that was happening to me and that I was merely being used as bait to get Larry back into China. It wasn't likely, I thought, but it could not be ruled out entirely. I might have slipped up somewhere along the line and, as in 1988, not noticed signs of a trap closing around me. So I told Larry earlier that when he came out of the terminal if he saw me and I waved, everything was all right. If I looked away after making eye contact with him, I told him, he should immediately turn around and go into the terminal again and book a return flight.

His flight arrived on time. It was already dark by that time and it was snowing heavily. I was still anxious and a bit uncertain. I stared at faces around me in the crowd for someone I might recognize, someone who might be an agent of the MSS, someone who might return my look and betray his true reason for being there. But no one paid me any attention. Then I saw Larry coming out the door. I waved to him and the soldier stepped forward and grabbed his suitcase. Larry rushed to me and embraced me. 'Welcome to China, again,' I said.

Larry kissed me on the forehead and said, 'Are you real? Is it really you? Is this really happening?' We held each other tightly for several seconds. Then we walked to the car and our driver took us to the Swan Cindic. We were in China, together again, for the first time in thirteen months.

Larry brought me many belated birthday and Christmas presents – clothing and shoes. He'd also brought a small gold wedding ring for me. But, he reminded me, 'I can't slip this on your finger until we are really married.' I knew for sure when I saw his face and his smile and heard his voice again that I was doing the right thing and that I loved him. I had been right to trust him to bring me to a new life.

He told me about the campaign against him in the Center by the MSS and the Chinese co-director soon after my disappearance. It had been trying, he said. But he was sustained in those difficult times by a faith in me. He said he knew, deep inside, that I'd never written the document the Chinese insisted they possessed. And when the Americans demanded to see it, the Chinese responded by telling them it was classified. Only the Chinese co-director had been allowed to see it and he, in turn, merely described it to the American officials. When the Americans demanded some hard evidence of Larry's alleged transgressions, the Chinese co-director responded by telling them that 'the charge is so serious it requires no evidence.' In order to defuse the situation, the American administrators promised Larry his full salary if he agreed to leave the Center. They also provided a letter praising his teaching at the Center and exonerating him of any wrongdoing. He accepted the arrangement and left Nanjing.

We talked late into the night. I confessed to him that I'd set up a very romantic image of him in my mind, like a little girl who dreamed about a prince who would come on a white horse and take her away. He told me he was just like that and he'd left his horse and lance at the airport in San Francisco. After we'd laughed he told me that I was the hero of our story, that I was the one who'd suffered, I was the one who'd been detained and interrogated and questioned. Perhaps, he suggested, I'd been the one who saved him. Now he was returning the favor. 'We were both reckless,' he said. 'And we were both innocent,' he assured me. 'If anyone has done anything wrong, it was me. And I'm here to make it right, now. With your permission.'

We had been friends for more than three months in the Center. Since that time I knew him best through his letters, through words on paper, and through our phone calls. My optimism and hope were based on those things. But as I listened to him and watched his expression and read the sincerity in his voice and felt his arms around me, I knew my optimism was justified.

Before returning to my own room I told Larry to get a good night's sleep because we'd be getting up early in the morning to catch the train to Zhenjiang. There was so much going through my head at the time, and so many fears. I expected everything to come crashing down at any moment. I was still looking over my shoulder.

At the Shanghai train station in the morning we waited in the cavernous lounge for foreign travelers. When Larry had been there a year earlier, there had been thousands of foreigners waiting for their trains. Now, in the wake of Tiananmen, there were just the two of us.

All that day, when I was with him, I felt safe for the first time in more than a year. He was so confident and so strong. His laughter was so uplifting and his embrace so reassuring. He was convinced that there was a solution for every problem we might confront. All we had to do, he advised me, was to continue to trust each other and we could do anything. I believed that he would allow no one to pull us apart this time. I believed he would die for me, if it came to that. And I would die for him.

So I tried to be apart from him as little as possible.

We arrived in Zhenjiang at four o'clock in the afternoon, hired a cab and went to our hotel. Larry was given a room on the fourth floor in one wing and I was given one on the first floor in another wing in a dormitory room for translators and tour guides working for foreigners. We had dinner in the hotel and talked long into the night. We walked a few blocks away to Jinshan Park and watched the men fishing with birds, and bought souvenirs from the street merchants.

I expected to be married on the following morning. But suddenly everything became very complicated. We took a taxi to the marriage registration bureau and were notified there that the clerks had discovered my former work unit was the PLA. They were indignant. 'Why didn't you tell us?' they snapped. 'We can't give you a certificate now. We have to have a letter from your institute saying your background is cleared.'

I panicked. I'd been far too optimistic. Now I would never be able to leave China and I would probably spend the foreseeable future in prison.

In a desperate gamble, I called the General from my hotel. He said he'd see what he could do. But the person who was in charge of providing the clearance was his archenemy – the Colonel. When I finished talking with him, I thought it was over and I'd been outmaneuvered.

But when I told Larry of the new difficulties he was unfazed. He said if it didn't work out this time, he'd return during the summer and we could be married then. I didn't tell him but my own feeling was that this was probably an all-or-nothing situation. If I failed this time they'd watch me much more closely. My veil of secrecy would be gone for good.

I knew the Colonel would never allow me to marry Larry. I felt as if I was standing at the edge of my own grave. Then I remembered the name of an old friend of my paternal grandfather. The man was a former mayor of Zhenjiang. He was retired but still had some influence in the city. Grandfather had helped his family decades earlier and he had never been asked to repay the favor. I went to him and told him I was Mr Xu's granddaughter and I needed help. He agreed to do what he could.

The clerks from the marriage bureau, in the meantime, had called the Institute in Nanjing on January 8 to get a report on me and clearance for marriage to a foreigner. They were put through to the office of the Colonel. Exercising one of the prerogatives of power, he had left the Institute to spend holiday vacation with his family in Beijing and he would not return for several weeks. His assistants took the message and said simply that they had information on me but could not release it without the approval of the Colonel.

Grandfather's friend went to the marriage bureau and told them that he would personally vouch for me. Then he asked them, 'What if the PLA does not respond to your inquiry? What will you do then? Keep this American friend waiting forever?' He suggested to them, 'If the PLA has not said no, will you accept that they don't object to the marriage?'

They thought about this novel proposal. Grandfather's friend reminded them, 'How can we keep an American professor waiting because of our slow bureaucracy? We must preserve a good image of how the government works here. If Xu Meihong was not eligible to marry the American professor, the PLA would have said so.'

The marriage bureau officials accepted this argument but they decided to wait a little longer. They said that if on the afternoon of Saturday, January 13, they had still not heard from the PLA, then I could be married. I was so nervous that I could not sleep for days. Then, late Saturday afternoon I received a phone call from the marriage bureau. They had heard nothing from the PLA. As promised, we could get married at 8 A.M. on Sunday 14 January.

This was more than luck. It was a miracle.

Larry was so happy and excited at the news and I was too. But at the same time, I was extremely worried and nervous. To me this was a matter of life and death. Every minute was critical. What if the Colonel called his office (or his assistant called him) and found out that Larry and I were trying to get married? I was sure the Colonel was determined to destroy me, let alone stop the marriage. I even doubted if it was true that the Colonel was away from his office. It could be an excuse used in order to buy more time to catch us quietly. I dared not communicate my fears to Larry. I didn't want to spoil his feeling of happiness.

On Saturday night we went to a large restaurant and enjoyed our last dinner together in Zhenjiang.

We decided that Larry should leave China with our marriage certificate as soon as we were married. I didn't know when I might ever see him again. So, I told him, I wanted us to become husband and wife – to have our wedding night before the wedding.

I went to his room that night. I drew the curtains, locked the door, listened for noises in the hallway. Then I took a chair and tilted it against the door handle. Larry started to laugh and said he felt as if he was doing this under siege and wanted to know what the plan might be if Ninja warriors came down the side of the building on ropes and broke through the windows. We started laughing at my caution and my transformation of the room into a fortress. I still thought someone would come along to destroy all of our work even at this late moment.

But they didn't.

The next morning we arose at six. It was still dark and it was snowing. Zhenjiang was a small city with few foreign visitors. I discovered when we were checking out that there were no taxis at that time of the morning and the taxi drivers did not have phones at their homes and could not be summoned. The marriage bureau was five miles away and there was no direct bus to go there. We had to walk that distance in the snow carrying our luggage.

But we had no choice. Larry insisted on carrying both of our bags and we started walking as fast as we could toward the heart of the city. He kept looking at his watch and I was talking to myself, saying, 'I can't believe this could happen. I can't believe we won't make it there on time. God, help us.'

Larry had brought no gloves with him. We had walked for almost thirty minutes and I was afraid we were not going to make it when I saw a man coming toward us on a large tricycle he used to transport vegetables around the city. I signaled for him to stop and told him I had an emergency and needed a ride. He agreed to take us all the way to the marriage bureau for five yuan. I tried to bargain with him and Larry said, 'My God, what are you arguing about? I want to get married this morning. Give him a hundred yuan but just get us there on time.'

The cyclist was an old man and did not look very strong. So I got on the back of his tricycle and Larry put both bags on and then jogged beside the tricycle so the man could go faster. We arrived at the marriage bureau at 7.55 A.M.

We hurried into the main office of the marriage bureau and the first thing the two clerks told me was 'We're sorry. We cannot give you the certificate today.' When I asked why, they said that Larry's certificate of singleness – which I'd given them earlier in the week – was from only one American state. The document said Larry had not been married in California in the past twenty-five years. They asked, 'What if he was married before that time? What if he was married in another state? You cannot marry him, because we are not sure if he is qualified to marry.'

I could hardly believe that all our planning could fall victim to this nonsense. I asked them to look at the copy of his tax return, which showed he had filed as a single man. But they didn't understand English and seemed adamant. Finally, we arrived at a compromise. I had Larry write in English in large letters 'I AM NOT MARRIED' and sign his name. Then I translated it into Chinese just beneath his words. Incredibly, this created another problem. Larry's hands were so cold from the trip to the bureau and he'd been carrying two suitcases most of the way. The building was also unheated and now he found he could not close his fingers around the pen. He tried again and again to hold the pen, even attempting to grasp it with both hands. But it kept falling out of his fingers. He muttered, 'My God, after all we've gone through to get here, now this!'

The clerks had seen this problem before. They poured water from a steaming kettle into a large cup and had Larry place his hand over the top of the cup and hold it there for a minute. The heat from the water loosened his muscles. Finally he could write, but just barely. He scratched out his name under the words. Then I signed as a witness and the document was stamped.

Then, almost unbelievably, we had to go through a question-and-answer session. They asked us when we met, how long we'd been in love, how we fell in love. I had to laugh now and then, but this was the standard procedure. They asked us about a dozen questions and treated us like kids. When they were finished, they moved to the side of the room and conferred with each other for several seconds. Then they returned to us, smiled and said, 'Congratulations, you are now husband and wife.'

I handed each of them two cartons of Marlboros that we'd purchased the previous afternoon and they pushed them back twice before accepting them. They gave us each in return an orange. Everyone was pleased with the morning's proceedings.

We were handed our marriage certificates and we shook hands with the clerks and departed. Outside again, Larry embraced me. Then we kissed and held each other tightly in the cold morning air. 'We did it,' Larry said. 'Now let's get the hell out of here before these guys change their mind.' We ran down the stairs to the street, where we found a taxi to take us to the train station. As we were going to the station, Larry suddenly said, 'I forgot something,' and reached into his pocket and pulled out a small blue envelope, opened it and took out the ring he'd brought from Hong Kong. He held my hand gently and then slipped the ring onto my finger. 'Congratulations, Mrs Engelmann,' he said. 'We're almost home.'

ix

We had breakfast together at a small restaurant across the street from the station. We held hands and laughed while we ate and recalled events of the hectic morning. I said I wished the ceremony could have been a little bit more special, but Larry told me it was the most wonderful morning and the most glorious wedding ceremony he'd ever seen and said he could never have dreamed any of it up. When he got home he was going to have trouble making people believe it.

On the train Larry held me close beside him all the way back to Shanghai. I was glowing with optimism now. I couldn't help but think I was almost out of China. Almost home.

When we arrived at the Shanghai airport we had an early dinner of cake and ice cream – our wedding cake, Larry called it – in a restaurant in the terminal. It was the most beautiful cake and ice cream I'd ever eaten. We had one hour left. But as the minutes ticked past I began to cry. I saw some American girls waiting for the plane. They seemed so free and I envied them. I wanted out of China with my husband so badly now.

Larry put his copy of our marriage certificate in an inside jacket pocket and then buttoned it closed. I feared that the customs inspectors might try to take it from him. I still thought there was a chance we would be stopped.

Larry paid our bill and then helped me put my coat on. Music was playing in the restaurant and after I'd buttoned my coat, Larry asked, 'How about a dance after dinner?' Before I could answer he put an arm around my waist and lifted my left hand into the air and danced me around and around out the door. I noticed the waitresses and the cashier turn and watch us, but Larry was oblivious to their attention and was humming with the music and holding me tightly as though we were in a ballroom somewhere surrounded by other dancers. He lifted me up when he'd finished and kissed me and told me,

'Don't be unhappy. We'll be together soon. Just try to stay optimistic, no matter what people tell you.'

'I'll try,' I promised.

I was not allowed in the international terminal without a ticket and a passport. We embraced and then we kissed each other again. Larry whispered, 'See you in California!' Then he turned and walked into the terminal. I watched through the glass doors as he approached the customs desk. Just as he put down his bags all the televisions in the terminal suddenly came on and began showing a Donald Duck cartoon. The customs officers looked up and nodded to the departing passengers and waved them through so as not to interrupt their viewing of the cartoon. I noticed Larry pat his jacket pocket as he walked into the departure lounge and disappeared from my sight.

I waited for two hours for my train. I kept my copy of the marriage certificate in a pocket inside my jacket to prevent a pickpocket from taking it from me. I shared my train compartment with a group of people who smoked, ate salted chicken and drank beer all the way to Zhenjiang. But somewhere, deep in my heart, for the first time in more than a year, I felt happy and safe.

X

On Monday morning, in Hong Kong, Larry xeroxed copies of the certificate, then faxed them to a friend in the United States who had envelopes and letters addressed to California senators Alan Cranston and Pete Wilson asking for their help in getting me out of China. Copies also went to several California congressmen, including Tom Campbell of Palo Alto, who was interested in U.S.–China relations, and to prominent members of Congress and to the Secretary of State, the Secretary of Defense, and the President and the Vice President. Larry told me that he was going to make as much noise and cause as much trouble as he could until I was safely by his side.

On January 15 I visited the Public Security Bureau in Danyang with my marriage certificate and requested a passport.

The officer in charge recognized me. He glanced up at me with unconcealed contempt and said, 'Oh, yes, I bet you would like a passport. Where would you like to go? Perhaps to America? Why don't you go home and stop wasting my time?'

'Yes, I'd like to go to America,' I told him.

'And what would you like to do there?' he asked derisively.

'I'd like to join my husband there. I'm the wife of an American citizen.'

His mouth dropped open and the cigarette he'd been holding between his lips fell to the table. He stood slowly and unsteadily, staring at me all the while. I saw the color drain from his face. I thought he was going to faint. His lips moved but no sound came out. My words rendered him dumbstruck.

I reached into my pocket and slowly withdrew my marriage certificate and handed it to him. He examined it carefully and saw the signatures and chops on it and realized it was not a forgery.

There was nothing more he could say. We both knew it. He sat down still holding the document, opening and closing it and putting it close to his eyes and then further away. When he'd recovered he spoke in a low tone, almost a whisper. 'What have you done?' he asked. I didn't even try to answer. He muttered something to himself under his breath over and over again. Then he said I'd need a letter from my husband inviting me to America and a letter from my mother and father giving me permission to leave China.

'I am twenty-six years old. Are you telling me I need my parents' permission to join my husband?'

'This is most unusual,' he kept repeating to himself, 'most unusual.'

I repeated my question, and he snapped to attention again and said, 'Even if you were sixty you would need their permission. That's the law.'

I returned home and thought about it for a day. I'd told my parents nothing about my divorce and nothing about my remarriage. The less they knew, I believed, the safer they would be. So I composed a letter and signed my parents' names with my left hand to disguise the writing. Larry provided the required documents by express service within days. I then returned with all the documents for the Public Security man. He told me, 'This will take at least three months. Don't come back until then.'

Larry called every day to check on my progress. I found I had used up all of my connections and influence in Danyang, but still I heard nothing from the passport office. Then I was notified that a letter had been received from the PLA in Nanjing stating that under no circumstances was I to be allowed to obtain a passport or to leave the country.

I received regular visits from the local MSS and from military representatives to inquire about my marriage – how it had been done, who had been paid, what influence had been used. They had all the paperwork and documentation and it was all legally signed and stamped, they could see. They encouraged me to be a good citizen and annul the marriage and promised there might be some form of rehabilitation available for me if I did. I simply repeated to them that I only wished to join my husband in America.

Larry succeeded in getting both California senators as well as Congressman Campbell to write to the Chinese Embassy expressing concern at his inability to get me out of China. They wanted to know why there was a delay. Larry called the State Department and spoke with the young man serving on the China desk, Patrick Freeman, who, Larry discovered, was a graduate of San Jose State University. When Larry told me that he laughed and said he knew that fate had to be on our side. When I asked Larry why these people were being so kind and spending time on my case he replied, 'Because that's the way it's supposed to work.'

Things seemed to be progressing for us until late June. Then I was summoned to the Public Security Bureau and told they had conferred with representatives from the PLA. The Army had decided that my familiarity with intelligence methods and operations meant that allowing me to go abroad would endanger state security. As a result, I was denied a passport and could not apply for one for seven years. By that time, they claimed, my knowledge of the security apparatus would no longer constitute a threat.

I called Larry and told him this time I was willing to end the marriage rather than have him wait seven years for me. He became increasingly impatient. 'Damn it,' he said. 'This is not going to take seven years. They are bluffing. Don't believe them. Just stop listening to them. This will not take seven years. No way.' We planned to meet in Guangzhou in two weeks.

His words comforted me but I knew of no method of getting out of China without the passport.

In July, Larry flew to Hong Kong, did some research for a book he was beginning on the plight of the boat people and then took the train to Guangzhou, where I met him. He'd made reservations for us at the White Swan Hotel in Guangzhou. We visited the American consulate, which was located near the hotel, to fill out the papers required for the issuance of my visa for America. Larry remained convinced that as long as he stayed in touch with senators and congressmen and continued to pressure Chinese diplomats in Washington through them, the Chinese government would relent and I would be released in a short time.

Then one afternoon beside the hotel pool, Larry took out a notebook and opened it and asked me to study what he'd drawn inside. He spoke in a low voice and we sat far away from others at the pool. 'Look at this,' he said. 'Make yourself familiar with it.' He'd drawn a map of the northern half of Vietnam, the Gulf of Tonkin (Beibu Wan), Hainan Island and the coast of China up to Hong Kong. 'I've interviewed hundreds of boat people in the camps in Hong Kong. The stories are pretty much the same. About ninety percent of them in the camps are from northern Vietnam, most from around Hanoi.' He drew a line with his pencil. 'They come this way out of Vietnam, across the South China Sea. They land on the northwest coast of Hainan, here,' he said, pointing to several places along the island. 'They buy supplies on the island, stay there several days, pay off the local authorities. Nobody bothers them if they move on. I talked to them in Hong Kong and in California, where many of them resettled. Here's what I want to do. I'll come back to Hong Kong at Christmas. Then I'll fly to Hainan and we can meet in Haikou, as if we are vacationers. Then we'll go to the coast, here, and wait for boats. When a Vietnamese boat shows up to get supplies, I'll buy us a place on the boat.'

I was amazed by his plan – to make us both boat people.

'Can you do this?'

'Of course I can do this. Chances are we'd be picked up by a ship in the South China Sea. I'll alert the State Department and the consulate in Hong Kong. They'll be waiting for us.'

'What if we're caught by the Chinese guards?'

'Great!' he said, and laughed. 'What a news story that will be. American citizen and his Chinese wife try desperately to escape from China as boat people. If we're caught, the news will go around the world. We can't lose – unless the boat sinks,' he said. 'But that won't happen.

'Are you willing to try?' he asked.

I thought about it for a moment and looked into his eyes. He was completely serious. I trusted him. 'Yes,' I said. 'I'll come with you.'

'If we do it, we'll have a great tale to tell our children. And if we don't make it,' he said, placing his hand on my hair, brushing it gently, 'we'll still be together. And I want that.'

He agreed to go over the map and dates with me before we parted. 'I really think we're going to embarrass them into letting you go,' he said. 'I just have a feeling we will.'

I flew back to Shanghai and Larry took the train to Hong Kong. We held each other for a long time, not knowing when we'd see each other again or what desperate measures we might be forced to take at the end of the year. 'This can't go on,' he said. 'I can't keep saying goodbye to you. The next time I leave China, I am not leaving without you. I promise you that.'

Back home, I was visited by the MSS people the day after I returned. They asked if I'd had a good time in Guangzhou. I told them I had. They asked why then I'd cried several times when Larry and I were talking. I said because we were apart. 'Get used to it,' they said, and gloated.

In October, Larry's book on the fall of South Vietnam, *Tears Before the Rain*, was published. He began a ten-city book tour to promote the book. In putting together the publicity folder that went to newspapers and radio stations around the country, Larry had the publisher, Oxford University Press, include a page on his marriage to a 'former PLA officer, Xu Meihong,' in Zhenjiang, China. And the statement that she remains in China and he is currently working to bring her to America. He appeared on several regional and national radio programs, including Monitor Radio in Boston and NPR in Philadelphia and Washington. Always, after discussing the book, the interviewers had questions about Larry's wife and his difficulties in getting her out of China. With the American public still interested in Tiananmen and relations with China, this story of Chinese vindictiveness, and the mysterious cloaking of reasons for preventing someone from leaving the country, caught the public eye. Larry even included a note in the acknowledgements of the book thanking me for helping him understand much of the material he'd collected. 'Finally, thank you, Xu Meihong,' he wrote, 'who helped me organize and transcribe much of this material during my stay in China. Our long conversations concerning the stories in this book, the nature of Asian Communism, American foreign policy, China's role in Southeast Asia and the future of the region provided me with many hours of provocative and enlightening dialogue. Meihong eventually paid a high price for our friendship. Her dreams and fears and her fate helped me understand some of the bitterness and the behavior of those who won and lost in Vietnam, and why they fought.' Larry had written the statement before we'd found each other again in August 1989. He told me later it demonstrated how important our long walks and talks had been in Nanjing and how deeply he regretted my disappearance and the role he might have played in my suffering.

He also continued to send out requests for individuals to drop a note to the Chinese embassy saying they were concerned about the Chinese policy of refusing to allow the wife of an American citizen to leave. Among others he sent notes to Brent Scowcroft, Henry Kissinger, former Presidents Gerald Ford and Jimmy Carter, Winston Lord and his wife, Bette Bao Lord, General William Westmoreland, people within the DIA, the CIA, the State Department and people at various think tanks and universities around the country. Congressman Campbell and Senator Wilson continued to keep him posted on their queries to the Chinese Embassy and the State Department.

In the midst of the book tour, when Larry was in Washington, he received a call from Patrick Freeman at the State Department telling him that someone in the Chinese Embassy would like to see him. Larry went to the embassy on Wednesday, October 24.

Larry was led to a conference room inside the embassy in northwest Washington. He smiled when he saw a poorly disguised two-way mirror. He was greeted by Wang Maoheng, the First Secretary of the embassy. Mr Wang was gracious, Larry found, but at the same time he had many more questions than answers.

'Dr Engelmann,' he began. 'I sympathize with the plight of you and your wife. And I'd like to help you. But I do not understand why she is being detained in China. Do you have any idea?'

'No, sir, I don't. That's why I came here. I thought you might be able to tell me.'

'All I can tell you is that it has something to do with her former work unit. Do you know what that was?'

'I have some idea. She was in the PLA, I believe.'

'Did you ever meet anyone else from her unit?'

'No, I didn't.'

'Did you ever meet her commanding officer?'

'No.'

'Did she introduce a general to you while you were in Nanjing in 1988?'

'No.'

The question-and-answer session lasted for half an hour. Mr Wang concluded in the end, 'I don't know what is going on. You know her unit has control over her permission to leave. So I am not sure what I can do. Perhaps you can assist me and I can provide information that might help.'

'I don't know how,' Larry said. 'That's why I'm here. I thought you could help. My wife is no threat to anyone. She merely wants to be here with me. We don't understand why your government is preventing that.'

The First Secretary closed his folder and placed it on a table next to his chair and stood. He extended his hand to Larry and said, 'Dr Engelmann, I sympathize with your plight. I will do all that I can to help you be reunited with your wife. If you come across any information that might be of use, please call me here.'

Larry told Patrick Freeman about his conversation at the Chinese Embassy and about his plan to bring me out of China as a refugee in a Vietnamese boat. Freeman at first thought he was joking. Larry said he was serious, and he was going to do it with or without the cooperation of the State Department. He said he wanted the Department to inform the U.S. consulate in Hong Kong and to have them alerted to the fact that he would be coming there with a boatload of Vietnamese probably later that year. 'Mr Engelmann,' Freeman told him, 'we really can't encourage you to do this and I hope you will reconsider. This is very serious.'

'I am very serious, Patrick,' he said. 'And it is going to happen.'

Within days David Chang from the U.S. consulate in Shanghai, who also had been working hard on my case, was in touch with Larry by phone and fax. He reported that he'd spoken to the Public Security People in Danyang and they were not straightforward about my case. Chang said he planned to pressure them more by traveling to Danyang and confronting them face to face. Larry said this was just the kind of pressure we needed to put on the Chinese. He thanked Chang and said he'd never forget what he was doing for us.

Meanwhile, I flew to Beijing and went to the American Embassy to seek help there. I spoke for a long time with Katherine Dee Robinson, who was helpful and encouraging. She said she would work on the case and stay on it until there was a better solution than my waiting seven years to get out of the country.

On the morning of December 10 Larry received a call from Patrick Freeman. 'Have you heard from your wife?' he asked.

'Not for a couple of days,' Larry said. 'Why?'

'Something is happening in China,' he said.

'What? What is it?' Larry asked.

'Don't get your hopes up. It could be bad. Or it could be good. We don't know. All we know is that the Chinese government has indicated that they will resolve her case but they didn't say how.'

Larry became apprehensive. 'Oh, Jesus, what do you think they'll do?' he asked. He feared I'd be rearrested on some trumped-up charge and disappear forever.

'I really don't know. But if she calls you, call me back immediately.'

A few minutes later Larry received a fax from Katherine Dee Robinson in Beijing indicating the same thing. 'Mr Engelmann. I have not been in touch with your wife, but the Chinese government has indicated they will resolve her case within the next few hours. Please get in touch with her and let us know what she knows about this.'

He'd planned to call on Wednesday morning and there was no way to get in touch with me before then since I didn't have a phone at home. But I called him on Tuesday evening and told him the news.

'What's going on?' he asked. 'Are you OK?'

'The Public Security people came to my home this morning.'

'And?'

'And they've been instructed to give me a passport. I'm to leave the country as soon as possible.'

'Oh, God, we've done it,' he said. He told me to make the plane reservation to San Francisco as soon as I could and to call him back every day with a progress report.

'It's very strange,' I told him. 'They told me that the order for issuing my passport came directly from the Party Central Committee in Beijing. Nanjing has been bypassed. I don't know why. I don't know who ordered this and they don't either.'

'Don't worry about that. We can worry about it later,' Larry said. 'Just buy a plane ticket when you receive your passport and get out.'

One week later I had my passport. When I picked it up at the Public Security headquarters the officer in charge was furious. He said this was highly unusual. He tried to ask me questions about friends in Beijing, but I wouldn't talk. Then he reminded me, ominously, 'You may be leaving China, Xu Meihong, but I want you to remember always that your family is still here. Don't forget that, ever. Your family is still here.'

I turned and walked out the door.

The next day I flew to Guangzhou and got my immigration visa from the U.S. Consulate there. Then I bought a ticket for a flight from Shanghai to Los Angeles and then on to San Francisco. I was scheduled to arrive on December 29 at 12.30 P.M. I called Larry with the good news.

He was so happy he could hardly speak. Yet both of us were still cautious. We knew that the extension of the permission to leave had come from some unknown government official – high in the government, obviously. And it could just as easily be canceled. I would not be safe, he concluded, till I was in the United States.

'I'll be waiting for you in San Francisco,' he said.

'I'll be there,' I said.

There was a slight pause, and then we both spoke at once: 'I love you.'

'Don't be late,' he said.

'I won't,' I promised.

'It looks like our Hainan–Hong Kong cruise will have to be canceled,' he said. 'That would have been an adventure.'

'I think we've had enough adventures for one lifetime, Larry,' I said. 'No more.'

ELEVEN

Another World

Peach blossoms float on water.
There is another world, better than this one.

— LI BAI

i

My flight landed in Los Angeles on the morning of December 29, 1990. I passed through customs and got my first look at America in the airport terminal. It seemed that everyone was smiling and happy. I caught a connecting flight to San Francisco later that morning. As soon as we touched down I took a small mirror from my purse and looked at myself to make sure I was presentable after such a long journey. I applied a little lipstick and powder and ran my fingers through my hair and examined my face in the mirror. I noticed my grandmother's fingerprints on my forehead and touched them gently with the tips of my own fingers. I was trembling slightly, I noticed, from anticipation. I took several deep breaths and tried to calm myself.

As I left the plane, the flight attendants bid me farewell and wished me luck. I walked down the long skyway to the terminal. In the distance I saw a crowd of people waiting for the arriving passengers. I searched for the familiar face of my husband and saw him suddenly emerge from the crowd and approach me, arms outstretched, smiling broadly, his eyes glistening with tears.

I dropped my bag and reached out for him. 'Welcome home,' he said. And then he put his arms around me and lifted me into the air.

That night I returned the silver bracelet to Larry. We decided that neither of us would ever wear it again. We'd keep it and someday give it to our children and tell them where it had been and what magic it worked.

For several weeks after my arrival I awakened in the middle of the night crying and in a cold sweat. I sat up in bed, trembling and utterly terrified because of a nightmare that I was still in China, questioned day and night with my life hanging in the balance. On those nights Larry sat up beside me, embraced me, dried my tears and assured me that everything was all right and that I was safe and no one could harm me again. He promised that nothing would ever separate us again. Nothing. Then I'd lie down again and fall asleep, peacefully, in his arms.

And so my old life ended and my new life began.

ii

Three years after I left China, I received a letter from Lin Cheng telling me he'd left the PLA and had remarried. The moment I read those words I cried. I knew that someday this news was sure to arrive. And I was equally certain that I would be as saddened as I was happy for him. I will always love that handsome cadet who won my heart in Nanjing in 1984 when both of us were still so young and red and intoxicated with the dreams of youth.

The General was arrested shortly after I departed from China. Eventually, he was cashiered from the PLA. Then he disappeared. I have no idea where he is today.

All of the Twelve Pandas left the PLA. Three of us live abroad today. The others remain in China. I keep the picture of us from our graduation day in my bedroom. And I often look at that picture and remember them, wishing each of them a happy life.

iii

Each year on September 1 when the new semester begins at the Nanjing Institute for International Relations of the PLA, the new recruits are gathered in a large auditorium and given a lecture detailing the history, heroes and successes of the Institute. The young cadets are told what will be expected of them and the part they will play in promoting the hegemony of the greatest nation on earth. And then, as a warning, one of the Institute's rare but instructive failures is mentioned. I have learned from several former cadets that my story is told to the new students as an example of what might happen when an innocent young soldier fails to heed the lessons of her training and ends up making an imprudent decision with potentially cataclysmic results. The lights in the room are dimmed and a picture of me in my cadet's uniform is projected on a large screen. A somber speaker tells the wide-eyed recruits the tragic story of 'Xu Meihong, a naive village girl from Jiangsu province, who showed great enthusiasm and promise when she arrived here. She worked hard and became a class leader and was commissioned as a first lieutenant. Much was expected of her. But during an early assignment she allowed herself to be deceived by an American agent. As a result, she betrayed her country. Before she could do serious damage to China's security, however, her deception was discovered. Because of her youth and her prior record of service to the PLA, she was shown mercy following a tearful confession. The damage she might have done was, thanks to her subsequent cooperation, successfully contained. Her life was spared. But she was cashiered from the military and exiled to the countryside for reeducation through hard labor. She died there in the winter of 1990.'

Like all of the other stories told to fresh and eager PLA cadets in China, this one is true.

AFTERWORD

The Stuff that Dreams are Made of

Larry Engelmann
July, 1999

The friends who met here and embraced are gone,
Each to his own mistakes.

— W.H. AUDEN, 'The Crossroads'

S he was always a dreamer.

From the moment I met her I realized that Meihong Xu was a young woman whose head was filled with dreams. During our walks in the autumn of 1988 in Nanjing, she was most animated when talking about her hopes for the future, the places she wanted to visit and the things she wanted to accomplish. She said she wanted to see the whole world – America, Europe, Africa, the rest of Asia – everywhere. She loved the stories I told about my home, my life in California and my travels. I saw her eyes fill with wonder when I told her what life was like outside China. And sometimes, when I'd say something amusing or surprising about a faraway place she'd exclaim, 'Oh, I want to go there. I want to see it for myself.' And when she said that I'd always assure her that some day she would.

I didn't know for a long time that she was watching me and reporting our conversations to someone else. I also didn't know that she was shielding me, protecting me, trying to keep me out of harm's way. And I didn't know that she continued to protect me after her arrest. I didn't know.

What I did know for certain was that she was the most engaging, energetic, articulate and intelligent dreamer I'd ever met in my life. She was absolutely unforgettable.

Following her disappearance from the Center I heard several rumors of what happened to Meihong – some mystifying, some confusing, some horrifying. Someone reported that a friend had seen her in Beijing in mid-December with a group of PLA officers. She'd obviously been reassigned, they said, and promoted to the rank of captain. Another account said she'd tired of her life at the Center and had rejoined her husband at the National Defense University. Still another alleged she had been arrested, removed from the Center in the middle of the night, and executed.

None of the stories could be verified. When I asked other students to find out where she'd gone, I was warned that merely asking about Meihong would bring me trouble. 'Just forget her,' was the most common advice I was given. 'Get on with your life and forget her.'

American officials also seemed happy just to forget the disappearance of the young woman. It was a matter for the Chinese, they said.

But I didn't forget her. I couldn't.

I left Nanjing in February, 1989. I never returned to the city.

I moved to Hong Kong and finished my book on the Vietnam War. I planned to return to Beijing as a tourist in mid-June, but the Tiananmen Massacre on 3–4 June altered my plans. I returned to the US but I kept wondering about Meihong. In a notebook I listed all the things I knew about her, what she'd told me and what I'd observed. I tried to remember what her voice sounded like, the touch of her hand, the way she threw her head back when she laughed. I could not get her out of my mind. I knew I would never rest peacefully until I found out what had really happened to her.

During my first week of teaching at San Jose State University in the August of 1989, I received a telephone call from a Chinese student at the University of Kansas. He said he had a message for me from Meihong. And a phone number. The moment I heard her voice that afternoon on the phone, I knew what I had to do. I returned to China in January, 1990, and married Meihong. Despite the tremendous difficulties we confronted from the Chinese government, before the year was over she was safe in California.

Three months after Meihong arrived in California we experienced a setback. We planned to celebrate the start of our new life by having a child together. But in March Meihong suffered a painful and serious miscarriage. She was hospitalized for two days. I sat beside her bed and watched her sleep during that crisis and thought I might actually lose her – after all we had been through together. The experience was a nightmare for both of us. Meihong suffered both emotionally and physically. It took her several weeks to recover her strength and her spirit. I didn't realize for a long time how deeply hurt she was by the experience.

We postponed starting a family. Meihong enrolled in San Jose State University, tried several majors and eventually entered the MBA program. She graduated as a top student in the spring of 1995. She was hired as an international marketing specialist for a computer company. She was sent back to China for a week that summer as a representative of the company and she was dispatched as an American representative to the international NGO women's conference in Beijing in August. I was very proud of her accomplishments.

In 1994, after much encouragement from our friends, we set out to write the story of our romance. Each day we'd sit down together with a tape recorder and talk about our lives. Only then did I learn the full story of Meihong's harrowing experience following her arrest. Eventually we taped more than 90 hours of material. I transcribed the recordings and began the task of organizing and writing the story of our lives and our love. We had faith that the story of our eventual triumph would inspire others. Love, determination, loyalty and faith had indeed moved mountains, we found.

I think writing the book held us together, just as adversity had pushed us together in 1988 and 1989. But at the same time I sensed a growing uneasiness in Meihong. A melancholy and a sadness that had not been characteristic of her in China. We had discovered our similarities in China. We discovered our differences in America.

Meihong had never lived independently. She had grown up in a tight-knit family in the village of Lishi. Then she had been inducted into the PLA where her every move was monitored and subject to criticism. She married while still in the military, divorced and then quickly married again.

After gaining a sense of safety and security in America, she found the constraints of marriage too confining. She told me several times of her desire to make her own decisions and to become more self reliant. On the morning of 7 February, 1998, Meihong told me she was moving out of our home in an effort to give herself some breathing room and time away from me so she could search for answers to her lingering unhappiness with our marriage. I tried to talk her out of leaving but was unsuccessful. I helped her pack her belongings and watched her drive away.

I thought for the next several months that she would return. When I saw headlights in the street late at night I was convinced it was Meihong coming home. But it wasn't. She did not return.

Meihong wanted a peaceful and simple life. She said she could not find it with me.

During the spring and summer of 1998 we met on a weekly basis to edit and complete this book. Very often as we read this narrative aloud we cried and embraced and comforted each other. Meihong told me she cried so many times that summer that she had no tears left. Still, we did not reconcile.

But this is not an unhappy ending. Meihong continues to prosper in her career. She has a bright future. She has already found dignity, respect and self confidence in America. She is respected by her colleagues, loved by her friends, admired by all who know her. She is energetic, intelligent, selfless and ethical.

We speak on the telephone occasionally. I still have the ability to make Meihong laugh. We share a common sense of humor. And when we talk we recall something good, something wonderful, that we'd shared. But there is no going back to it.

I tell Meihong that I still love her. That I always will. That if I had to do it all over again – go back for her and take the risks I took to get her to the US – and I knew ahead of time it would end this way, I would still do it. We shared seven wonderful years together. They were the best years of my life. They were a gift to me, I believe, from God. A compensation, perhaps, for a good deed.

Meihong keeps the silver bracelet I locked around her wrist in December, 1988. And she knows that should there ever again be a time when she needs a rescuer, I will be there. Always.

I pray she will find the happiness and the peace she has been seeking for so long. She has sacrificed much in her life. She has suffered much. God owes her happiness and peace.

When I think of Meihong – and I think of her every day – I remember her the way she was those autumn days in Nanjing when we took our walks and talked about America and the future. I remember how happy she made me by lifting me out of my dark moods and how happy I seemed to make her. I loved the way she talked about her dreams and how she was so determined to make them come true some day. She inspired me. She amazed me. Neither of us could see into the future and know the price we'd pay for our conversations, our friendship and then our love. Nor did we imagine that, in time, her dreams would come true. And so would mine, for a time.

I have not changed my mind about Meihong Xu over the years. My impression of her remains today what it was in Nanjing in the autumn of 1988. At that time, as I watched her and listened to her tell me of her great dreams, she became to me the stuff that dreams are made of.

I am a lucky man. I have been blessed. When I went to China in 1988 I had no idea what fate awaited me there. I never expected to meet the woman of my dreams in Nanjing – but I did. And I certainly never expected to be given the opportunity to rescue her from a grim life, marry her and bring her to America. But I did that, too. The years I spent married to Meihong were the happiest of my life. And she will always be the great love of my life.

We were divorced on 6 January 1999.

And so my old life ended and my new life began.

If you enjoyed this book here is a selection of other bestselling non-fiction titles from Headline